MANAGING EDUCATIONAL CHALLENGES

A Global View

MANAGING EDUCATIONAL CHALLENGES
A Global View

Dr. Hemlata Talesra
Dr. P.K. Dashora
Shima Sarupria

AUTHORS**PRESS**

under the auspices of

Rajasthan Council of Educational Administration and Management (Affiliated to Commonwealth Council of Educational Administration and Management)

Worldwide Circulation through Authorspress Global Network
First Published 2002
by Authorspress

E-35/103, Jawahar Park,
Laxmi Nagar, Delhi-110 092

e-mail: authorspress@yahoo.com
quantum_soul@mantramail.com

Typeset in NewCenturySchlbk by Chitra Computers

Managing Educational Challenges: A Global View
ISBN 81-7273-092-6

Printed in India at Tarun Offset Press, Delhi.

Preface

When we have entered the 21st century it is rather far more important at this juncture to look around us and identify a path which can lead all of us to a destination which provides a systematic, harmonious, co-operative, and a happy society. The most important tool which we all will be needing and using to achieve our desired goal and shape the future is 'education'. Education, right from the pre-primary to the university level, should not merely be transmission, acquisition and retention of information but it should be capable of making any person a full person, a holistic person with a pragmatic and positive attitude imbibed with certain values which are cherished by a civilised society. This Herculian task can never be accomplished without proper and systematic thinking, churning of varied ideas, and sharing of experiences from all over the world.

The present attempt of collecting and discussing the experiences and opinions of renowned educationists from all over the world and publishing the well synthesized ideas in a book form to benefit all those who are directly or indirectly concerned with the arena of education is, in fact, a fruitful outcome of the activities of Rajastan Council of Educational Administration and Management (RCEAM). Twenty-two articles covering a wider spectrum of different issues pertaining to the institutional planning, management and other related aspects contributed by eminent scholars from all over the world have been identified from the papers presented in the international conferences on 'Education and Global Challenge' held at Hobart, Tasmania, Australia during September 2000 and on "Institutional Planning" held at Banswara, Rajasthan, India, besides a few articles collected by RCEAM.

The editors express their heartiest thanks to all the contributors who have shared their valuable views in the form of their papers. The co-operation and encouragement received from all the members and executives of RCEAM were the only source of motivation and energy. RCEAM and the editors will be satisfied if those who are in the field of education find something useful in this book.

Editors

Contents

1

Government Educational Administration Policies, 1984-1994: A Case of New Zealand

—*Jo Howse**

INTRODUCTION

During the past six years, New Zealand has been subjected to the most radical and comprehensive reforms in its educational history. In the mid-1980s, a fiscal crisis, reflected in an increasing overseas debt and rising inflation, led to demands for accountability in all sectors of New Zealand society. New Zealand had become "one of the more highly indebted countries in the OECD" (*Government Management*, Volume 1, 1987, p. 229). The National government, under the leadership of Sir Robert Muldoon (1975-1984) with an escalating overseas debt, had "gradually lost credibility in its traditional power bases, the agricultural and corporate sectors, by being so interventionist and yet could not control the frightening growth of external debt" (Macpherson, 1993, p. 247). Its fiscal policy of subsidies and heavy state borrowing contrasted sharply with other OECD countries which privatised state assets and businesses. The National Minister of Education, the Honourable Merv Wellington, led an educational standards debate which focused

**President, CCEAM, and Head of Centre for Professional Education, Auckland Institute of Technology, New Zealand.*

on a presumed need for higher standards in teaching and learning, and a curriculum which required urgent revision to ensure the delivery of basic teaching subjects (Codd, 1990, p. 193).

Educational reform and equal opportunities for women, Maori, Pacific Island Groups and the working class (Gordon, 1990, p. 179) were major platforms in the manifesto of the fourth Labour government which came into power in July 1984. A Curriculum Review Committee was set up in November 1994 and included the wider community as part of the new government's consultative style. The Opposition Spokesperson on Education, Ruth Richardson, forcefully promoted the view that education should join the market economy. Local control, teacher accountability, decentralised financing, national standards of attainment and a voucher system were the suggested ways to achieve this (Snook L., 1990, p. 317). Notions of accountability, educational standards and teacher competence were emerging.

The *Treasury Report, Economic Management* (1984) was the blueprint for the radical economic reforms "that were to transform the New Zealand economy: deregulation of finance, floating the dollar, abolition of exchange controls, corporatisation, GST, reduced income tax, family care and so on" (Jesson, 1988, p. 43). The *Treasury Report* (1984) foreshadowed the radical changes to follow in education, by commenting on the failure of education to deliver the skills required in the reformed New Zealand labour market. "The poor performance of the education sector has adverse effects on the adjustment of the labour market directly and indirectly on the performance of the overall economy" (*Treasury*, 1984, p. 268). It went on to speak about the perceived capture of education by the middle class and expressed deep concern for equity. "For instance, there is suggestive evidence, at least, that the education system is poorly adapted to Maori and Pacific Island students and devotes too few resources to special educational needs" (*Treasury*, 1984, p. 249). The *Treasury* analysis strongly influenced the Lange government, as events in parliament accelerated public concern.

Changes in New Zealand society were occurring on all fronts and the average New Zealander was subjected to the rapid and sometimes traumatic economic measures as part of the reform process. From the late 1980s into the 1990s, redundancy and unemployment impacted directly on the lives of many New Zealanders. Downsizing occurred at middle and senior management levels while many large and well established companies went into receivership. Many adults were forced to retrain and to return study and this increased considerably the demand for polytechnics to provide short and long term academic and technical courses.

In August 1987, the Labour government was re-elected and Prime Minister Lange himself took on the education portfolio. He announced that educational reform would be high on the agenda. The dropping of the Honourable Marshall from the education portfolio was of concern to educators as they saw it as an attempt to reduce consultation, limit negotiation and to contain the influence of interested groups such as primary and secondary teacher unions.

PICOT REPORT (1988)

Taskforce to Review Education Administration was established in July 1987 and released on May 10, 1988. It was chaired by the successful supermarket entrepreneur, the Brian Picot, and the members were Peter Ramsay, Colin Wise, Whetumarama Wereta and Margaret Rosemergy. The terms of reference of the *taskforce* covered all sectors of educational universities. Picot was to report directly to the Ministers of Education, Finance and State Services. The terms of reference for the task force were to examine:

a) the functions of the head office of the Department of Education with a view to focusing them more sharply and delegating responsibilities as far as is practicable;

b) the work of polytechnic and community college councils, teachers college councils, secondary school boards and school committees with a view to increasing their powers and responsibilities.

c) the department's role in relation to other educational services;

d) changes in the territorial organisation of public education with reference to the future roles of education boards, other education authorities, and the regional offices of the Department of Education;

e) any other aspects that warrant review.

The taskforce will endeavour to ensure that the systems and structures proposed are flexible and responsive to changes in the educational needs of the community and the objectives of the government.

It will identify any costs and benefits of its recommendations and recommend the nature and timing of any necessary transitional arrangements.

> The taskforce is to make recommendations which will ensure the efficiency of any new system of education administration that might be proposed. (*Taskforce to Review Education Administration*, 1988, p ix).

The *Picot Taskforce* did not question or develop government policy on education and worked on the assumption that the state was to be the principal funder of formal education, that education was to remain compulsory for 6-15-year olds and that the provisions of the Treaty of Waitangi were to be observed (p. 3). A widespread concern detected was that the delivery of education was failing in many ways. The *taskforce* decided that creation of more choice in the system would ensure greater efficiency and equity, and that a cooperative partnership should develop between the community and the learning institution (p.4). The importance of cultural sensitivity was recognised, not only in relation to the Maori people under the obligations of the Treaty of Waitangi, but also for all cultures in New Zealand (p. 4).

The *Picot Report* was released on May 1988, in a television presentation to the public of New Zealand by Prime Minister David Lange and Brian Picot. The following concern with regard to the coordination of the polytechnic sector was raised:

> One of the more serious concerns raised with us is the large number of young people who leave school without any qualification and who are, all too frequently, thoroughly disenchanted with formal learning of any kind. We believe the secondary schools and the polytechnics have a major role to play in co-operating to ensure that this group of young people continue with their education and develop skills and abilities which will make them attractive to an increasingly discerning labour market (*Taskforce to Review Education Administration*, 1988, p. 72).

The release was timed to coincide with the beginning of school holidays. The decision to allow only seven weeks for public response was widely criticised. Three different documents for early childhood, primary and secondary, and tertiary education were then released to clarify implications by sector. (See Figure 1.1).

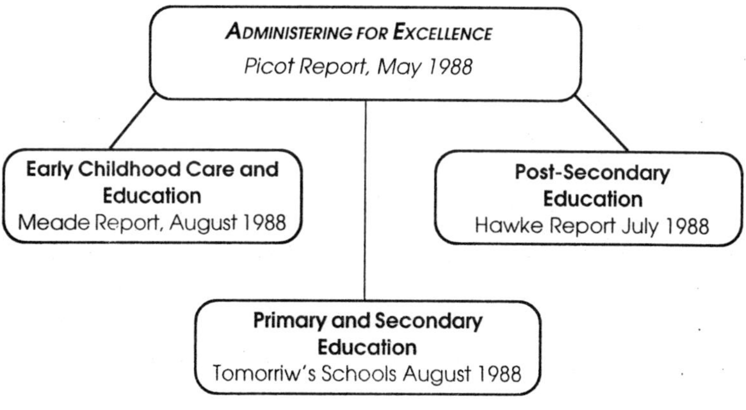

Figure 1.1: Review of New Zealand Educational Administration

All of these reports were 'green papers', that is, policy proposals. After a period of four months for largely symbolic consultation, the government issued a 'white paper' announcing its decisions, *Tomorrow's Schools*. The latter was written in the Prime Ministers office, without any significant research or consultation with the Department of Education or the primary and secondary teachers' unions. The government marginalised educators from policy and decision making at the national level while, according to Codd (1990, p. 201), the influence of Treasury and the State Services Commission (the government's agent in the public sector) increased considerably during the period of restructuring. The deconstruction of the old Education Department was marked by the establishment of the new Ministry of Education, the Education Review Office (ERO) and the New Zealand Qualification Authority (NZQA).

Other earlier reviews relating to polytechnic education and training were the *Probine Fargher Report, The Management, Funding and Organisation of Continuing Education and Training,* (March, 1987) and the *Tertiary Reviews*, *Report on Submissions to the Tertiary Review* (February, 1988). These reviews and others relating to universities, social policy, research and non-formal education were limited to specific areas. The government required a more comprehensive report to link the various reviews already completed to the Picot Report.

Professor Hawke was commissioned to clarify the implications of the *Picot Report* for the PCET sector. *The Report of the Working Group on Post-Compulsory Education and Training* (1988) was presented to Cabinet as a 'green paper.' The government's decisions on PCET were published in the white papers' *Learning for Life: One* (1988) and the revised version *Learning for Life: Two,* (1989). The revision occurred after the government consulted widely with people involved in PCET education.

Although the Labour government lost the election in 1991, the education reforms initiated by the fourth Labour government were sustained by the incoming National government. The *Todd Report* (1994) advised the new government on the funding of future growth in (PCET) education in the fight of the rapidly increasing student population. The sequence of reports in the PCET sector is set out in Figure 1.2 and then discussed in detail.

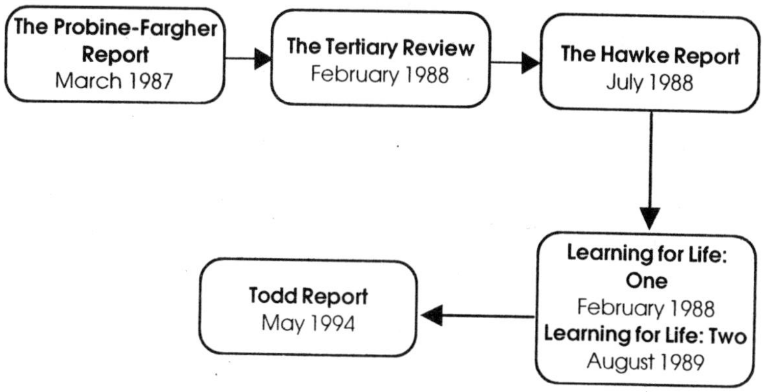

Figure 1.2: Reviews of tertiary education and training

PROBINE-FARGHER REPORT (1987)

The Probine-Fargher Report, The Management, Funding and Organisation of Continuing Education and Training (1987) took a wide view of continuing education and training addressing significant issues such as the :

a) The low participation rates in post-compulsory education
b) The inadequate supply of people with technological skills
c) The highly centralised and interventionist style of management
d) The constraints on an entrepreneurial approach to the delivery of services

e) The lack of coordination in the delivery of education services

f) The need to provide special help to the socially disadvantaged groups such as the young unemployed, Maori, women, aged, residents in rural areas, migrants, the physically and intellectually disabled and the socially isolated. (Probine and Fargher, 1987).

The Probine-Fargher Report identified the key role of the 22 technical institutes and community colleges in vocational studies and training as contributing to the economic growth and development of New Zealand.

> But the technical institute system also has another role, the promotion of education for personal enrichment; and, increasingly, the technical institute and community college sector is being used by the Government as an important instrument of national policy in relation to labour market adjustments, social equity issues of access and equal opportunity, and the transition of young people to adult life (Probine and Fargher, 1987, p. 1).

A major concern was the increasing number of young people who were leaving secondary schools not only disillusioned about education, and low in self-esteem but also without qualifications, jobs and access to education and training. This offered strong support to the claims of the Picot Report. Many young New Zealanders needed a second chance to be educated, and polytechnics were available and best able to provide this opportunity. Young people needed to upskill and train to give them access to an increasingly competitive job market and the chance for social advancement. *The Probine-Fargher Report* focused on a new 'education underclass' emerging and estimated that it constituted some 10 to 20 per cent of school leavers who left school early because they were disenchanted with the school system (p. 11). The Working Party acknowledged that 'equity' was being addressed with bicultural initiatives in technical institutes and community colleges.

Maori Liaison Tutors were being appointed, courses were being offered off campus on *maraes* and in consultation with the local people or *whanau* (p. 14). However, *The Probine-Fargher Report* (1987, p. 14) observed:

> many young Maori see the technical institutes and community colleges as an extension of that same secondary school system which they left harbouring a feeling of resentment and relief to be out of it all.

TERTIARY REVIEW (1988)

The comprehensive review of tertiary education continued with the circulation of two discussion documents by the Department of Education. These publications sought infor-mation and comment on issues of concern from both the general public and those organisations directly involved with tertiary education: *Further Education and Training: Who Should Pay?* (1987) and *Tertiary Education in New Zealand, Issues and Comment: Have Your Say* (1987).

A recurring theme in the *Tertiary Reviews* was the inequity in New Zealand society with limited access for minority groups such as women, Maori, and Pacific Islanders to tertiary education. A concern in several papers was the basic tertiary assistance grant of $41 per week compared to the access training allowance of $109 per week and the youth unemployment benefit of $100 per week. This marked discrepancy was considered anomalous, inequitable and a disincentive to higher education (pp. 20-22). It was recommended that the five-year entitlement to tertiary assistance grants be retained or increased (pp. 25-26). Many submissions strongly opposed the application of user-pays and/or student loans in tertiary education on the grounds of equity, except in specific circumstances (pp. 31). There was a majority view that education vouchers should be opposed on the grounds of equity and economic grounds (pp. 40) and strong support for income support for post-compulsory school students (pp. 38-39).

A shared theme of *the Probine-Fargher Report* (1986), *the Tertiary Review* (1988) and *the Picot Report* (1988) was to increase the participation of disadvantaged and minority groups in tertiary education. Link, foundation and bridging programmes, which provide access to the mainstream courses in tertiary education, were supported by all reports, and that polytechnics remain the main providers of these preliminary programmes. *The Tertiary Review* also recommended the reform of the Access programme (pp. 116-118).

The government now required consolidation on all the tertiary reviews completed in just over a year. This was the task assigned to the Post-compulsory Education and Training Group chaired by Professor Gary Hawke, Institute of Policy Studies, Victoria University.

HAWKE REPORT (1988)

> *Polytechnics:* provide a wide spectrum of vocational education and training from pre-employment to professional training and retraining, provide opportunities for personal enrichment as part of social development including some social and vocational research and criticism, and act as repositories of expertise and knowledge in those areas (*Hawke Report,* 1988, p. 15).

The policy reviews of tertiary education and training between 1987 and 1988 were summarised by the Post-compulsory Education and Training Group convened by Professor Hawke at the behest of the Lange government. The *Hawke Report* (1988) related these reports to *the Picot Report*, and set out to define the decisions required from government, and to recommend what those decisions should be (p. 3).

Equity, a recurrent theme in all the tertiary reviews summarised above, was also emphasised in *the Hawke Report*.

Polytechnics were expected to make PCET more accessible to disadvantaged groups. Minister Marshall (1986) indicated strongly that the Labour government wanted to see more Maori and Pacific Island people participating in regular full-time courses in institutes and greater participation of women in non-traditional areas of vocational education and training (pp. 88-89).

Equity issues, such as the participation of disadvantaged groups and equal employment opportunities, addressed in earlier reports, were to be monitored by the Review and Audit Agency in terms of an institution's charter provisions (p. 58). It was argued that this would help avoid unnecessary barriers to the progress of students to and through further education and training. It was also proposed that the Ministry of Education and Training would not approve charters of tertiary institutions unless they had adequate management systems to achieve objectives relating to the use of public funds and assets for the provision of education and training, as elaborated in the report. The principal responsibilities of councils were, it was recommended (p. 80), to appoint and reappoint chief executives and to review plans and processes to ensure that the assets and funds of the institutions were used to the best advantage in terms of statutory objectives and charters. *The Hawke Report* was received by the government, and after 24 months of consultations, released two white papers now reviewed: *Learning for Life: One* (1988) and the revision, *Learning for Life: Two* (1989).

LEARNING FOR LIFE: TWO (1989)

> A Polytechnic is characterised by continuing education including vocational training which contributes to the maintenance, advancement and dissemination of knowledge and expertise, and by research, particularly applied and technological research, which aids development (*Learning for Life: Two*, 1989, p. 16).

Learning for Life: *One* (1988) and the revision, *Learning for Life*: *Two* (1989) were the government's policy statements after two years of intensive reviews of post-compulsory education and training. They outlined the comprehensive changes to the organisation and delivery of post-compulsory education and training. The government made a decision to revise the original policy document, *Learning for Life*: *One,* (1988) months later with the revision, *Learning for Life*: *Two*, (1989) after wide consultation with the many groups of people involved in post-compulsory education. The changes were linked to those in Tomorrow's Schools which dealt with primary and secondary education. They also linked with the changes outlined in the *Meade Report* on early childhood care and education. PCET was defined as education and training beyond the age of 15 and the delivery remained split between the school and post-school sectors. The institutional administrative reforms in *Learning for Life*: *Two* (1989) applied only to post-compulsory institutions, referred to as post-school institutions, such as the present universities, colleges of education and polytechnics. The reforms were based on the following principal features (*Learning for Life: Two*, 1989, p. 8):

a) Institutions were given independence and freedom to make operational and management decisions
b) The Ministry of Education was to be set up as a policy ministry to provide comprehensive policy advice on education and training and would not be an operational department.
c) There would be a new mechanism for government funding based on a common formula and a new approach to achieve funding.
d) There would be changes in the funding of research and scholarship from that of teaching.
e) A National Education Qualifications Authority (NEQA) would be set up to provide a comprehensive and integrated approach to the validation of qualifications in schools and in vocational and advanced academic areas.

f) To encourage greater participation in post-school education and training for under-represented groups.

g) To actively encourage excellence and to maximise the educational potential of all members of the population. (*Learning for Life* : Two, 1989, p. 8)

Equity was acknowledged (p. 13) by reference on the importance of PCET providing a pathway for Maori to achieve social and economic potential. Full participation by Maori in the spirit of the Treaty of Waitangi was declared (p.13) to be an important objective of post-compulsory education and training, yet no new programmes were proposed.

To summarise this section, between 1987 and 1989, the Labour government completed extensive reviews of tertiary education. Over the same period, the enrolment of students increased in polytechnics and universities while there was a decline in colleges of education. The rapid expansion of polytechnics and the funding implications of this escalating tertiary student population became a major concern of the National government.

TODD REPORT (1994)

A Ministerial Consultative Group (MCG) chaired by Jeff Todd, a senior partner of Price Waterhouse Ltd., reported on the *Funding Growth in Tertiary Education and Training Report of the Ministerial Consultative Group* (MCG) (1994) (termed the *Todd Report*). It identified the key issue as the sharing of the total costs of formal tertiary education and training between students, and trainees and the government (p. 25). A wide range of organisations were invited to submit their views on relevant issues while other submissions were a response to the discussion paper on funding growth in tertiary education. The MCG consulted with interested parties from tertiary education and training sectors, inclusive of students, Maori and Pacific Island representatives (p. 8). The submissions reflected the broad and common vision New Zealanders had of the role of education in their society. Two options emerged for the future funding of tertiary education.

> Option A reflects viewpoints that, as a result of recent education changes, considerable progress has been made in expanding tertiary education and training with previously unparalleled increases in participation, and that the existing funding arrangements are sound. It proposes that a combination of measures, including marginal increases in private contributions and changes to increase the diversity of education and training opportunities should be sufficient to provide for projected increases in participation.
>
> Option B is based on a view that under-representation in tertiary education by Maori and low income people should be addressed quickly. Increased targeted assistance funded through higher private contributions by those students who can comfortably afford to do so by reference to their lifetime earnings is proposed. Efficient and effective outcomes are best ensured by empowering student purchasers and promoting competition between providers (Todd Report, 1994, p. 22).

The *Todd Report* recognised the government's five-year cycle, and that it had successfully implemented most of the reforms recommended in the *Probine-Fargher Report* (1986), the *Tertiary Reviews* (1987) and the *Hawke Report* (1988). The educational reforms had changed the patterns in enrolments in post-compulsory education, especially of mature-aged students and groups previously under-represented, most notably women, and Maori and Pacific Island Groups (*Todd Report*, 1994, p. 1878) as shown in Tables 2.1, 2.2 and 2.3.

The *Education Amendment Act* (1990) provided tertiary institutions (25 polytechnics, seven universities, two wananga and five colleges of education) with greater responsibility for educational administration. The Act declared (1990, p. 31) that it was the intention of parliament that academic freedom and autonomy of institutions were to be preserved and enhanced.

> as much independence and freedom to make academic, operational and management decisions as is consistent with the nature of the services they provide, the efficient use of national resources, the national interest, and the demands of accountability.

Table 1.1: Percentages of women in tertiary education programmes

	1973	*1983*	*1993*
College of Education	71.3	80.9	80.5
Polytechnic	N/A	34.7	49.8
University	35.9	48.0	52.5
Total	N/A	45.3	52.8

Table 1.2: Percentages of Maori in tertiary education programmes

	1991	*1993*
Colleges of Education	17.2	10.3
Polytechnic	7.8	10.9
University	6.7	8.4
Total	7.6	9.6

Table 1.3: Percentages of New Zealand Pacific Islands students in tertiary education programmes

	1991	*1993*
College of Education	4.5	3.4
Polytechnic	2.3	2.9
University	1.8	2.3
Total	2.1	2.6

The *Todd Report* examined the central policy dilemma; the challenge to fund the increased growth in tertiary education in a sustainable manner. Difficult choices had to be made between either an increased government contribution or an increased private contribution (p. 15).

The fourth Labour government during two terms (1984, 1987) released two extensive reviews of post-compulsory education in the *Probine-Fargher Report* (March, 1987) and the *Tertiary Review* (February, 1988). These two reports were linked closely to the *Picot Report* (1988) and consolidated by Hawke (1988). The *Hawke Report* consulted widely post-compulsory education interest groups and this consultative process was reflected in the revision of the original policy statements *Learning for Life: One* (1988) as *Learning for Life: Two* (1989).

2

Education—The Global Challenge: Issues of Professionalism in Community Centres in New Zealand

*—Greg Whitecliffe**

INTRODUCTION

The transitions of cultural change become evident to us when expressions appear in public venues and auditoriums, visual media or are promulgated in print media. Sometimes the *avante garde* expressions shock and repel us; sometimes they become instantly fashionable and successfully commercial for the creators. Less understood by the public is where such transitions of culture emerge in the first instance, where they are honed, refined or developed through experiment. Most think artists, designers and inventors just spring their creations upon the public and market fully formed, packaged and developed. In some instances this is true, particularly for seasoned professionals and accomplished specialists. Equally so is the reality that many inspired developments never get past the drawing board or the creators' imaginations. Some developments are trailed in less broadly appreciated settings; sometimes they succeed, sometimes they fail. Sometimes in less sophisticated settings such ventures nevertheless add to or

**Fellow, Royal Society of Arts, New Zealand.*

influence further initiatives in the fields and contribute to the cumulative transition of cultural change.

My preliminary doctoral research has been in the nature and role of Community Art Centres in New Zealand and the issues of professionalism; these centres of community activity are proving to be 'first base' settings where new inspired, developing and rekindled cultural expressions are emerging. The activities of community groups, their education programmes, exhibitions and cultural events seldom make the headlines, seldom feature in the emergence of new cultural change, yet they are considered by some as one of the bridgeheads of such change. Those in administration of such community centres, their roles and responsibilities are extraordinary if not surreal when one considers the place they have in the development of culture.

The issues as questions I want to examine in this paper are:

1) What constitutes a 'community centre', how may they be defined for New Zealand in particular, and to a degree in other societies?
2) What activities, particularly in education, evident in such Community Centres, are important to observe and understand?
3) What challenges face these administrators and managers of community centres, particularly in the changing technological environment?
4) What is the place of community centres in the wider global change of education?

Along the way, I hope to pose some of the obvious outcomes and/or solutions to these issues/questions. Although my research focuses primarily on the issues of professionalism and the role of managers, their roles are bound up in the realities and dynamics of cultural change. This paper is thus a precis as a discussion of some of the issues that are yet to be examined in more detailed research over the next year or two. I have deliberately eliminated specific references, quantitative findings and quotations, to focus more specifically on the key issues as a discussion paper.

The Community Centre

In New Zealand, there are an estimated 500 community centres. They occupy a special place in societal groups, often the centre of local activities. The town hall of previous years has re-emerged with a new focus. Even the antiquated RSA (Returned Services Association) Halls are taking on new appearances. In New Zealand, marae (Maori village centres) and the meeting houses have an increasing role in formal education programmes, rather than just repositories of cultural heritage.

Thus the concept of a community centre, is different and under constant change. Preliminary research indicates this phenomenon is replicated in many developed countries. In the United Kingdom, United States, Canada, Australia and a number of Scandinavian and European countries, the value and importance of community centres has been recognised, and local or central (federal) funding has been augmented to support the activities. In New Zealand, some scattered examples of such support does emerge, bu as yet the value has not been well understood to promote any cohesive policy (or national policy).

The fact that community centres are defined in so many ways—community centres, art centres, museum halls, cultural centres, maraes, town halls, church halls, society halls, school halls (primary or secondary), memorial halls etc.,—leads to considerable confusion as to their implicit or explicit roles in a defined societal group. Some are identified specifically as to the activities or groups associated. For example, ethnic groups may 'brand' a centre, and religious groups may determine similar branding. Nevertheless the activities in contemporary times are increasingly geared to inclusive engagements rather than exclusive clustering. For example, church halls are being used for prenatal education, kung fu instruction and stage acting for television as well as prayer groups and choir practices. The multifaceted activities have been driven mainly by financial needs of the centres to cover overheads, but more often than not by the desire of community groups to utilise the available space that is less expensive than professionally equipped and managed venues. This dichotomy of financial imperatives is an issue that emerges often in the management; increasingly a challenge for the quasi-professionals in charge of management.

In New Zealand small towns and provincial centres have these halls as venues for all levels of society, from school groups for pantomime productions, retired citizens for housie on Wednesday nights, indoor bowls for leisure sports, night school for nationally funded education programmes and still serve as civil defence headquarters and gathering places for town meetings, young farmers, playgroups, etc. Many have small museum collections as part of the local history. In the larger provincial cities and the main urban centres, community Centres occupy niches within suburbs, within retail centres or in association with sporting fields and complexes.

Immigrant groups find homes in community centres to rekindle or retain their cultural heritage. Folk art classes, language nests and ethnic events are commonplace, usually without formal structures (i.e., accreditation or benchmarking). To preserve their culture, immigrant groups typically work in shared schedules at such centres. Church halls are the most typical, where separate religious seminars give way to segregated cultural activities in after hours.

Community arts centres have emerged as increasingly more sophisticated centres where exhibitions, performances, events and education programmes are developing with new benchmarks of societal value. Community arts centres have the greatest profile of all community centres, with the greatest involvement in educational programmes. The New Zealand

Qualifications Authority (NZQA) has registered a vast number of such centres as centres where approved and accredited (and funded) programmes can occur and citizens can obtain recognised qualifications. Art centres are forming a significant role in New Zealand's cultural development, particularly with the benchmarking in the last 10 years. With the sophistication of displays, performances and education programmes, art centres move from the periphery of offerings to more mainstream. Nevertheless the recognition of these centres and the collation of statistical information and database management is absent. *Creative New Zealand*, the government-funded body for the arts, has no registers, lists or contact details for any community centres in New Zealand. There is a complete lack of understanding or interest in the places they have in cultural development, despite the fact that government recognition by the NZQA and the Ministry of Education is taking place.

Community arts centres are often the place where experimental art forms and new emerging artists first display/perform their work. Pubic recognition is at its best scattered, but evidence suggests a growing appreciation of the place of such public showings in the broader picture of contemporary arts.

Community centres are growing as places for groups to visit, this is the position gathered in exploratory research. The programmes of activities are becoming more numerous and increasingly sophisticated. The perceived budgets are growing (albeit mainly localised). Publicity attached to events and activities is evident. For example, over the last six years the number of newspaper clippings of articles focused on 'arts activities' in community centres has grown by 48 per cent.

Despite all this the relative anonymity of community centres nationally is clear, particularly the lack of centralised account of community centres or their activities. The connections between informal and formal education programmes as part of a national scheme of community-based educational activities is also missing. New Zealand's cultural decision-makers are engaged in the quest right now to define cultural management imperatives, develop policies to determine the value of the arts in society. Yet the mention or recognition of this vital source as one bridgehead of cultural development is not part of their consciousness.

Educational Activities

Graduates in the arts who are interested in education pursue teaching qualifications as the next step. However, a fair percentage of those interested in education prefer adult education. The difficulties they face in getting that first position in the tertiary field are obvious, the primary one being lack of teaching experience in their discipline. Adult education teaching qualifications are just emerging in New Zealand, with a handful of postgraduate degrees and numerous short course night school certificate programmes.

Young graduates find community arts centres (and indeed all community centres) are places where they can 'cut their teeth', develop personalised pedagogical practices and hone their methodology. It often suits the community centres as well; young untried teachers have less remunerative expectations and the centre managers are able to finance education programmes accordingly.

The central issue here is a balance between enthusiastic semi-professional artisans and the amateur untrained or untried teachers. A balance is also between economically viable offerings versus the risk of substandard delivery and product for the consumer. The price of programmes is a gauge of level and expectations to some degree. Community centre-based education programmes are invariably up to a third less in cost than the comparable programmes offered in polytechnics, private accredited specialised colleges (PTE's—Private Training Establishments) and university Community-based programmes. Location has a lot to do with choice, as community centres are conveniently placed for its client base. However, choice by cost is often a primary motivation for people making the first step in second chance learning or extra mural interest learning.

Education programmes offered at community centres vary considerably. As already mentioned they range between informal and formal (NZQA accredited). Options are immense and vary throughout the country. These community centres sometimes devise programmes around the unit standards framework (specific benchmarked NZQA unit standards). These learning units are designed to be portable units and readily transferable. These option plus *link* modules (portable learning units between secondary and tertiary) are on the increase outside formal educational institutions (polytechnics, universities, colleges of education, wananga and private institutions). Exploratory research findings to date indicate around 10 per cent of community centres are offering formal (NZQA accredited) education programmes. Most others offer some form of informal programmes.

First step learning units are offered less and less by state institutions as PTE's occupy that niche in post-secondary education. It is relevant to add here that community centres become registered as PTE's, despite the fact that they undertake many activities that are not strictly educational. Educational programmes occur mainly as night schools and occasionally receive other forms of funding from local and government agencies, e.g., Work and Income New Zealand.

What is important in all this is the relative absence of understanding of the critical role community centres play in the provision of formal and informal education. No major research or account has been made of the impact of education offered in these settings. No separate register exists, no thorough analysis of the relative success or failure of programmes for users and no real value is placed on the community benefits either.

Administrators

Community centres have always operated within the New

Zealand context on the margins of communities. Until recent times they were informal gathering halls for bazaars, fairs, town meetings and occasional public activities. Most smaller communities have developed beyond the incorporated committee-based volunteer organisations to have administrators providing an organisational management of growing activities within the community. The level of commitment of these administrators vary considerably, from part-time volunteers (unpaid) to full-time paid employees of controlling authorities: societies, town councils or foundations. Salary bases, from preliminary research, suggests modest incomes (less than $30,000 pa) but multiple duties as part of the job descriptions. Most administrators answer to volunteer committees or councils, and operate tight and perpetually marginal budgets. Yet through all this there is a perception, at least, that community pride is drawing an increasingly sophisticated range of expectations on the administrators. Often these administrators are alone, operating with little help. This is forcing these quasi-professionals to seek critical upskilling to keep ahead of expectations. Their stewardship of the cultural development (retention and/or presentation) is being taken seriously by all stakeholders in the community. Websites for community centres are springing up across the country. Administrators are enrolling in management courses part time and they appear regularly at *travelling seminars* on sponsorship, fund-raising and educational management forums. Communication by e-mail and in-house computer-based productions of newsletters are common features today.

Since a small number of community centres operate government EFTS (Effective Full Time Student) funded tertiary programmes, accountability for government finance (under the Government Finance Act) and quality assurance management practices are encouraging more rigorous reporting. This appears to be spilling over to those community centres which operate outside formal systems. Administrators are caught up in this process and gone are the days of amateurs administering loosely fronted programmes. Commercial practices, from the

Consumer Guarantees Act, the Fair Trading practices and the Copyright Act have direct impact on the operations of these centres, and the working approach and responsibilities of the administrator, regardless of the formality of educational programmes.

The complete machination of new demands is at odds with the poor remunerative rewards for administrators. The degree of professionalism of these individuals is subject to greater scrutiny, not only by the communities they serve, but also the bureaucracies that they are accountable to. Issues of professsionalism emerge as accountability of public (local) resources come under scrutiny. These administrators without appropriate training or tertiary credentials are being passed over for those with credentials and track record of administrative activities for communities.

The challenges are formidable; however, evidences to date suggest that the occupations are treasured greatly. Working alongside the community is one part and being a respected member of the community is another aspect that makes up the many intrinsic rewards that appear to substitute for the modest material rewards. One administrator commented to me recently that her community regularly filled her larder with fruit, vegetables and a side of lamb which seemed to compensate for the pittance she received for working upwards of 60 hours a week at the community centre.

The Place in Wider Global Challenge of Education

Community centres are the testing grounds for new initiatives in education, and regularly offered pilot programmes in a plethora of domains. From the weird and wacky to the mainstream, education programmes at community centres provide the educators and students with a chance to try new things at a minimal investment, without complex enrolment/ registration aspects, and yet, given the degree of accreditation sometimes now available, still add those experiences as part of the record of learning for an individual. As community centres around the world take on an increasingly formal role in providing 'second chance' community-based education (or *enabling* education) their role as crucibles of development will become more and more obvious. In New Zealand, at least, there is a growing appreciation of their role and contribution. It is hoped in New Zealand that policies, centralised funding and greater recognition will follow.

As testing grounds, the extremes of educational offerings also engender considerable experimentation in delivery focus. Evidences suggest that this aspect is the most exciting element that spills over into formal educational institutes as individual teachers move into state-funded institutions and others following their experiences at community centres. Creative programmes utilising low-level resources and self-help systems provide an innovative environment to test the resourcefulness of these new educators. That in itself is a productive moulding that engenders positive outcomes for the community and wider educational practice.

Since the economic imperatives are so critical education in community centres takes on differing expectations of both educators and students. Without the broader subsidised structures, programmes live and die by their popularity or otherwise. Funding has a way of subverting this realism and community centre programmes running at the margins have to be viable. Popular programmes that run successfully at community centres end up fairly soon being offered in public institutions (state-funded). The reverse is not always the case. Uneconomic programmes at state-funded institutes often continue well beyond economic viability measurements, being cross subsidised between the other more successful programmes. The challenge is to recognise that community centres provide the bridgehead to economically successful programmes, driven by the fashion interest and public consciousness (i.e., clear demand factors).

Administrators of cultural development in the broader realm of cultural heritage gather their experiences in a variety of settings. Formal education for arts administrators is not common. Community centres are settings where such training and experiences happen. The development of professional skills, albeit piecemeal, can occur in these settings. The challenge for the global community is to recognise that this is the case, and that the place of administrators in community centres should be brought in from the periphery to the centre. Professionalism of the administrators need to be understood and they, being the administrators and controlling authorities, need to properly illustrate their value to the community they serve, to advise central governments that their value to society warrants the inclusion in the understanding of cultural development. Professionalism is needed from the legislators and policy makers to incorporate community centres in the make-up of resource allocations. The controlling authorities should also be professional enough to value the organisations that are in their midst and work to identify their central place in the culture of that community.

Conclusion

Community centres occupy a special niche in New Zealand society. Their activities and their contribution to the development of culture is unmapped and poorly understood. Within the vast variety of community centres, community arts centres are the bridgehead for the development of the arts-related education programmes. Understanding the nature of all types of community centres, their variable functions and roles is difficult. How they are managed, how they fit into the daily life of a community is equally complex. However globally, community centres have a place in the development of the communities. The links between their funding, the activities and the development of culture are being understood. In New Zealand, there is some ground to make up in this understanding. The value of community centres will become more of an issue as groups within society seek to enhance, retain and share their unique characters. Cultural identity, cultural heritage and cultural differences are emergent paradigms.

As all this happens community centres are coming of age, the antiquated recreational halls are being gilded by sophisticated technology, wired on line and networked to the national shoal of activities. Administrators at the helm of these, at times, fragile entities, face some awesome tasks in bringing communities into the cyber community. Despite considerable disadvantages and poorly remunerated careers the administrators value their place in the enterprise development. With growing anticipation new professionalism will emerge, a result of the quest for both administrators and communities to bring focus to their own values and the cultural treasures they manage, where uniqueness and individuality are prized above replicated sameness.

As the eyeglass comes on community centres in the 21st century the view will be more comprehensive than in any previous age.

REFERENCES

Braden, S., (1998), *Artists and People,* London: Routledge and Kegan Paul.

Burnham, Linda and Durland, Steven, (1998), *The Citizen Artist,* NY: Critical Press.

Carr, D. et al., (1985), *Local Recreation and Community Development Scheme: an Analysis of the Distribution of Funds by Local Authorities,* 1982/3 *and* 1988/84, Wellington: Department of Internal Affairs.

Cummings Milton, C., and Katz, Richard, (1987), *The Patron State Government and the Arts in Europe, North America and Japan,* London: Oxford University Press.

Di Maggio, Paul. J., (1986), *Non-Profit Enterprises in the Arts,* NY: Oxford University Press.

Karp, I., Kreafer, C. & Lavine, S., (1992), *Museums and Communities—The Politics of Public Culture,* Washington, USA: Smithsonian Institute Press.

Klamer, Arjon, (1996), *The Value of Culture—on the Relationships between Economics and Arts,* Amsterdam: Amsterdam University Press.

Ministry of Cultural Affairs, (1995), *New Zealand Cultural Statistics 1995*, Wellington: Ministry of Cultural Affairs.

Mitchell, W.J.T., (1992), *Art and the Public Sphere, USA:* University of Chicago.

Rowen, Arlene, (1993), *Art in the Public Interest,* NY: Da Capo Press.

3

Indian Education: Priorities in the New Millennium

*—Hemlata Talesra**

We have just stepped into the threshold of the new century—and the new millennium faces the great challenge of adapting education to the changing needs of the society. With the scientific and technological advancement taking place in leaps and bounds, change is inevitable in all walks of life. In today's competitive world, varied sources of information are trying to educate the future generation on a wide spectrum of knowledge. Today, the transmission of information and explosion of knowledge is very fast and it is very urgent to take immediate steps to make the education more useful and relevant.

Kofi Annan, UN Secretary General, highlighted the priorities of education for the new century in his message to National Commission on Human Rights on the occasion of Human Rights Day, December 10, 1999: "As we cross into the new century, let us all do our part to advance understanding and defeat racism of embracing diversity, by teaching tolerance and by treating every human being with the dignity he or she desires. It only requires humanity to live up to its name".

In order to fulfil the requirements of the new millennium successfully all nations must determine the extent to which

**Secretary General, RCEAM, Professor and Head, Deptt. of Edu. Planning, Management and Administration, Vidya Bhawan G.S. IASE, Udaipur.*

their educational systems are preparing the next generation for successful participation in the existing enterprise. For this it is essential to understand the requirements, possibilities and problems of a country, and prepare an alternative plan based on the challenges of the new millennium.

The Kothari Commission (1963-66) visualised a society which was free from superstition, fatalism and passive resignation in the next millennium. The Commission wanted a scientific outlook to become part of our way of life and culture. For this it emphasised the need for educational reconstruction. An educational revolution is needed for this purpose. Digital age transforms all walks of life with new information revolution and changes our way of work, to learn, think, communicate our choices and decisions.

The following priorities may be suggested in Indian education to fulfil the requirements of the new millennium:

Education should Represent Growth

The new millennium represents growth in the area of technology and human development. The paradigm will be shifted to advanced technology information society, industrial society, long-term planning, creative learning and decentralisation from traditional educational system.

Skill-based Learning

For the new era skill-based learning should be emphasised. Learning should be based on hardware and software. There will be global thinking in education. The teacher should be fully acquainted with the different teaching skills and they can use them successfully in the classrooms.

Continuous Improvement

In the education process continuous improvement should be achieved through different methods of learning theory and practical aspects should be interlinked and enriched by experiments and innovations. Time to time a systematic evaluation should be done to know the achievements of students, institutions and teachers. Improvement should be based on the totality of education.

The notion of life-long education should be examined. The focus should be on the quality of education, and fulfilling the needs of the learners.

Inculcation of Values

To make education more meaningful, inculcation of values through education has to be stressed upon for school children in most formative and sensitive period in their life. Hence, it is the most appropriate time for the inculcation of values in life which will enable the child to have a proper direction (*disha*) in life. An analysis of the four most desirable goals in human life, according to the basic Indian philosophy (*dharma, artha, kama* and *moksha*) would practically encompass (economic self-reliance) all the values that have been identified in different parts of the world, following different approaches. The growth of a developed millennium society is simultaneously linked to the evaluation of acceptance and adherence to values in human life. Education is one of the most significant vehicles to achieve this synchronisation. The significance and importance of the teachers' role in inculcating values among their pupils are understood and well appreciated. The teachers on their part need to realise the immense potentialities of various interactions that take place in the classrooms and outside and exploit these in developing and inculcating such values as would form the foundation of a democratic, secular and integrated nation. In addition to this, the teachers by serving as role models in terms of their own scholarship, creativity, behaviour and personal qualities like love, honesty, integrity of character, etc., may inculcate values without having to expend any extra or conscious efforts. Despite the best of intentions, policies and decisions, value education is lacking in the education systems of today in the developed nations and even more so in the developing countries, and this is the urgent need for new millennium.

Raising Efficiency

The administrative system in education is virtually on the collapse. Unless new alternative delivery systems are devised all stages of education in the country will continue to suffer tremendously; its quality will remain and it will not be in a position to meet the emerging challenges of the twenty-first century.

Community Involvement

The local community can effectively discharge its role and functions in educational management at every stage. Community involvement in the decentralised management of school education throws light on the problems involved in policy and implementation. Assigning powers and functions to the community must necessarily be based on the abilities, motivation and track record. As suggested by the Education Commission and National Policy school committees at the village level can help in more effective running of school education.

Utilising All Resources

One recent notable demand has been the advocacy of quality improvement in schools by utilising all resources of a school to foster the development of all its children. The principles of sharing, joint exploration, networking, collaboration and continuity, together with progress, should be reflected in the overall management of the school. However, the reality is that the reform in Indian education for quality improvement is still a distant goal. There are numerous barriers in reforming schools which incorporate new demands and changes. It is, therefore, crucial to identify and examine the obstacles in the new millennium, so that an appropriate methodology and strategies can be developed that are not only theoretically sound but practically viable in managing change effectively in the education system of the country.

Balance of Control and Change

Lack of balance of control in practically all the educational institutions needs to be clear in relation to control of resources, role and functions of various participating members, centralisation vs decentralisation, financial autonomy of various departments, roles/functions, time schedule as related to roles, duties and responsibilities networking between departments and existing structures, communication and feedback, monitoring and evaluation. Work task requires a confident, well-trained staff, prior planning and staff preparation. For the new millennium, the following should be the priorities:

1. Quality improvement
2. Sustained commitment
3. Building of structures and capabilities
4. Identification of required linkages
5. Availability of needed resources
6. Actual implementation
7. Developing community role in planning, implementation, assessment and monitoring/evaluation of desired changes.

Continuity in Education Changes

Systematic change requires continuity in the programme, strategies and outcomes of the institution. Some important points should be kept in mind for systematic change:

1. Strengths and weaknesses of the institution
2. Vision in core values for betterment

3. Priorities, goals and strategies for change
4. Structure and need of the institution to reach the identified goals.
5. The new skills and resources required to attain the desired changes.

Recognising the need for effective change and the difficulty in doing so-called for the identification of exposition of barriers inhibiting effective changes based on qualitative research data. This in turn facilitated the development of a suitable methodology for the successful implementation of change.

Priority to Improvement—Different Components of Education

The education system consists of the components of curriculum and syllabus, textbooks and learning materials, physical facilities, principals, teachers, non-teaching staff, parents and students. The following knowledge are considered as inputs, the physical facilities and learning material is used through well-designed instructional process and the changes in behaviour of the students are measured and these students become output at the end. In this process of providing education, teachers and principals/administrators are very important.

Multi-pronged Approach

Education in the new millennium should be dynamic; and dynamic education needs an administrative system. This requires following multi-pronged approach including *inter alia*:

1) Decentralisation of administration and greater involvement of community,
2) Networking of institution,
3) Modernising inspection and supervision system,
4) Autonomy and accountability,
5) Performance-oriented management,

6) Strong management information system,
7) Greater private initiative, and
8) Raising competencies in educational administration.

Non-formal System

Taking into consideration the experience of the government system and experiments of non-government forums, the non-formal system of education emerged as an alternative to formal schooling. The concept of non-formal system evolved from the manipulation/modifications of some of the features of school education resulting in redefining the clientele group, the site, the objective, the curriculum, etc.

Non-formal system of education did not try to develop an existence independent of the formal schooling, it is complementary parallel to formal schooling. In the new millennium this system will cater to the educational needs of those children who fail to benefit from the full-time schooling facilities specially at the primary level.

Increased Government Funding and Support to Private Educational Institutions

Recent years have brought a global upsurge of interest in privatisation. The interest has been evident in all sectors of the economy and society, including education. Privatisation has been widely advocated as a mechanism to improve efficiency, cater to pluralistic preferences, make institutions more accountable and reduce government expenditure.

In Tanzania a big part of government resources is devoted to education, especially primary level on the grounds that it is important to achieve universal literacy and minimise social inequalities.

In China private schools have emerged as part of marketisation. On the basis of researches it in found that private schools are more efficient then government schools.

They are more personal and respond to consumer wishes as well as being more careful about how to spend the funds. In the new millennium these effectively-run privately institutions are giving better achievements of the students.

Stress should be given on Primary Education

In the new millennium, India will overcome the problems of universalisation of primary education, and the most important programme to be implemented in the new millennium is to improve the quality of primary education and to reduce stagnation and wastage to the minimum. To achieve this, a number of steps ought to be taken. The schools must be provided professionally qualified teachers and better equipments. The methods of teaching should conform to the psychological requirements of the students. Their parents should be educated in rural area regarding the importance of education. In the new millennium India requires better primary education that will bring the other desirable things within the easy reach of the Indians.

Abolition of Illiteracy

One of the biggest challenges still faced by our country is illiteracy. A lot has been achieved in this front; while Kerala has almost 100 per cent literacy, quite a few states have 80 per cent literacy rate. Still a lot needs to done by the people of India and we should take the help of technology in achieving 100 per cent literacy rate.

Education System should be Revised

In spite of a huge network of formal, non-formal, open and distance education system in India, a large proportion of the population is illiterate. It is a well established fact that because of rigid rules and regulations of school admissions many children cannot enter the school. If they enter, either they soon drop out of the school due to household duties and other reasons.

The present school curriculum has failed to attract the children and parents for schooling as well as continue their interest for schooling for a longer period because the school has been proved to be a place for punishment as a prison and hospital where inmates have no choice. The examination system has lost its credibility, accountability, reliability and validity among the people because of malpractices and corruption. Therefore, the whole education system of India should be revised and based on the need and culture of the Indians.

The Commonwealth Foundation's report, *Citizens and Governance: Civil Society in the New Millennium* (September 1999) is an important initiative to provide a new thinking about the education of the new millennium. This report is based upon the answers of thousands of citizens from 47 Commonwealth countries to the following questions:

1. What is your view of a 'good' society? To what extent does such a society exist today?
2. What roles are best played by citizens and what roles are best played by the state and other sectors in such a good society?
3. What would enable citizens to play their role in the development of society more effectively in the future?

Behind these three questions lies a central issue—what kind of society do citizens wants the future generations to live in? This involves the need and type of education for those pupil who will form good society. The dream of a good society includes the active roles of citizens.

In undertaking the journey into the next millennium, they may feel disillusioned and disappointed about the present but not hopeless or helpless about the future. While many citizens are not able to comprehend or conceptualise their roles in the big pictures they know they want to play their part, whatever it is. And some at least have the confidence and commitment that comes from already being engaged in small scale and local action. Others are motivated by the selfishness, individualism and 'uncivil' citizen action they see going on around them. In the next millennium, education should develop the commitment, confidence and responsibilities in the future citizens, who are studying in schools.

The realisation of a good society requires mutual and complementary actions by governments and citizens alike. This is the outline of a new consensus for the next millennium which has three key features:

1) A strong state and strong civil society
2) A deepened democracy and democratic cultures
3) An enlarged role for citizens.

In the new era education has the responsibility to adopt the above consensus on a priority basis. Through education we should develop a strong civil society where citizens:

1) are aware and informed
2) understand their rights and responsibilities
3) behave as active citizens in the family and community
4) show solidarity, generosity and mutual support towards fellow citizens
5) participate in local associations and organisations to work on a common public agenda
6) demonstrate assertive, caring and ethical leadership
7) are enabled and encouraged to engage and connect with public institutions, officials and leaders of public concerns
8) are not passive, apathetic or self-centred.

Citizens who know their rights and obligations through education play a very important role in the country and contribute their talents, energies and resources to develop the society.

4

Quality of Teaching and Preparation Time in Schools: Some Perspectives and Rationale

*—Chandralekha Rawat**

INTRODUCTION

Whatever might be called about the teachers and their teaching, as though they are synonymous, only a handful of people would disagree that the work pattern and workload both have changed extremely over the period of a decade. Certainly, teaching is no more viewed what it used to be. New subjects are continuously being added, curriculum programmes, and syllabi are constantly changing. As innovations in other fields multiply, demands and pressures on teachers increase. Teachers' job responsibilities have become more extensive. Ask teachers and they say their roles are not clearly defined. For those who are bothered they are less sure if they are getting better or worse. For others it makes little difference because they believe in their old rudimentary systems. Under such emerging realities where those who want to change are not skilled and where teachers don't want to change what is required is:

**Principal, Cambridge Court High School, Fellow, University of Cambridge, UK.*

> professionalisation and intensification . . . because teaching has become a more complex and more skilled job.
>
> *Andy Hargreaves (1994)*

But, Marxist theories would portray teachers' job as more routinised and de-skilled as they are not trusted to exercise their expertise of discretionary judgement in classroom. Still teachers are more and more controlled by set programmes to teach mandated books and curricula and piecemeal approach of instruction. Under this view, it is expected of teachers to change with the changing times. As one of the English teachers in Cambridge Court High School says:

> I am always being told by my principal about my job responsibilities. I have to know where my students are and what they're doing. I have to programme for all different abilities in my classroom It's not a simple matter of saying, "Today, I am going to read a story on pg. 26!" What my job demands is? Who can read this story and what am I going to do with the kids who can't? And how do I go about getting these students to answer in complete sentences at that age group, while I am getting this child who's sitting in my class and can only read of class one level? And also about what am I going to give this person to read, because I have to be there to read with her, but I also have to be there to help gifted or the weakest lot of students?

In the light of this statement and discussion held with other teachers it can be said that the changing composition of teachers' classes over the years then has had implications not only for discipline and stress but for the complexity of programming and preparation too. In the same context another set of teachers comments:

> If it was just about the teaching it is alright. But we . . . are accountable to parents and the principal in this school for everything . . . like curriculum, assessment, examination, child psychology, . . . if anyone gets hurt in the class and out on the field, it's teacher's responsibility . . . and its many more responsibilities.

Hence, accountability to parents and administrators increased the sense of pressure for a number of teachers. Accountability, in private schools in India as in other countries, has also brought a lot of form filling and paperwork. Also, more accounting for what is being done, has been done, and is intended to be done, for the benefit of parents, administrators students and community is continuously demanded.

These rising demands on and expectations of teachers certainly amount to strong support, training and culture within which they work, and attitudinal change on the part of the administrators and they themselves. When further nudged about their job one of the few relatively old teachers says:

> . . .I am 54 now. I have got 25 years of experience of teaching. But never in my life have I done so much of paperwork as in the last 10-12 years. Half of my time I spend in completing documents. . . . Its enormous accountability to parents, principal, inspectors, and more to it colleagues whom you don't want to displease.

Also according to Flinders (1988) teaching as compared to other occupations is:

> . . . an open-ended activity. If time and energy allowed, lesson plans could always he revised and improved, readings could always be reviewed again, more text material could always be covered before the end of the term, students could always be given more individual attention, and homework could always be graded with greater care.
>
> *Flinders D. J. (1988)*

Clearly, Flinders expects a teacher's job to be student-oriented, rather than holding them accountable to many other aspects of teaching. But in present circumstances this is not the virtual reality of teaching.

As in the eye of one of the colleagues, teaching is totally an unpredictable job. She comments:

> Every morning is new for me. As I enter I have to see the principal for knowing which job has to be done at priority. It is all so confusing. My job is not clearly defined, not even for a month . . . other than these jobs . . . I require more time to do justice with my students. At the moment I spend only half of my duty hours with my students.

From our discussion it is obvious that teachers necessarily deal with uncertain and unknowable and diffusely defined aspects of teaching. So, we explored the possibilities of improving quality assurance techniques in the most formal and Informal ways to deal with such unpredictable jobs and also having researched with the teachers for six months, I, as an action researcher and principal, gave my colleagues an additional hour by reducing the number of classes they took. This time was 'exclusively' used to prepare for their classes. We called it off 'preparation time for teaching'.

WHY PREPARATION TIME?

The time and effort these teachers commit to their preparation and teaching comes not so much from grudging compliance with external demands but as from dedication of doing the job and providing effective care within a work context that is diffusely defined and has no clear criteria for successful completion. This 'internally generated' dedication in the context of a diffusely defined occupation seems to be in what both Woods and Nias call professional and vocational 'commitments', commitments that are grounded in the kinds of meanings and purposes that teachers attach to their work.

Teachers reported that increases in preparation time had offered important benefits on the quality of their work in general and their instruction in particular. Colleagues pointed out that more preparation time was important in reducing stress at home and in school, especially with students in their classes. It helped restore something to their lives outside teaching, enabling them to give a little more time to their families, their leisure and themselves. Together, these two things helped improve teachers' temperament in the classroom. They argued, improving the quality of interaction with students and classes due to extra time given, they had better temperament. Teachers now also proved to develop and improve the school culture.

In addition to relieving stress and creating space in other parts of the teacher's life and also in addition to making existing work easier, that is, preparation time for many teachers, also helped them to do things better. It enabled them to be more organised and to be better prepared for the next class.

Preparation time, according to some teachers, also allowed them to do more things, to take on a wider range of activities than they had before.

As one of the faculty members pointed out:

> . . . Now after having an additional hour I planned more excursions and visits for my students. In short, my teaching has become more practical.

For many teachers, the importance of preparation time was to be found not in time for extra-curricular activities, but in the extra investments they could make in the business of instruction within their own classes. For these teachers, preparation time helped them to become 'innovative' and improve appropriateness of their pedagogy.

LIMITATIONS OF PREPARATION TIME

Increased preparation time did not necessarily guarantee the processes of association and collegiality among teachers. Time itself was not a sufficient condition for collegiality and collaboration. As Flinders remarks:

> . . . isolation is an adaptive strategy because it protects the time and energy required to meet immediate instructional demands.
>
> *Flinders D.J. (1988)*

The same can be said of teachers' individualistic uses of preparation time that they used to prepare for their next class or the activities to be organised. Clearly then, while preparation time could enhance the working of the staff it could also divide them to watertight compartments that would take them away from collaborating.

It was observed that during preparation time teachers preferred to sit in resource rooms and libraries, rather than with their colleagues. Hence, in any case preparation time did not 'automatically' improve the conditions for collegiality and collaboration.

Preparation time was considered too precious and scare to waste on activities like relaxation or personal life conversation with colleagues. There was simply no time for chatting. There were too many things to do. As one teacher puts it:

> . . . I never had any time to chat. Once I made the mistake by starting a personal talk with my friend in the school, I wasted a lot of my time which I could have used to prepare for three more classes.

Preparation time, therefore, did not automatically assist the 'process' of binding the staff and their association with community or the students at large.

Ironically, for some teachers the law of diminishing returns set in, where further additions to preparation time reduced rather than enhanced the quality of classroom service provided, because the extra time drew teachers away from their classrooms too much and they were more busy in accumulation of resources, planning and organisation, but 'little' time was given for implementation of planned lessons.

However absence of preparation time inhibits association among teachers, its presence by no guarantees such association. More than this, the kinds of association that are created in the spaces afforded by preparation time may not always be those that enhance teacher development—personal or professional, and empowerment.

Preparation time has its limitations as well as its potentials. Beyond a certain point increases in preparation time reduced rather than improved the quality of service provided to students, as teachers were drawn away from their own classes into other areas of work.

Lastly, when preparation time was used in the context of collaborative setting, this created an increased number of meetings and additional work that teachers' work longer time, and subjected them to further administrative control instead of releasing them to develop things themselves. Even Barth (1981) points towards unanticipated ironies of complex bureaucratic systems which hold within them only yet more problems for every new solution that is offered.

Time then can be; and has seemed, an easy solution to the problems of change. Perhaps, the confidence expressed in the solution of increased teachers' time away from class has, to some extent, been a result of the perceived likelihood of its implementation.

In any case, against the tendencies towards increased workload and pressure to which preparation time during the research has contributed significantly the advent of preparation time has introduced a measure of compensation and easement in Cambridge Court High School where it was tried and tested for repercussions have to be worked upon and tested for the future benefit of the teaching community and the organisations where they are associated.

PREPARATION TIME, CURRICULUM DEVELOPMENT AND SCHOOL EFFECTIVENESS

This research study has shown that the job responsibilities of teachers have dramatically changed over the period of a decade. Preparation time comes as a boon to help overloaded teachers to improve the quality of teaching. But,

> The extent to which pupil learns in the schools is the function of many different conditions, of which the teachers' mode of operation is only one. . . . The teacher factor may well account for only a small amount of the differences in achievement.
>
> *Millman (1981)*

Subsequent studies (e.g., Purkey and Smith 1983; Mortimore *et al.*, 1988) show that certain 'internal conditions' of schools are associated with higher levels of achievement by students. Differences in student outcomes are then at least in part attributable to the strength of teaching factors that contribute to school effectiveness.

Reynolds (1982) however emphasised that schools have different levels of influence on teachers and students, and comments:

> Schools can be differently effective or ineffective for different types of pupils. . . . There are huge differences between departments or faculties in their effectiveness judged on examination results, which means that even within school exist some areas of teaching practice which are ineffective. The converse is also true.
>
> *Reynolds (1992)*

It is clear, therefore, that the assessment of school effectiveness and curriculum are not an exact science. The process of monitoring teacher and school effectiveness are 'complicated' by many internal and external variables which may not always be in the control of the schools themselves.

School improvement and curriculum development are then problematic. Most of the factors related to school improvement are subjective and complicated and difficult to measure; some of these factors are interactive; some have indirect yet strong effects; and some have direct yet weak effects on school outcomes, student achievements and teacher outcomes (Mc Dill and Rigsby 1973) but they may be seen as prerequisite to build a climate of 'success' that is conducive to growth. (Rosenholtz 1989 cited by Owens).

Modifications undertaken in the Indian National Policy (1992; 35) and National Policy on Education (1986) demonstrate the need to reorient the content and process of teacher training centres. However, Shrivastava (1994) states:

> An effective curriculum can neither be evolved in a vacuum nor without a strong foundation. This base and the ethos is provided by the social, economic, political, cultural, scientific and technological developments and by the environment they jointly create.
>
> *Shrivastava (1994)*

Obviously then, what we require to do is to take the 'holistic' view of the internal and external environment which is important to develop the quality of the 'whole' school.

CONCLUSION

Implicitly it has been shown that 'preparation time' is no panacea. It lends no guarantees. It provides only opportunities. Preparation time can be used for purposes other than its proponents, and the organisational contingencies surrounding its implementation can yield a range of unintended consequences that easily be explained within the parameters of the labour process theory.

It has also been argued that in order to assure quality in our teaching pedagogy and school system the senior authorities and teacher education colleges need to cross the functional boundaries and view the school in relation to its environment as a whole and then to develop a curricula for teacher training colleges. This approach also suggests that improvement in the quality of teaching and learning requires a simplified model that is necessarily accessible by all the teachers, students and community.

Perhaps the quest for quality in education means that it is time for us to raise our heads from the current quality assurance tools like inspection, bureaucratic set-ups and other performance indicators that do not motivate teachers to work collaboratively and bring changes in their attitudes; and begin to develop a more strategic perspective.

Our colleges which train teachers need to be more proactive in future and develop a package that brings an attitudinal change amongst the futuristic teachers. This research-based paper has also shown that it is in the hands of principals or managers of the school to provide a work culture that will necessarily help the teachers to 'change' not with grudging compliance but with a tender care that will be effective against all odds. Perhaps, principals before taking such challenging jobs, need to undergo a 'leadership' educational course. This will help the teachers to learn the process of learning, and bring about long-term benefits to the organisation where they work.

REFERENCES

Andy, Hargreaves, 1994, *Changing Teachers Changing Times—Teacher's Work and Culture in the Post-modern Age*; Cassell.

Barth, R.S., 1990, *Improving Schools from Within: Teachers, Parents and Principals can make a Difference*, San Francisco, Jossey-Bass.

Flinders, D.J., 1998, 17-28, *"Teacher Isolation and the New Reform"* Journal of Curriculum and Supervision, 14 (1)".

Dill, E.L and Rigsby, L.C., 1973, *Structure and Process in Secondary Schools; The Academic Impact of Educational Climates*, Baltimore: John University Press.

Millman, J., 1981, "Student Achievement as a Measure of Teacher Competence" in Millman. J. (ed.), *Hand Book of Teacher Evaluation,* Beverly Hills: Sage Publication.

Mortimore, P., et al., 1988, *School Matters: The Junior Years*, England: Wells, Open Books Publishing Ltd.

National Policy on Education (1986), With modification undertaken in (1992), New Delhi, Ministry of Human Resource Development, Department of Education.

Purkey, S., and Smith, M., 1983, "Effective Schools: A Review", *Elementary School Journal*, Vol 83., pp. 427- 452.

Reynolds, D., 1982, "The Search for Effective Schools", *Organisation*, Vol. 2., No 3., pp. 215 - 237.

Rosenholtz, 1989, Cited b. Owens, R. G., 1987, *Organisational Behaviour in Education*, New Jersey: Prentice-Hall.

5

KI TE ARA TUATORU: Towards a Third Way in the Administration of the School Sector in Aotearoa New Zealand

*—Ken Rae**

INTRODUCTION

This paper comments on the potential impact on the leadership and administration of New Zealand's schools of the initial education legislation of New Zealand's second MMP government. The new administration comprises a coalition of the left, of the labour and alliance parties. It came to power after the election of 30 November 1999 and is governing with support from the Greens.

The Education Amendment Act 2000, which passed into law after its Third Reading on 6 July, was described in the purpose section, section 3, as:

An Act

a) to change the rules concerning enrolment schemes for schools, in particular by requiring that the enrolment scheme of every ordinary state school must identify a home zone for the school.

**CCEAM, FNZEAS, formerly Senior Policy Analyst in the Ministry of Education, Wellington, New Zealand, past-National Secretary, NZEAS.*

b) to abolish bulk funding agreements, for the payment of teachers' salaries.

c) to strengthen the arrangements for the governance of schools.

d) to simplify the rules about tertiary students associations.

e) to amend provisions in order to make them consistent with the Human Rights Act 1993.

The Bill, after introduction, was sent to the Education and Science Select Committee for the hearing of public submissions. The two lightning rod elements of the legislation attracting strongly conflicting points of view were purposes (a) and (b). This paper will focus principally on (a), the issues of enrolment schemes and compulsory home zones supplemented by balloted entry for those schools requiring a scheme because they are threatened with overcrowding.

From 2001 the boards of trustees of any school requiring an enrolment scheme will designate a home zone. When adjacent schools are threatened with overcrowding their zones will be contiguous. Students living in the zone will have an absolute right to enrol at any time. If there are more applications than there are places available—after all zone students have been enrolled—priority will be given to those enrolling in special programmes offered by the school, then to siblings of current pupils, then to siblings of' former pupils. If in any category there are more applicants than places, then election will be by ballot conducted under instructions drawn up by the Secretary of Education. All schemes will require the approval of the Secretary.

When reported back by the Select Committee the definition of special programmes had been enlarged to cover—in addition to programmes providing Special Education, Maori language immersion classes, and specialised programmes countering educational disadvantage—a new group of programmes with a significantly different approach in order to address particular student needs, which would not be viable unless they could draw from a catchment area beyond the schools' home zone. Entry for such programmes will be determined by an organisation or process that is independent of the school. Major representations had been made to the Committee on behalf of a course in performance music at a suburban school which fed into the orchestras of Christchurch. The Select Committee reported that at present 18 per cent of New Zealand schools require enrolment schemes.

To comment in passing on the other major issue, bulk funding of teacher salaries has been a focus of divisive debate in New Zealand education policy for a decade. It was proposed as a key feature of devolution of management responsibilities to school level the 1999 *Picot Task Force Report* on the reform of New Zealand's educational administration, and in the subsequent *White Paper Of the Fourth Labour Government, Tomorrow's Schools*. Due to pressure of tight timelines a workable bulk funding salaries formula was not achieved by changeover date of 1 October 1989. This arose from the difficult problem of 'loser schools'—those faced with terminating staff under bulk funding because of above average numbers of teachers at the top of the salary scale.

Dr Lockwood Smith, Minister of Education in the National Government, elected at the end of 1990, won approval for a three-year bulk funding trial, which was joined by 70 volunteer schools in 1993. The trial was thrown open in 1996 and joined by a limited number of additional schools. In the 1998 budget the National government provided $200 million in new funding over three years, to provide for an enhanced grant based on salaries at the top of the relevant salary scales. The modified scheme was joined eventually by 840 out of 2,700 state-integrated schools (approximately 30 per cent of schools catering to 40 per cent of pupils).

In June 1998, at the time of the modification, the Labour party announced its intention if elected to abolish what it described as an unfair, divisive, and unsustainable policy. The legisation passed this year provides for bulk funding of teacher salaries to cease in all but a few exceptional cases at the commencement of the 2001 school year. The funding allocated for promoting bulk funding will be distributed across all schools, with calculations on a base, per pupil and decile-loaded basis (based on the socioeconomic status of the surrounding community), and will be paid into their operational funding

Boards of trustees will have increased flexibility in the use of operational funding for the employment of teachers, possibly even on a permanent basis, an interesting contrast with 1989 legislation which strictly controlled this process in the interests of equity. The restriction was intended to prevent wealthy school 'poaching' teachers, then in scarce supply, at the expense of schools in less wealthy suburbs who would be unable to afford equivalent financial support to their schools.

Purpose (c) increased the power of the Minister to intervene in cases where a self-managing school board was in difficulties from which it would not recover unassisted. It was also served by sections providing for larger multi-school boards, possibly regional structures in more rural districts, and for boards with constitutions approved by the Minister which departed from the standard model. That standard model continues to emphasise that the majority of each board of trustees will be elected representatives of the parents of the students at the school or (in some cases in future) schools for which it has governance responsibilities.

Any non-standard governance structures under the present government will likely be driven by a concern to implement its policy of 'Closing the Gaps', countering disadvantages. Under an alternative administration the same provision could however leave room for the alternatives being promoted by the previous government in 1999, as in its discussion paper, *Legislation for Learning* (1999). I suggested to the Year 2000 NZEAS conference that this document should be studied carefully to see if it was promoting the development of alternative school structures analogous to the English 'grant-maintained' phenomenon (Rae, 2000, p. 18).

Purpose (d) was a reversal of legislation enacted by the previous government, which had implications for student representation on university and other tertiary councils and for the provision of student services formerly provided by the associations. Purpose (e) is best thought of as remedying a technicality.

A Third Way

My title proposes exploration of a 'Third Way'. The concepts of a Third Way, for New Zealand education and for New Zealand society and politics more generally, are derived from an anthology of analysis and commentary by academics and trade union officials, which was published some months before the November 1999 election and entitled *The New Politics: a Third Way for New Zealand* (Chatterjee et al, 1999). The text was an endeavour to broaden the options of New Zealand voters and politicians. For 15 years both groups had been confronted with a single TINA (There is No Alternative) message on economic, political and social 'reform'.

That policy was identified by New Zealanders as 'Rogernomics', after its initial proponent, Hon Roger Douglas, the Minister of Finance of the fourth Labour government, was elected in 1984. A later variant, promoted by the first Minister of Finance in the National government elected in late 1990, Hon Ruth Richardson, and marketed by sharp reductions in benefit levels in the 1991 budget, was subsequently labelled 'Ruthenasia'.

The 'reform' policies pursued under both administrations were marked by a desire to reduce state expenditure and to move to budget surpluses which would be used to reduce debt, a concern to control inflation, an emphasis on use of market forces to bring greater efficiency to the provision of state services, a drive to free trade and free movement of capital and investment flows, and by 'reforming' industrial relations with the creation of a 'flexible' labour market.

Similar policies promoted by the World Bank, the International Monetary Fund, the US Treasury and the Federal Reserve were in 1990 labelled 'The Washington Consensus' on economic development, by the United States economist, John Williamson. From that perspective the First Way is that of Western capitalist democracies, their development now accompanied by the increasing globalisation of transactional organisations, electronic communication and instantaneous international financial transactions. The Second Way is the command economy model of the Communist East, discredited since the collapse of the Soviet Empire and the fall of the Berlin Wall.

The Third Way is that associated since with the 'New Democrats' of the United States, the Social Democrats of Western Europe, New Labour of the United Kingdom. There is a search by Third Way leaders of the last decade, such as President Clinton, Prime Minister Tony Blair and Chancellor Gerhard Schroeder for a new political economy of continuing but sustainable growth, reduced welfare dependency with empowerment through appropriate education policies, and reduction of unemployment to bring greater inclusion and fairness.

Eichbaum in paper in the Chattergee et al text identifies the June 1999 Blair/Schroeder statement, *Europe: The Third Way: Die Neue Mitte* (The New Middle) as one of the more substantive statements of the Third Way as a political project and policy programme' (1999, p. 53). Harris, in the introductory essay in that text, finds some shortcomings, however in the theoretical model of Reich (1999) in the United States, and Eichbaum later critiques that of Giddens (1998) in the United Kingdom.

Joseph Stiglitz, former World Bank Vice-President and Chief Executive Officer, contributed the preface to the anthology. He wrote:

"The past several years have witnessed an enormous amount of emotional debate surrounding the 'Washington

Consensus', the set of development prescriptions that until recently dominated development thinking. This caricature of successful development—a straight recipe of open markets, free trade, unfettered capital flows and minimal government intervention, all in the service of GDP growth goals—has been largely discredited in the last several years... [He cites the inappropriate remedies for the 1997-98 Asian crisis, and the shrinking of the Russian economy as a result of the free market approach advocated there].

"The Washington Consensus never addressed the deeper and equally important questions of our ultimate goals in development. And in focusing on more immediate objectives those subscribing to the Washington Consensus took privatisation and trade liberalisation as ends in themselves, rather than as means to more sustainable, equitable and democratic growth.

"What we have learned since is that this recipe alone ensures neither growth nor stability nor equity .... Successful development relies on the pillars of education and health: only with these can a country develop, attract and build modern industries, adopt new growing technologies rapidly in the rural sector, and enable its people to learn, to accept and help engender this transformation.

"At its heart, the new development strategy must involve meaningful ownership and participation—which not only have inherent value, but also increase the effectiveness and stability of development policies". (1999, pp. 7-10).

Stiglitz's comments resonate with the conference theme, Community Building in a Global Context, and the role of education, and those in leadership positions in education who share in the responsibility for building inclusive, healthy and sustainable communities. Appropriate education will be the empowering factor for the participants in the societies and economics of the future, and the source of human capital that will promote their sustainable growth.

The well-being of the citizens of those communities will spring from their informed participation in democratic government, and from their sense of ownership when that participation results in equitable outcomes because their society's policies are interacting appropriately with economic forces at national and international levels. It is thus a global as well as a community level challenge that faces the scholars, the researchers and the leadership of our educational institutions in the new century.

THE THREE WAYS IN NEW ZEALAND

The comments certainly resonate with New Zealand citizens who are now aware that the 15-year regime of 'reform' that conforms to the Washington Consensus has brought little gain from the years of pain. Those years have increased inequality dramatically within New Zealand society, the top 10 per cent of families being better off in 1996 compared with their position a decade before, the next 10 per cent holding their own, and the remainder of the population experiencing a decline in their fortunes (*Statistics New Zealand*, 1999). Studies by Professor Chattergee indicate that for the bottom 40 per cent the falling spending power 1984-96 is more than three per cent, for the bottom 10 per cent a staggering 8.7 per cent. These are very large numbers (comment by Dalziel, 1999, p. 67).

New Zealand has been left with an ongoing adverse balance of trade ($ 8.5 billion in the year to March 2000, 8.2 per cent of GDP), as a consequence of the disruption of the manufacturing and exporting sectors by removal of tariffs and fluctuations in the currency, and as a direct consequence of overseas purchase of New Zealand companies and, in particular, the privatised formed state enterprises. Payments overseas of interest and dividends in the year to March 2000 totalled over $6 billion. In the year 2000 the nation's overseas debt, now overwhelmingly private sector debt, ($109.1 billion) exceeds our annual GDP ($104.25 billion) (McLoughlin, 2000, pp. 53-55).

In the Chatterjee et al text, both Philpott and Dalziel chart the lag in New Zealand growth since 1984. New Zealand had previously enjoyed growth comparable to that of Australia. Philpott calculates the loss of national income from GDP over the 15 years of reform at a staggering $12,000 per head of New Zealand population, more than one-third of the average per capita real income. (p. 94). Dalziel calculates New Zealand's lost national product over 15 years at $ 215 billion, 'equal to more than two years production in this country' (p. 66).

Chapman (1999) has analysed the changes of the 1980's as destabilising interruption of our political culture, managed by an elite convening in Wellington and drawn from both the state and private sectors. At a deeper level there has been growing opposition to the ongoing years of pain, because the policies have been driven by an ethos that is fundamentally disempowering and demeaning. The world view of Rogernomics and Ruthenasia, and the Washington Consensus, diminishes our feelings of and for a common humanity, as we are reduced in states to mere buyers and sellers in a world of ever-widening market relationships, with ultimately our history, our culture and our ethnicity denied.

Community or cooperative endeavour, any action particularly on the life of weaker members of the community, has been likely in New Zealand to be stigmatised as an 'intervention', able to be justified only in the event of identified 'market collapse'. The dominant theories of the last 15 years have discounted the value of those relationships of trust, those investments in 'social capital' that are required to provide the glue that binds any society together. Ultimately, these theories threaten people's faith in the democratic process itself. Hazeltine (1996) recently labelled this dominant perspective of 'the rational utility maximiser', homo economicus, as the 'selfish shit' theory of human motivation.

In New Zealand, it could be argued that our First Way was that of 50 years' duration commencing with the election of the first Labour government of 1935, which brought New Zealand out of the depression experience by immediately nationalising the Reserve Bank, by establishing social security and subsidised medicine by 1938, by building greater manufacturing capacity behind tariff barriers, and directing from the centre the extensive building up of the national infrastructure of roading, airways, housing and hydroelectric power. This First Way was pursued after 1949 by centre right National governments. It was sustained by overseas exchange gained from the produce of New Zealand farms that had a guaranteed access to markets in the United Kingdom.

In 1960, 85 per cent of exports went there. Diversification was required as Britain sought entry to the EEC and an alternative was sought in Closer Economic Relations (CER Agreement) from 1970 with Australia. In the 1990's more than 20 per cent of exports went to Australia, out biggest market, and very similar proportions to North America, Japan and East Asia, the EC including the United Kingdom, and the rest of the world. The First Way came under increasing stress from the oil shocks of the seventies, with world economic adjustments, a sluggish economy and increasing unemployment all contributing to budget deficits. There was also the self-inflicted wound of the generous national superannuation scheme offered as an inducement by the National party in the 1975 election campaign.

The First Way of the 'managed economy' reached its apotheosis under Prime Minister Muldoon's National government in the early 1980's, when he sought to beat these challenges by a two- year wage and price freeze. This ended only with his inability to write a budget in 1984, a foreign exchange crisis, and his defeat in the snap election of 14 July, 1984, resonant dates both of them. The election of the fourth Labour government of Prime Minister Lange abruptly ushered in New Zealand's Second Way, the era of the 'reforms' of Rogernomics and Ruthenasia. As for Europe, the United Kingdom and the United States, in the year 2000 a Third Way producing greater equity, inclusiveness and sustainability is now required.

New Zealand's election returns of 30 November 1999 were the more difficult to predict because the labour campaign seemed to be going out of its way in macroeconomic policy to avoid spooking 'the markets', local and international, by any financial unorthodoxy. The Labour Party however certainly made clear, to the business, financial and entrepreneurial interests who had benefited from the previous 15 years, that it had two lighthouse policies, reform of the 1991 Employment Contracts Act (ECA) and reinstatement of management by a state corporation of a no-fault Accident Compensation regime as it had been instituted by the Third Labour Government in 1974.

The ECA had significantly reduced the rights of workers and unions in negotiating conditions of service. According to Dalziel the new labour market flexibility had resulted in disappointing increases in worker productivity when New Zealand's statistics under a confrontational regime were compared with Australia's, with its strategy of an national industrial accord under the Hawke government (1999, p. 73). The ACC regime had been thrown open to market competition only months before the election, in pursuit of a policy paradigm proposing that greater efficiency and equity would be derived from increased exposure of a public service monopoly to market forces. This thesis had lost credibility with significant sectors of the population.

THE THIRD WAY IN NEW ZEALAND EDUCATION

In education the First Way of 50 years evolution (and accretions according to the 1988 *Picot Report*) was swept away by the 1989 administrative reform. No central or district structure survived 1 October 1989 unchanged. In the Second Way a range of more focused bodies replaced the former multilateral Department of Education. In particular the former Department Inspectors of Schools disappeared and the Education Review Office emerged with a strong auditing bent, particularly under new leadership from 1993, as it measured school leadership and performance against Charter under-takings to the Crown of each school's board of trustees, and reported on their other obligations under a range of legislation.

Under the National's Education Minister, Lockwood Smith, this Second Way of education reform extended to curriculum and assessment policy, and with abolition in 1991 of a requirement for enrolment zones moved increasingly to promotion of an education market as the means to institutional responsiveness and national competitiveness.

As is noted below the Second Way was marked by increasing disparity between schools, the emergence of three tiers of schooling in metropolitan areas (Hughes et al, 1996). Gaps increased in the qualification and retention statistics between the different ethnic groups in New Zealand, particularly those of the indigenous *langata whenua*, the Maori students 920 per cent of the school population), and those of Pacific students 97.6 per cent) when compared with the majority Pakeha (those of European descent) population. (The 5.9 per cent of Asian students perform on a par or better than the Pakeha majority.)

The 1999 Labour campaign had lighthouse policies also in education—the reduction of the burden of tertiary student loans, the removal of bulk funding of teachers' salaries, and a guarantee to every child to attend a neighbourhood school. These latter two policies would require legislative change.

Tabling of the new government's bill in March, and hearings before the Select Committee from May to June, kept the lightning rod policies in the media and before the public. Those opposed to the changes have claimed that they are an infringement on school choice and school level self, management, two cornerstones of the education reforms pioneered by the fourth Labour government in 1989.

As I prepared the final draft of this paper a letter appeared in *The Dominion of Wellington* of 19 July 2000.

"The Minister wants to return to zoning so that all children can attend their local school; in itself this is a laudable objective; the problem arises when the local school is a poor one and the child cannot get into another.

"The reforms will reduce parental choice and the flexibility schools have had to adapt to their communities' needs. The reforms will also remove much of the incentives that schools and principles have to perform and improve. Zoning by guaranteeing a school's roll removes one of the key incentives to perform.

"No doubt Labour by taking so much more control of schools thinks its reforms will create a fairer education system. Unfortunately what it will actually do is foster mediocrity and stifle excellence."

The writer and I probably have differing perceptions of the Third Way that lies ahead for New Zealand's education system.

Earlier Provisions Governing Enrolment Schemes

From 1978 in any district in which a student could conveniently attend more than one secondary school the Department of Education negotiated a district enrolment scheme with the boards of governors (Rae, 1991). The aim was to control enrolments and avoid excessive fluctuations in roll numbers, and the consequent changes to staffing entitlements which would impact on a school's curriculum structures, and to minimise avoidable terminations of teachers in times of a national teacher shortage.

Negotiations with the boards of the district schools, conducted by the regional superintendent of education, produced schemes with a pattern of home zones which required enrolment at a designated school, and usually contained agreed but limited quotas for out-of-zone students, together with the criteria to be used in filling those quotas. (Other choices were available for those prepared to enrol their children at a private school 4 per cent of enrolments—or an integrated school—9 per cent of enrolments).

These district schemes established the catchment zone and likely roll numbers for each school. The out-of-zone numbers could be adjusted annually to support new or under-subscribed schools. Each scheme was brought into force when signed by the Minister of Education. In practice, informal meetings between principals and boards (which even pre-1989 usually contained a majority of elected parents' representatives) to produce draft schemes often preceded the formal consultation convened by the regional superintendent. Parental choice was significantly constrained in the interests of system level priorities.

The reality of irregular placement over the years of secondary schools across New Zealand cities forced an amendment within two years by which schemes could be solely numbers-based, with enrolments determined on the basis of agreed criteria written into the scheme. An appeal to the courts later produced a ruling that criteria-based schemes still needed to provide for all students to reasonably conveniently attend a school (*Brown v Minister of Education [1985] 2 NZLR 356).*

In 1989 the changes in the legislation were intended to increase parental choice. They provided for the Ministry to establish a maximum roll for every secondary school and permitted all schools to enrol up to that capacity. It was a time of declining enrolments nationally and therefore some surplus accommodation. Enrolment schemes (still for secondary schools only) were to be put in place only when family choices placed pressure on a school's capacity and threatened it with overcrowding. Each school scheme was to be established by the Secretary for Education after consultation with the board of trustees.

A scheme had to include a home zone, which gave to residents of that zone an entitlement to enrol at the local school (but unlike the 1978 regime did not require that they so enrol). There was legislative provision for siblings and hostel students to be considered as in-zone enrolments. If out-of-zone enrolments exceeded the number of places available after in-zone enrolments had been completed, selection in the interests of fairness was to be by ballot. (For primary schools the pre-1989 situation continued to apply; the roll of a school could be closed to further enrolments by the Secretary—formerly this had been the responsibility of the relevant district education board—and families were expected to approach the neighbouring school).

The dominant sentiment in 1989 was for encouragement of choice-enrolment schemes which were seen as a side issue required only to tidy up around the edges. A significant policy gap emerged in the rush to implementation of the new provisions in 1990. The new home zones were presumably to be different in kind from the old contiguous zones of the former district schemes, but how different? The bureaucrats decided to kick for touch, and make only minimal changes to existing zones for 1991, pending policy decisions by the government.

In the event, the 1989 legislation provided for enrolments only for the 1991 school year. Hon Lockwood Smith, the Minister of Education in the new National government elected with a large majority in November 1990, had during the campaign stressed the need for maximum possible choice in the interests of a more effective education system, and the need for further reduction in the role of the central bureaucracy. He had been particularly scathing of 'education by lottery', i.e., the use of the ballot to determine some enrolments.

In 1991, a bill sponsored by Dr. Smith to amend the Education Act provided for the transfer of responsibility to the school's board of trustees for devising and managing an enrolment scheme, whenever required. Schemes no longer would have to have a home zone. The amendment reduced the role of the Secretary to certifying that a threat of overcrowding existed. That certificate would permit the board of any school, now both primary and secondary, to put an enrolment scheme in place—and to specify the means by which it would choose which students could enrol at the school.

The Select Committee of the day perceived a gap in the provisions. In reporting the Bill back to the House it recommended that a reserve power be created, so that the Secretary could require an enrolment in cases in which the operation of one or more enrolment schemes had meant that the student "would not be able reasonably practicably to attend any state school of the appropriate class" or that their operation "would be so disadvantageous that giving a person preferential treatment is justified" (section 12B).

Since 1992 and up until the 1999 school year, these provisions were in force for enrolment schemes, where required. Of recent years up to 400-plus state schools (out of 2700) have been authorised by the Secretary to institute and operate an enrolment scheme in 1997, these schemes covered the enrolments of 32 per cent of the student population (*Minister of Education*, 1998, p. 46).

Critics of the 1991 changes suggested increased choice was unlikely to be equally available to or equally exercised by all parents, and in the case of the oversubscribed schools, would be exercised by schools rather than parents. In developing enrolment schemes since 1991, some school boards have indeed exercised this greater choice of students, by decreasing the emphasis on the student's place of residence and increasing the emphasis on other criteria as the basis for the selection of students.

In June 1994, 37 schemes out of 269 did not have zones, and four of those 37 made no mention of proximity to school as a criterion. In June 1997, 78 schemes out of 414 did not have zones and 13 of the 78 made no mention of proximity to school as a criterion. Few of the 78 however made proximity an explicitly predominant criterion.

In 1994, in a parliament evenly balanced after the 1993 election had reduced the government's majority to one, the government member for the Eden electorate called for the revisiting of enrolment scheme policy. In Auckland in particular, the provision of school places was falling behind demand, because of fiscal constraints imposed by central government on all capital investment in times of stable overall national enrolment numbers—and because of the loss of the pre-1989 education bureaucracy and its planning structures.

A shortage of accommodation was more likely to occur in any area where population growth was being intensified by increased immigration and infill housing, as was the case in the Eden electorate. The member had received representations from families, particularly those moving during the school year, that they were encountering difficulty in enrolling their children in a local school, or indeed any school within convenient access. She had also received representations from boards of trustees that the responsibility for coordinated action, in the face of a shortfall in total places available, was not readily apparent to them.

In 1995 the Minister of Education was authorised to consult with other political parties, and an agreement was reached on significant changes to the 1991 enrolment scheme legislation. There was no return to zones as an obligatory part in any scheme, but enrolment scheme provisions should in future be underpinned by a priority principle: no enrolment scheme or amendment to a scheme can be agreed that has the effect of excluding a student who could reasonably conveniently attend the school unless the student can reasonably conveniently attend another state school (that is not an integrated school).

Further, a school board of trustees, before preparing an enrolment scheme or proposing amendment to a scheme, would need to discover and consider the views of the parents of students at the school, the people living in the geographical area in which the school is situated and the boards of other schools that the board thought might be affected by the scheme. Thirdly, the Secretary for Education would in future be required to agree to each school enrolment scheme. In the event, the government moved to minority government status and no legislation was introduced.

After the 1996 election, the first under MMP rules, the Coalition Agreement of December 1996 reflected the concern of the junior coalition partner New Zealand First, that "the concept that priority of attendance at neighbourhood schools will be given to those living in the local area".

A 1997 Education Amendment Bill, introduced by a new more pragmatic Minister of Education, Hon Wyatt Creech, initially as a catch up after a major break from any education legislation, did however address three major issues, and included enrolment schemes. (It also revisited suspension and expulsion provisions for the first time since 1978, and addressed the need for a new and appropriate legislative foundation for the National Curriculum Statements being progressively introduced to implement the national Curriculum Framework sponsored by Dr. Lockwood Smith in 1993.)

The Bill modified to some degree the decisions of the pre-1997 government. It had a chequered passage through the House. It was originally reported back as planned in June 1988, but then delayed because of dissatisfaction from backbenchers, in particular the member from Eden. As finally passed through Committee and Third Reading stages in the last week of the session in December, it contained significant additional duties for the Secretary in resolving disputes or stalemates in the development of enrolment schemes, and in winning agreement between contiguous boards with possibly conflicting goals for their schools. It also reflected the diffi-culties for a minister who wished to remove enrolment scheme disputes from the political arena by designing challenge-proof procedures, but had backbenchers who thought 'zone' an unspeakable four-letter word.

So the legislation contained a more generally expressed underlying principle, incorporating two criteria, for the designing of enrolment schemes by boards, and their approval by the Secretary. These are to be found in the purpose clause (new section 11 A) which underwent an interesting reshaping between June and December.

The purpose of an enrolment schemes is:

a) To avoid overcrowding or the likelihood of overcrowding of schools, at the school to which it applies; and
b) To enable the Secretary to make reasonable use of the network of schools.

The amplified purpose clause provides more flexibility in the exercise of the Secretary's discretionary power to approve schemes. Its expression also reduces the likelihood of legal challenges to the Secretary's decisions and any consequent uncertainty for parents, students and boards about their enrolment decisions. Other material in the purpose clause, as reported back in June, was moved in December with some additions to a new section entitled 'Principles governing content and implementation of enrolment schemes' (new section 11 B).

1. When developing, adopting, amending, and implementing an enrolment scheme, a Board must, as far as it can, ensure that the enrolment scheme:

    a. Excludes from the school no more prospective students than is necessary to avoid overcrowding at the school.

    b. Reflects the desirability of students being able to attend a reasonably convenient school.

    c. Enables the Secretary to make reasonable use of the existing network of schools, by taking into account the location and capacity of other schools that are reasonably convenient schools for students in the general area served by the school.

2. When developing, adopting, amending, and implementing an enrolment scheme, a Board must, to the extent that it is reasonable and practicable to do so

without derogating from the principles in subsection (1), ensure that students can attend a school of their choice.

These two sections encapsulate the tensions and ambiguities forever inherent in the management of enrolment scheme/ school choice policy. Maximum choice is desirable, attendance at a local school where that is, the school of choice is desirable, development of enrolment schemes, where required, by the local board or boards rather than by a distant bureaucracy is desirable. But, especially at a time when school rolls are once again increasing, importance by the Secretary to maintain and expand the network of schools within the finite limits of Vote-Education is given. With the requirement of compulsory enrolment at a school, ready access to at least a convenient school should equally be given. And this right for some will, of course, very likely conflict with and reduce the choice available to others

The two opposition parties, Labour and Alliance, were critical of the legislation in that it failed to guarantee access to the nearest or local school by compulsory use of home zones—and in contradistinction to 1990 that appeared to mean in 1998 contiguous zones, a position maintained by the Labour party as it campaigned for the 1999 election. Although home zones were not explicitly required by the government proposals, boards could have introduced home zones if they so wished, and this was agreed in their consultations. Some schools have found them the most convenient form of scheme.

In fact, in 1999, the Ministry in consultation with the sector developed guidelines for enrolment schemes for the school year 2000 and, to provide a universal right to attend at least one state school, the requirement for home zones became explicit. And those zones where required were to be contiguous, but could overlap (which gave some families a double entitlement and a guaranteed choice).

Some boards and their principals in the press (*NZ Education Review*, March 26, 1999) contested the changes, as the initial round of consultations under the new procedures proceeded to reshape existing schemes. Eventually, one board of trustees of a prestigious boys school in Auckland, because the legislation did not specify home zones and even though the Secretary's rules had been reached after extensive consultation and had won widespread agreement by trustees, principals and teachers organisations, did hold out for a wide 'zone of influence' from which it could entertain applications for enrolment.

It undertook to not act unreasonably in a manner that would involve the invocation of the Secretary's reserve powers, and in the event no such difficulty arose. The example of a school demanding and getting administrative freedoms unavailable to others was picked up by 'prestigious' schools in other metropolitan areas. It was also picked up by the Labour and Alliance political parties as they entered the 1999 campaign.

The year 2000 legislation goes beyond the demands of the 1989 model in its requirement for home zones, in fact, beyond what proved practicable in the pre-1989 era. It restores the ballot concept of the 1989 legislation, but with added procedural safeguards to ensure fairness and transparency. It provides amplified priorities which were found in practice to be lacking in 1990 and for which draft legislation was being prepared.

It is much less ambiguous than the previous legislation in its expression of its purposes (section 11 A):

a) to avoid overcrowding or the likelihood of overcrowding at [a] school.

b) to ensure that the selection of applicants for enrolment at the school is carried out in a fair and transparent manner.

c) to enable the Secretary to make the best use of the existing networks of state schools.

Schemes must ensure that they do 'not exclude local students' and "no more students are excluded from the school than is necessary to avoid overcrowding." Zones will be quite unambiguous so that "any given address is either within or outside the home zone". (section 11 E (1). The Secretary has a comprehensive power to issue instructions and guidelines on the operation of schemes (section 11 G), and may alter scheme zones to make best use of the networks of schools (section 11 E (2) (c)).

6

Institutional Planning: Concept, Process and Techniques

*—M.M. Kapoor**

INTRODUCTION

If you are appointed as head of an educational institution, how would you begin your work? Would you like to know the purposes or objectives for which the institution was set up? The progress made so far by the institution in the attainment of those objectives? The resources and constraints experienced by the institution and the feedback that may be available from a formal or non-formal evaluation of the programmes undertaken by the institution? Your answers would certainly be in the affirmative. When you make your future plans about the institution, this information would certainly be useful in making realistic plans.

This module will set you thinking about institutions. After studying this module, you should be able to:

i) Precisely define institutional planning;

ii) State the objectives for which an institution has been set up;

**The late M.M. Kapoor was Senior Fellow, National Institute of Educational Planning and Administration, New Delhi.* *Editors are thankful to Mrs Kapoor for permitting to publish this paper.*

iii) Identify the needs of the institution and problems faced;
iv) Assess the available resources and constraints on resources;
v) Determine priorities among different needs of the institution;
vi) Select the most viable among alternative strategies for fulfilling a task;
vii) Formulate an institutional plan;
viii) Visualise steps in the implementation of the plan;
ix) Monitor the progress of implementation; and
x) Use feedback to revise and restructure the plan, if necessary.

What is Institutional Planning?

The idea of institutional planning is not a new one in the field of education. Irrespective of the fact whether there exists any system of educational planning in a country or not, some kind of planning activity goes on within the institution. Every member of the faculty plans course-outline and every student his programme of study. Every institution prepares a timetable and also an annual budget. And yet, something always seems to be missing as each one has been partly planning instit-utional activities. It is never possible to view the total institution at any time. There is no system of comprehensive planning through which academic and administrative activities are linked with the guiding purpose of the institution. This way plans become separated from the life of an institution.

INSTITUTIONAL PLANNING CONCEPT, PROCESS AND TECHNIQUES

To achieve educational objectives in a creative, orderly, and economically sound manner is a task demanding also those of the future, together with creative and persistent effort to implement programmes. Planning is an all encompassing activity that depends on party-state and nation, and involves public and private, and large and small institutions. If done well, the result could be a nation educated to breadth, depth and quality not previously envisioned.

Institutional planning may be described as a systematic approach to prepare comprehensive plans for educational development at the institutional level. It is necessary to understand what the institution is, where it stands, what it wants to be and how it can achieve its goals. The plans, thus prepared, would provide a blueprint for an institution for improving and developing its activities within a national or regional framework, based on the well identified needs and resources of an institution, with full participation of all the concerned parties, i.e., the head of an institution, its teachers, parents, students and community to which it caters to.

The aims of institutional planning are basically the same as the aims of educational planning but immediate objectives and the specific purpose of the programme of its action at the institutional level differ in order of priority and degree of importance with respect to the sub-regional, regional, state or national programme.

Need for Planning at Institutional Level

Educational planning should be done at all those levels of administrative set up where decisions are taken, i.e., at the national, state, regional, sub-regional and institutional levels. No comprehensive programme of educational development can even be put across unless systematic planning is done at all these levels. And the most important level at which all the plans are operationalised or which serve as a foundation stone for all other levels, is that of an institution. In fact, institutional planning is recognition of the role of practitioners of education in the process of educational planning in a country.

Scope and Coverage

In order to determine the scope and coverage of programmes under institutional planning, one has to look into the objectives for which an institution has been set up. These are generally listed in the prospectus (if any) of the institution or may be available in records relating to the period when the institution was set up. These may also be inferred to some extent from the activities in which the institution is engaged in.

After proceeding from the objectives, we need to analyse the tasks involved in achieving the objectives. Identify major problems faced by the institution and thereby determine the various areas for planning at the institutional level.

These areas would cover both quantitative and qualitative aspects of development of an institution in respect of its curricular, co-curricular and extra curricular activities. There is just an indication and can be adapted/adopted to meet the varying requirements in a changed situation:

i) Student services
ii) Faculty improvement
iii) Building and equipment
iv) Extension and other programmes
v) General administration
vi) Financial management

The various activities covered under these areas are given in annexure I. This grouping of activities can be done either for various programme areas or for various organisational units, e.g., administration, library, etc. It is suggested that at the planning stage, activities may be grouped according to the programme areas and at the operational stage, responsibilities for implementation of various activities may be assigned, according to the organisational set-up.

The nature of these projects can change according to the level of and the type of an institution or institutions. On the basis of an analysis of the institutional plans carried out in one of the Districts of Rajasthan (Amjer District), the various types of projects covered are listed in Annexure II.

Process of Institutional Planning

The process of preparing an institutional plan can be explained in the form of three stages of planning:

a) Normative stage : It involves determining what ought to be done;

b) Strategic stage : It involves determining what can be done; and

c) Operational stage : It involves determining what detailed steps needs to be taken in order to achieve an agreed objective.

It is suggested that the following main steps may be undertaken under various stages of planning.

i) Establishment of objectives, mission and goals.
ii) Identification of problems and needs.
iii) Assessment of resources.
iv) Determination of priorities.
v) Formulation of plan.
vi) Finalisation of plan.
vii) Workplan for implementation.
viii) Monitoring and evaluation.
ix) Revision of plan.

The steps in the planning process as outlined here are only for clarity and convenience of practitioners. In reality, they represent points on a continuum rather than steps of a chain reaction. Any stage may be an entry point to the planning process, provided that the cycle is completed as an ongoing enterprise.

Establishment of Objectives

This is the most difficult step in the process of institutional planning as it involves establishment of clear and specific objectives to be accomplished. These objectives have to be derived from the aims of and purpose of the institute. Many institutes have a clear definition of their purpose/aims, whereas others have the most general overview of guiding ideals. Some institutional identity is more clearly visible in what the institute is actually doing. Primary programmes of an institution can be divided in these groups and of the purpose of the institute can be defined against them:

a) Academic
b) Para-academic
c) Extension

Under 'academic' objectives the type of courses/training programmes/research activities coming within the purview of the institute should defined. Under para-academic objectives various co-curricular and extra-curricular activities should be identified. And under 'extension services' objectives with regard to the understanding of various community related activities like adult education, literacy programmes, youth services, etc., should be given.

Identification of Problems and Needs

After the aims and objectives of the institute have been defined, the next step is to identify the problems and needs of the institute to achieve these objectives. For this purpose various objectives to be linked to various programmes are shown in Annexure II. This step would involve:

1) Making of projections:
    a) Enrolment projections;
    b) Staff requirements; and
    c) Building requirements.

2) Identification of problems and needs with respect to the various programmes and projects to improve upon the existing situation and to meet the future requirements.

Enrolment projections should be based on the past trend and on the future requirement in accordance with the objectives of the institute for various subjects and courses with detailed break-up into six: community, area, full-time, part-time, etc. These projections should be done at least for the next five years. On the basis of these projections, work out size and number of sections for various courses and classes. An example of an institution having one-year course with 385 enrolment and 10 various subjects has been given in three Annexures. In Annexure V-A, weekly teaching workload has been calculated. In V-B, the requirement of teachers with various subject combination has been worked out. The Annexure V-C contains the method of assessing teaching space requirements and application of use factor. It is just a hypothetical example to show the technique. It can be used not only to project future requirements but also to assess the teaching extent of shortage and surplus of existing teaching and space resources. The norms with respect to the class size, teacher-pupil ratio, subject combinations, workload of teachers should be based on the guidelines given by the university, boards, the concerned department, or based on sound academic principles and financial viability.

The second step at this stage is to prepare sub-plans for various programmes as given in Annexure I on the basis of the objectives of the institute and future requirements of enrolment, teachers and teaching spaces. It is suggested that the teaching staff of the institute be divided in groups to prepare sub-plans separately for various programme areas. These groups should make an assessment of the existing situation with respect to the facilities already available, extent of their utilisation, need for further improvement, etc.

There should also be a coordination group so as to avoid any overlapping or duplication of work among various groups. The following plan of action based on systems approach is suggested for preparation of the various projects:

1) Identify projects under each programme, the project of cycle sheds under the programme of student services. An indicative list is given in Annexure II.
2) Under each project analyse and assess the extent of facilities already available and identify the main problem areas. It would require very comprehensive analysis as problems, which are sometimes considered to be the major ones, do not always turn out to be the main ones. It would require isolation of the apparent problem areas through:
   a) Collection of relevant data; and
   b) Analysis of data

It sometimes takes a long time as most of us are problem blind. Isolation of the problem areas then follows the sequences of stops that allow one to spell out in precise detail the nature of the problems.

3) Once the specific problems have boon isolated, it is necessary to do a detailed comprehensive review of those areas and suggest tentative solutions to the problems. These suggestions should be separately made for:
   a) Improvement in the existing situations; and
   b) Development of new programmes in the future.
4) The various suggestions should be phased over timescale clearly indicating short-term and long-term stops required to be undertaken.
5) Suggestions where no financial implications are required should be preferred over these involving financial implication. However, in case of items under a later category, total requirement of funds should be worked out with recurring and non-recurring break-up.

Suggested outlines for preparation of various projects have been given in Annexure VI.

Assessment of Resources

The next stage is to make the assessment of the resources available and resources harnessable for development of the institute. The following steps are suggested for this:

1) First of all make an assessment of resources already available in the institute:
2) Study the departmental/government plans for educational development to identify the schemes under which the institute can claim grants for its programmes;
3) Find out ways and means where funds can be raised from the community and the students;
4) Think of special schemes through which funds can be raised, e.g., organisation of fairs, shows, etc.

Determination of Priorities

After knowing the direction of development and having identified the possible resources, the next step is to proceed to determine priorities based on alternative choices. For example, one may be faced with the alternative of having more books for the library or more equipment for the laboratory. For this purpose it is suggested that a working group of teachers and students may be set up which can go into various questions such as:

1) Allocation of resources among various programmes;
2) Allocation of resources to various projects within a programme; and
3) Working out yearwise phasing of project proposals, etc.

Formulation of Plan

Having determined the priorities, the next logical step would be to formulate the total plan of the institute. This step would not only involve target setting in terms of expansion, improvement and diversification, but also consolidation of various programmes and projects prepared by various groups. A suggested outline for preparing an institutional plan has been given in Annexure III. It can be used as a guideline to prepare a comprehensive plan by an institution.

Finalisation of Plan

The draft plan prepared by the institute may be finalised after discussion at various levels:

1) In the general meeting of the staff.
2) With the student representatives, parents and community representatives, if possible.
3) With various governing bodies of the institute department, university, board, etc.

On the basis of these discussions, a final version of the plan incorporating the various changes suggested at theses levels should be prepared for implementation.

WorkPlan for Implementation

Only preparation of a very good plan will not produce any result. To achieve the results, strategies will have to be worked out for skilful implementation. Two suggestions are made with this regard:

1) In implementation of the plan, involvement of every teacher is a must and of students, if possible, and
2) Preparation of workplan for implementation to control time and cost factors.

An example of Workplan Schedule for implementation of schemes with examples from selected activities in preparation of Timetables has been given in Annexure IV. Similar workplan schedules may be prepared for all other programmes and projects of the plan for effective implementation and control.

Monitoring and Evaluation

The workplan schedule is the most effective instrument of continuous monitoring and feedback for implementation of the plan. Regular staff meeting should be organised, particularly to assess the implementation of the various schemes as per the schedule. Every concerned staff member in charge of implementation of a scheme should present a brief review of the implementation of the scheme.

Various difficulties faced in implementation and suggestions made to overcome them should be thoroughly discussed in these meetings. An annual review of the institutional plan should also be prepared and circulated. The results of planning, whether positive or negative, must become a central part of the institute's information system.

While evaluating the success of an institutional plan, it is not enough to evaluate it in terms of achievement of targets but also in terms of participation of the various groups and creation of enthusiasm all around.

It is said that "planning is permanent", a plan is not, if a plan it is not. If a plan is not generating the anticipated results, it should be modified or discarded if nothing emerges out of it. In the light of the experience gained, the plans should be revised, modified and this much flexibility should be inbuilt in the plan mechanism.

Ground Rules for Preparing an Effective Plan

For an institutional plan to be effective, it is necessary to take into account certain factors at various stages of its implementation.

Best utilisation of existing resources

Institutional plans should not be prepared like a charter of demands. These should be prepared mainly from the points of view of best utilisation of existing resources. Emphasis should be on human efforts rather than on the additional resources we need, the institutional plan would merely become a charter of demands. Funds to meet these demands will not be available and this would lead to frustration.

In an institutional plan, the question to be asked to every institution should be "What can be done for hard work?" Education is essentially a stretching process and it has to stretch teachers and students to external discipline and the institutional plan is a tool which can be used for this purpose.

Participatory Planning

It is possible that the head of an institution may be so enthusiastic that he may himself prepare a plan for development of the institute. This will not be a right procedure. Institutional plan must be democratically oriented and should involve everyone concerned, i.e., principal, teachers, pupils, parents and the community. This is essential not only from the viewpoint of effective implementation but also for creating additional resources both in terms of men and material.

Project approach

Instead of waiting for the whole plan of the institute to be prepared, finalised and then wait for it to be followed both in preparation and in the implementation of institutional plans, these projects which do not require any additional financial inputs can be immediately implemented. It is also suggested that in the beginning, only those projects should be taken which can be implemented without much resistance. It is essential that various projects are carefully formulated with clear objectives and specific time schedule for implementation.

Role of principal

The role of the principal is very crucial for the success of planning at the institutional level. The head of the institution should look at the system of the institute as a whole, assess the strengths and weaknesses and then carefully create a feeling of readiness for change. Involvement of staff will depend entirely on the commitment and involvement of the head of the institute. The principal should have the capacity and perspective to clearly define the goals and tasks of the institute. Most of the principals are output-oriented and believe in schemes having immediate 'show effect'. Instead of this 'show business', the principal should go deep into the real problems of the institute, and believe more in the process than in the results only.

Realistic and Practical

An institutional plan should be realistic and practical rather than ambitious and utopian. Here our motto should be "not high aim but failure should be crime" instead of "not failure but low aim is crime". The plan may be very small but once it is finalised, there should be no excuse for its failure. One should insist on doing things with dignity, with pride in oneself and with success. If this is the spirit, an institutional plan can be successfully put on the ground.

Summary

Institutional planning should be seen as an exercise in preparation of a comprehensive plan for educational development at the institutional level. In preparing such a plan cognisance should be taken of the objectives of the institution within a broad framework of national aspirations, needs and resources of the institution, problems being faced and feasible solutions leading to attainment of the institution's objectives.

Plans should be realistic and practical, making full utilisation of existing resources. A participatory approach should permeate the entire exercise from planning to execution.

ANNEXURE I

Areas of Planning at the Institutional Level

Student services faculty improvement building and equipment extension activities and other programmes

Canteen Cyclesheds Water cooler Book bank	Growth of new faculty Organisation of seminars/work shops	Institute building Hostel building Playgrounds Recreation hall	Library improvement Laboratory improvement
Cooperatives Work experience Common room Union office	Discussions Adoption of modern teaching techniques Faculty evaluation (Self-assessment)	Teacher quarters Guest house	Institute's Magazine Extra curricular activities
Financial Assistance	Travel grants		Annual function
Health care Vocational	Teacher diaries Preparation of		National service scheme
Employment	Improved teaching		Adult education
Bureau	Aids		Involvement of community in institute's activities
Student study Homes Hostel facilities Non-resident Student centres Remedial classes for weak and under-privileged students Games/Sports Debates/Seminars, etc. Hobby classes Special coaching			

General Administration Financial Management

General Administration	Financial Management
Timetable	Raising of additional resources
Option provision	
Teacher's/Student's Union Activities	Running of activities on no-profit no-loss basis like canteen, cooperative stores etc.
Concessions	
Office administration	Timely payment of financial aid to students and other payments to staff
Discipline	
Examinations	
Publications	

ANNEXURE II

List of Projects Covered in Institutional Plans Prepared by Various Schools of District Ajmer in Rajasthan

1. Unit planning and testing
2. Use of diagnostic tests
3. Improving of financial use of school library
4. Starting housing system in the school
5. Construction of boundary wall by students and staff
6. Construction of classrooms in the school
7. Beautifying the school campus
8. Better planning of school laboratory
9. Allowing more time to students for experimentation in laboratory
10. Devices for correction of written work in languages and maths
11. Varied programmes of work experience
12. Starting subject teacher associations
13. Preparation and better use of teaching aids
14. Organised home assignment for summer vacation and long holidays

15. Various schemes of preparing wall magazines
16. Effective parent-teacher association
17. Academic reforms through school complex programme
18. Starting adult education centre
19. Provision of electricity in school
20. Improvement in English teaching
21. Special class for backward students
22. Introducing moral education
23. Planned staff meeting
24. Assisting the poor students in several ways
25. Running hostel for rural boys
26. Starting little children's lectures
27. Providing enough drinking water
28. Starting surprise and informed supervision of classes
29. Preparing school calendar and diary
30. Various activities for the professional growth of teachers
31. Reporting seminar activities in teacher's club
32. Stating tutorial classes under the guidance of head-masters
33. Tackling truancy
34. Introducing night classes
35. Procuring material donations from Rotary Club and Lions Club
36. Starting children's court programme
37. Projects for reading comprehension
38. Getting bullock cart from community for transport of school material
39. Getting furniture donations from parents
40. Planned use of films in classroom

ANNEXURE III

Suggested Outline for Institutional Plan

I. Introduction or background information

   1. Brief historical development of the institute
   2. Objective of the institute
   3. Description of the service area of the institute
   4. Curricular and training programmes
   5. Organisational structure of the institute

II. Situational analysis

   1. Quantitative aspects
      - 1.1 Enrolment (classwise/sexwise/with SC/ST break up for past five to 10 years)
      - 1.2 Survival rate, participation rate, graduation rate, etc.
      - 1.3 Teachers' profile
      - 1.4 Teacher-pupil ratio/classroom-pupil ratio
      - 1.5 Site
      - 1.6 Curricular offerings and enrolment in each course
      - 1.7 Others
   2. Qualitative aspects
      - 2.1 Staff development programme
      - 2.2 Administrative and supervisory programme
      - 2.3 Selection and placement of students
      - 2.4 Academic improvement programmes
      - 2.5 Research and evaluation
      - 2.6 Provision of extension services
      - 2.7 Others

III. Objectives/Targets/Strategies

   1. Assumptions for the future
      - 1.1 Possible change in population and labour force

1.2 Economic growth in the area

1.3 Social development in the area

1.4 Educational and economic plans for the government and their implication for the school

1.5 Need for education and training by the people

2. Quantitative expansion

2.1 Projection of enrolment by grade/level and course for the plan period

2.2 Projection of personnel requirements

2.2.1 Teaching personnel

2.2.2 Non-teaching personnel

2.3 Projection of land and building requirements

2.4 Projection of needed instructional facilities

2.4.1 Equipment including furniture

2.4.2 Supplies and materials

2.4.3 Library facilities

2.5 Extension projects

3. Qualitative improvement

3.1 Administrative structure and/or procedural reform

3.2 Curricular revision/reorientation

3.3 Provision of life or community experience

3.4 Placement and follow-up studies of graduates

3.5 Research and evaluation

3.6 Selection and school placements of students

IV. Programmes/Projects/Activities

Detailed plans for all the projects should be given separately along with work plan (Refer Annexure VI)

V. Costing of the plan (financial requirements) (total as well as projectwise break up)

1. Revenue expenditure

1.1 Salaries of personnel

1.2 Operational expenses (item-wise)

1.3 Other expenditures (give details).

2. Capital expenditure

   Expenditure for school projects such as building and purchase of equipments

VI. Strategy of implementation

1. Administrative approval of the plan
2. Ways and means of obtaining funds for programmes/ projects.
3. Further maximisation of the use of resources
4. Time schedule and target period
5. Alternative measures for contingencies that might crop up
6. Involvement of implementators and decision makers
7. Other measures

VII. Evaluation

1. Periodical reports and feedbacks
2. Actual inspection and observation of projects
3. Workplans, graph, pert.

ANNEXURE IV

Workplan Schedule for implementation of institution Plan

(Forming of timetable)

Activity breakdown	*Work implementation*				*Time schedule for implementation*							
	By whom	*In consalutation*	*To be enforced by*	*Final Decision*	*April* *I*	*II*	*II*	*IV*	*May* *I*	*II*	*III*	*IV*
1. Collection of necessary data (subject list, staff statement, accommodation, old timetable)	Vice-Principal	Principal	-	-								
2. Preparation of draft timetable	Vice-principal	Concerned faculty	-	Vice Principal								

(Contd...)

(Contd...)

3. Discussion on draft	Vice Principal	Heads of Depts.	Heads of Depts.	Vice Principal	
4. Finalisation of timetable	Principal	Vice Principal	Heads of Depts.	Principal	
5. Implementation of time table	Heads of Dep.	Vice-Principal	Concerned faculty	Vice-Principal	
6. Revision of time	Vice Principal	Heads of Dept.	Concerned faculty	Principal	*As and when necessary*

ANNEXURE V (A)

Method of Working out Teachers and Teaching Space Requirements at Institutional Level

(Institution with 385 students having one-year course)

Subject	*Size of section*	*No. of sections*	*No. of periods per week*	*Total weekly teaching load*
1. English	40	10	5	50
2. Science				
- Theory	40	10	5	50
- Practicals	20	20	5	100
3. Maths	40	10	5	50
4. Religion	80	5	3	15
5. Civics	40	10	2	20
6. Social Studies	40	10	3	30
7. Community Development	40	10	2	20
8. Industrial Arts	65	6	5	30
9. Physical Education	80	5	5	25
10. Home Science	40	4	5	20

Note : i) There are 40 periods per week

ii) Home Science is for girls and Industrial Arts for boys.

ANNEXURE V (B)

Requirement of Teachers in an Institution for 385 Students having One Year Course

	Subject	*Total weekly teaching load*	*Teaching periods per teacher per week*	*No. of teachers*	*Teachers required*
1.	English	50	20	2.5	English = 3
2.	Science				
	- Theory	50	20	2.5	Science = 10
	- Practicals	100	20	5.0	Maths
3.	Maths	50	20	2.5	
4.	Religion	15	20	0.8	Religion = 1
5.	Civics	20	20	1	
6.	Social Studies	30	20	1.5	Civics, Social Studies
7.	Community Development	20	20	1	Community Development = 4
8.	Industrial	30	20	1.5	Industrial Arts = 2
9.	Physical Education	25	20	1.3	Pgy.Edn. = 1
10.	Home Science	20	20	1.0	Home Sc. = 1

Summary:

No. of Teachers Required =	22	Enrolment = 385
Principal	1	Teacher: Pupil Ratio = 16:7
Total	23	

ANNEXURE V (C)

Teaching Space Requirements and its Weekly Utilisation by an Institution with 385 Students having One Year Course

		Type of accommodation					
Subject	*Total weekly*	*General class*	*Science labs.*	*Indust-arts room*	*Multi-purpose room*	*Field*
1. English	50	50	–	–	–	–
2. Science						
Theory	50	50	–	–	–	–
Practicals	100	–	100	–	–	–
3. Maths	50	50	–	–	–	–
4. Religion	15	–	–	–	15	–
5. Civics	20	2	–	–	–	–
6. Social Studies	30	30	–	–	–	–
7. Industrial Community Development	20	20	–	–	–	–
8. Industrial Arts	30	–	–	30	–	–
9. Physical Edn.	25	–	–	–	–	25
10. Home Science	20	20	–	–	–	–
Total	410	240	100	30	15	25
No. of rooms required		7	3	1	1	
Job Factor		86%	83%	75%	38%	

7

Institutional Self-Evaluation: A Module

—*N.M. Bhagia, A. Mathew**

I

THE CONCEPT

Institutional evaluation, *per se,* is not an innovation. The concern for establishing the principle of accountability in education, reflected in the National Policy on Education (1986), has renewed interest of educators and administrators in institutional evaluation. This has motivated educational workers to think of appropriate methods to plan and manage institutional evaluation more effectively.

The National Policy on Education (NPE) 1986 states that "an overhaul of the system of planning and the management of education will receive high priority." This emphasis on revitalising the system of planning and management of education appears to underscore the NPE's conviction that the success of revamping the educational system depends upon the degree to which the internal efficiency of the educational institutions could be increased. Establishing the principle of accountability in relation to given objectives and norms, which

**National Institute of Educational Planning and Administration 17-B Sri Aurobindo Marg, New Delhi.*

is one of the guiding considerations in the overhauling of the system of planning and management, is of particular importance to increase the institutional efficiency. The Programme of Action which elaborates the operational strategies speaks of "rigorous systems of performance audit against practical and objective performance" to be laid down and enforced through incentives and disincentives.

It is evident that the system of evaluation and appraisal of institutional performance is called upon to be more professional than the modes of evaluation we have had so far, especially inspection and supervision. This module is based and developed on the premise that (i) the system of inspection and supervision, although concerned with it, is not an adequate instrument for institutional evaluation; and (ii) for this purpose, participative self-evaluation of the institution is a better mode of performance audit for increasing institutional efficiency.

Institutional Evaluation

At the outset, the term 'institutional evaluation' must be distinguished from 'student evaluation' and 'teacher evaluation'—terms which are very often talked about whenever there is a concern for educational reforms and innovations. Student evaluation naturally follows student learning and teacher evaluation is an attempt to have an appraisal of teachers' activities in and outside the classroom. Both these terms are, therefore, restricted and limited to particular areas of evaluation in an institution.

The focus of institutional evaluation is the performance of the institution as a whole, and not the performance of individual students or staff members alone. Although, the connection between performance of individuals and performance of institutions is inseparable and highly dependent on each other, yet it is important to appreciate the distinction between the holistic approach of institutional evaluation and the individualistic approach of evaluating performance of students or the staff members, commonly known as staff appraisal or personnel evaluation. Institutional evaluation is, therefore, much more than student or personnel evaluation.

> Institution being multi-faceted, institutional evaluation encompasses all crucial facets related to institutional inputs, process and outputs or products.

Three characteristics of evaluation of an institution must be understood. First, it is empirical in process. It involves the systematic collection and analysis of data/information concerning the operation of an institution. Second, institutional evaluation is an attempt to determine the worth, merit and effect of an institution. The third, and the most important, evaluation examines whether the institution is achieving its objectives and whether its organisational climate is healthy.

When an institution is found ineffective, its revival is achieved by infusing new resources, a redefinition of its direction and a realignment of its functioning.

Evaluation can be threefold: (i) external (both in conception and execution), (ii) designed externally or jointly, but conducted by internal members, and (iii) designed and conducted internally (institutional self-evaluation). For various considerations as explained below, internal self-evaluation would appear to be the most effective, from the point of view of institutional efficiency and achievement of its goals.

Why Institutional Self-Evaluation?

Institutional development

Any institution that wishes to change and move faster towards its goals in a systematic manner must continually evaluate its own performance and assess the discrepancy between current operations and desired outcomes. This calls for developing and practising some system of self-appraisal by the institution.

Such a system will help in appropriate planning, resource allocation and effective management resulting in institutional development.

Promoting accountability

The National Policy on Education (1986) in its part-X states that an overhaul of the system of planning and the management of education will receive high priority. One of the guiding considerations for this purpose, the document points out, will be "establishment of the principle of accountability in relation to given objectives and norms." Institutional self-evaluation is a mechanism for promoting accountability in education.

Overcoming weakness of external evaluation

External evaluation, which has been in vogue for a pretty long time in educational system, has been getting weaker day by day. Several research studies have pointed out a number of weaknesses in the inspection system of schools. The studies show that the practice of inspection of schools and evaluating them is too haphazard and does not achieve the goals. There is a lot of window dressing at the time of inspection in schools and colleges and a tendency to cover up deficiencies. Many a time, inspectors fail to play an effective supervisory role because of the limitations of time and energy and lack of proper planning for inspection and proper cooperation from the teachers.

Prevalence and scope in India

Self-evaluation of educational institutions, including schools, is a widely accepted mode of institutional evaluation and appraisal in Western countries. This is due largely to the degree of autonomy they enjoy in matters of appointment of teachers, powers of the heads of institutions, decision-making processes, autonomy in designing curricular programmes and the management of the institution as a whole. Being under state control, the system of organisation and management of educational institutions, especially at the school level, is totally different in India. And, although decentralised at the district and block levels, the system of evaluation and appraisal is with the government and its local bodies. Thus, institutional self-evaluation as an alternative to this system of evaluation may seem less appropriate. But considering its advantages, if institutional self-evaluation is conceived as a complementarity to the system of inspection and supervision, then there is greater chance of meeting the NPE's objectives of enhancing internal efficiency of the institution as well as achieving the objectives outlined for each level of education.

Even in India, institutional evaluation, through the modality of grading of schools, as a complement to the annual inspection and supervision, has been accepted and adopted in many states and union territories and school networks under the central government, like the Kendriya Vidyalaya schools. These exercises are internal only in the sense that they are conducted by the head of the institution. They are intended to be an aid and not a substitute for the annual inspection and supervision. Although conducted internally, they are not exercises in institutional self-evaluation. Thus, there in a case for institutional self evaluation not only on its own merit as a form of appraisal and audit, but also as an aid to inspection and supervision.

That could be used as an independent, and in many ways as a more comprehensive and realistic method as is seen from the practices of the 'Public Schools' in India which are unaided but recognised and under private management. They do not have the system of annual inspection and supervision by the functionaries of the State/District Education Department. But does not affect the efficiency of the public schools. For, they do practice a systems performance appraisal and evaluation which are more in common with the attributes of institutional self-evaluation. The gains of institutional self-evaluation can, therefore, still be interwoven in the governmental educational system as an aid to the existing system of evaluation through inspection and supervision.

Advantages and limitation

Advantages and limitations of self-evaluation should be understood clearly in order to be aware of the positive gains as well as the possible criticisms by those who are believers in *status quo* or sceptical about the desired results.

Advantages

i) Internal self-evaluation is done with a fuller understanding of the context and dynamics within which the institution is working because it is carried out by those who are members of the institution.

ii) The experience and insight gained by the evaluators in the process of evaluation remains with the institution.

iii) It saves the time of the evaluators as they are conversant with the working of the institution whereas external evaluators would take time to familiarise themselves with the functioning of the institution.

iv) The evaluators by their knowledge and experience within the institution can straight away come to identify the bottlenecks and focus attention. This helps evaluation to be an in-depth rather than a superficial exercise.

v) As involvement helps increase commitment, those involved in evaluation will stand committed to change and that will make improvement easier.

Limitations

To be able to guard themselves against and in the interest of credibility, the institutional head and evaluators should also be conscious of the limitations of internal self-evaluation.

i) The relative isolation of one department from another which prevails in our educational institutions would easily disprove the assumption that internal self-evaluation team has fuller understanding of the dynamics within which the institution functions. Similarly, the experience and insights gained by internal evaluators remaining within the institution would hold good only if they are not transferred.

ii) Internal evaluators may find it difficult to raise sensitive issues as they are part of the system. Besides, the biases of an internal evaluation team may creep into evaluation and people may be on the defensive when asked for self-evaluation, especially those teachers who feel insecure in their knowledge as well as those in administration who are not honest.

iii) Internal evaluators may have insights into the process of their institution, but may lack a larger perspective of external agency whose members have experience of evaluating many institutions.

iv) If teachers' time is not properly budgeted in their academic calendar, evaluation would either cut into their instructional schedule or overburden them.

v) Pressures from outside for accountability might not be satisfied if internal self-evaluation is related only to the institution's self-determined objectives.

Points for Discussion

1. In what sense is institutional evaluation holistic in nature?
2. How does institutional self-evaluation help in establishing the principle of accountability as envisaged by NPE?
3. How can we overcome the limitations of institutional self-evaluation?

II

PLANNING CONSIDERATIONS

In planning the strategy for evaluation an institutional head would need to address himself/herself to five crucial questions:

i) What is the purpose of evaluation?
ii) What do we evaluate?
iii) How do we know what we evaluate has relevance and credibility?
iv) What do we need in order to be able to evaluate?
v) How do we determine our evaluation strategy?

Statement of Purpose

Institutional self-evaluation can be on the diverse aspects of the institution, viz., (i) its worth and merit, (ii) the extent to which its objectives have been achieved, (iii) assessing its process and functioning for progressive improvement, and (iv) to provide a knowledge for defending and validating the institution's functioning and achievement.

The second category of aspects of evaluation relates to the operations of functional process of institution which facilitate in achieving intended outcomes. These refer to structure and methodology of the institutional operation.

The success and utility of process or operation of evaluation depends upon the identification of right and critical variables or indicators. While it may not be necessary to evaluate every process indicator, we should be aware of the full list of process variables so that we may select the more critical ones.

Educational institutions normally have the following systems or groups; (i) Administrative or Governance system; (ii) Faculty; (iii) Students, (iv) Support systems; and (v) Academic programmes.

The major concerns of each of the subsystems are as under:

a) The system of governance is the heart of an institutional operation as it lays down the policy, and provides direction and guidance to the different subsystems.
b) The faculty is the backbone in an educational institution and their commitment to the education of the children as

well as the efficiency of the institution determine the quality of the institution itself.

c) The main stake of an educational institution is the students, the avenues for their learning and development.

d) The support systems, not so much their availability and adequacy, but their utilisation, can make all the difference to the efficient and effective functioning of an educational institution.

e) The instructional and other teaching-learning programmes, their designing and management involve a whole range of issues relating to the faculty, institutional goals, etc.

The relationship between and interaction of each of these subsystems of an educational institution yield a rich list of operation variables. The role of these subsystems, including the variables and their implications for the operational efficiency of the institution as explicated in greater detail in appendix, need to be appreciated.

Relevance and Credibility of Internal Evaluation

Evaluation should begin with an articulation of the rationale, goals, objectives, functions and tasks of the institution. Evaluation must be based on accurate and reliable information on the institution's internal operations and its impact both on the external environment as well as on the achievement of its goals and objectives.

Educational institutions should be sensitive to the changing needs of the community in which it serves, or else it would be in danger of fast becoming irrelevant. The information system of the institution should reflect its responsiveness to social and technological changes, and rising expectations. Evaluation must also bring out the institution's sensitivity to the expectations of the different clients it serves—students, parents, employers, who are concerned with the efficiency and quality of the services. To be relevant, evaluation must define the institution's role *vis-a-vis* the social milieu in which it functions.

A major issue of internal self-evaluation is its credibility in terms of the standards set and maintained in evaluation. The internal credibility of self-evaluation would depend upon the objectives and the reliable and efficient manner in which it is conducted. Internal credibility implies that the persons conducting the evaluation are both trustworthy and competent to perform the job.

In an environment where mutual trust and open criticism are institutional norms, objectivity has a fair chance of thriving; and where staff competitiveness and territorial defensive -ness are prevalent, objectivity would be a rare commodity. In such a climate, an independent evaluation unit may be required.

Internal evaluation is a credible activity only if information about the institution's functioning is readily available for internal discussion and decision making. Self-evaluation will command acceptance by the employees only if they are assured that their views are respected, reports are clear and timely and follow-up actions are in consonance with the decision of evaluation reports.

The degree to which internal evaluation convinces its external audiences about the impartiality, honesty and completeness in reporting, would determine external credibility. The common criticism that those involved in the programmes of an institution would have a vested interest in claiming its success can easily be weighed down by another possibility. Those who design the operations of an institution are likely to be more concerned about the validity and reliability of their own evaluation. Thus, from both points of view, there is need to make explicit controls for ensuring credibility of internal evaluation.

Even in Western countries where institutional self-evaluation is an accepted mode of assessment, there is this practice of external experts checking and verifying its reliability. There is also another method of combining external evaluation after every three to five years with the more frequent internal self-evaluation.

In India, where self-evaluation is still to gain the confidence of the Education Department and the public, there is a greater need for a periodic external evaluation to check realistic nature of internal self-evaluation.

The most vital component of internal evaluation is the technical competence and personal integrity of the evaluators and they should enjoy the reputation of being competent and honest.

Competence comes from training and training needs can be assessed and attended to by the technically more competent staff through in-house training. Technical competence and objectivity can be conveyed through evaluation reports, which explicitly state the evaluation procedures adopted, quality control used and methodology employed.

To sum up:

i) Relevance of internal evaluation depends on the impact which the institution has on external environment;

ii) Objectivity would be determined by the technical competence and personal integrity of those conducting evaluation;

iii) External credibility would be ensured by impartiality, honesty and completeness in reporting;

iv) Internal credibility would depend upon ready availability of information regarding institutional functioning and respect accorded to individual's views; and

v) Internal credibility would also hinge on the trust-worthiness of those conducting evaluation.

Evaluation Needs

It is precisely to ensure gaining the advantages and avoiding the disadvantages of internal self-evaluation that clarity is needed in respect of what is required for evaluation. The requirements for evaluation must be worked out within the framework and premise that it aims to minimise additional personnel and resources by using existing manpower and effecting savings arising from improvement in managing practices. It is with this perspective that the requirements in terms of time, personnel and financial resources have to be determined.

Personnel

It is vital that those who have to assume evaluation sales be identified and their roles legitimised. The skills and knowledge as well as the methodology and procedures used in evaluation should not be those of evaluation specialists, but be within the competency level of the personnel. If it is of a specialist nature, evaluation cannot become an institution-wise activity and it will lose the inherent value of participation by staff. Institutional self-evaluation should be conceived as a layman organisational activity, with skills that can be readily acquired by those involved in it. Even then, it is important at the planning stage, to identify the nature and scope of evaluation including the various tasks and competencies required. This would help assess the competence the staff possess and arrange for training needs to undertake evaluation, this would also validate the rationale that no new staff is required and that the existing staff can be prepared to undertake evaluation as a part of the institutional task. This will also help raise staff competence and experience in evaluation.

Time

Preliminary planning decision should be made regarding time to be allocated within the institution's and individual's calendar of activities. The timing of evaluation could be on a regular, periodic basis, monthly, quarterly, half-yearly or yearly or at critical points of institutional life—completion of a particular phase of a programme, like before the change of text books, etc.

Finance

Financial constraints are always a reality in planning, self-evaluation, unlike external evaluation; one is not expected to need large financial outlay because it is part of an institutional activity. In fact, evaluation which is expected to lead to a better performance and improved management, should result in considerable savings. But whatever financial requirements are envisaged for the initial states of the evaluation programme, such as for training, information collection and analysis, etc., should be provided for.

Evaluation methodology

The purpose, scope and technical standard of evaluation determine the kinds of methodology to be used. However, it would be useful for the evaluation staff to try out the evaluation programme in the formative stages, using questionnaire surveys, interviews and observations, workshop/conference methods, records study or a combination of all these methods before determining the methodology to evaluate the process. Some of the tools available for this purpose are included in the references.

Whatever be the type of evaluation and methodology adopted, it should not be over-sophisticated, making it difficult for use and application. That evaluation design is the best which allows the evaluators to make valid inference from the proper data available.

Information base

In building an information base, it would be necessary to consider an appropriate information management design. Information design is a way of identifying and arranging the available data in such a way as to indicate the operations and output of an organisation.

The basic questions to be addressed in the design of information systems are:

i) *Availability of data:* Data availability refers to the readily available information as well as those that would be generated depending upon the issues to be evaluated.

ii) *Accessibility of data:* Data accessibility is a little more serious issue. The data may be readily available but the question is whether evaluator has access to information concerning people, programmes, functions and management decisions. There are moral, social and political considerations of information and abuse. Thus, evaluator's and individual's right to discretion' need to be reconciled and evaluators need to adopt defensible procedures to have access to, as well as the use of data.

iii) *Kinds of tools needed to extract (collect and generate) data*: Data collection methods include questionnaires, job records, periodic returns, observation schedule and checklists. The selection of data collection methods, data base management programmes are capable of paying rich dividends in subsequent data collection and analysis.

Determine Evaluation Strategy

There are three approaches to finalise the evaluation strategy: (i) to get external experts to draw up the evaluation strategy: (ii) constituting a taskforce of internal members to formulate the evaluation strategy; and (iii) giving broad guidelines through seminars/workshops, conferences, etc., and have the strategy formulated by groups.

Each of these strategies has its own advantages and disadvantages corresponding to the reactions such types of evaluations would evoke. The third appears to be the most democratic in terms of participative planning, involvement and eventually commitment. But the one that is generally preferred is the in-house taskforce strategy.

III

MANAGING SELF-EVALUATION

In implementing institutional self-evaluation, four component tasks must be pressed into operation, viz., (i) Staff preparation; (ii) Installation; (iii) Information management; and (iv) Follow-up action.

Staff Preparation

Evaluation for improvement implies that it is pervasive activity of an institution, involving extensive staff partici-pation in performance appraisal and decision making as a conscious, willing and committed activity. Management may install and direct evaluation, but in self-evaluation for better performance on the part of the staff and institution, staff commitment to self-evaluation is critical.

To ensure that all members share a common perspective, and have the confidence to perform the tasks ahead, opportunities must be provided to staff members to discuss, debate, acquire the necessary competence and work out the areas of evaluation.

Staff preparation will vary according to the degree and depth of evaluation. Where an internal self-evaluation plan has already been formulated, the following sequence of activities would help the smooth flow of evaluation process.

i) Initial orientation and briefing the staff on evaluation strategy;
ii) Allowing time for staff members to study the evaluation strategy;

iii) Allowing staff to ventilate their misgivings and offer their alternative suggestions;

iv) Constant monitoring of evaluation's progress;

v) Fostered through continuing staff development and resources allocation for institution improvement.

Installation Component

Introduction of internal self-evaluation would need to take into consideration the following factors.

1. *Perception of utility:* Evaluation as an activity would be valued if it is perceived to have utility, in a personal sense, by staff members. It would be readily accepted if it is shown that it would not disrupt the normal life of the institution.
2. *Work schedule of personnel:* The scope of evaluation programme would determine the persons to be involved, the nature of involvement, time and the appropriate changes needed in their schedule of activities. If everyone is involved in evaluation, then, it is necessary to write workload into their work schedules. Extra efforts would be needed to motivate the staff to accept the 'new' tasks of evaluation.
3. *Visibility:* Evaluation should never be a covert activity of an institution, but it must be known to and seen by everyone. This is all the more essential if evaluation is programmed as a regular part of the institution's activities. Evaluation involves visible inputs and is identifiable by visible outputs which affect the majority of staff members. Its visibility, therefore, ensures that it receives due attention from all concerned at all levels of the institution. Visibility also means that evaluation activities are reported as scheduled to those in the institution and the community who have the right to know for prompt follow-up action.

4. *Clarity of task:* A common mistake of most institutions in installing evaluation is to assume that everyone involved in evaluation knows and understands what others are talking about. It is absolutely essential at the outset for the staff to have clarity of the operational definition of evaluation, at least on the three essential points:

i) The events to be evaluated;
ii) Some standards for judgement; and
iii) Using the judgement of worth or value for some action.

Information Management

The task of installing an information system includes (a) deciding about the mode of collection, centralised or decentralised, (b) collecting it without distortion, (d) analysing it, and (e) making it available for decision-making purposes.

Information should be collected not only on input and output data, but also on the day-to-day processes of the institution. Data relating to the day-to-day processes could be voluminous and its selection, collection, disaggregation and dissemination to relevant persons should be structured help to monitor the institutional functioning.

For data to be forthcoming for timely decision-making, data collection, selection and analysis must be considered as a specialised activity of an organisation. In all institutions, useful data for management have to be deliberately extracted from the ever accumulating records.

Follow-up Actions

Evaluation is meant to facilitate intelligent decision-making. Hence, evaluation reports are not to be shelved, but its findings should be put to good use relating to the following issues:

i) Whether the institution actually works.

ii) How the institution actually works.
iii) Whether it operates satisfactorily.
iv) Whether it utilises its resources optimally.
v) Whether it is cost effective.
vi) Whether it can be improved upon.
vii) By what means can it be improved upon.

IV

CONCLUSION

The culture (norms and values) which an institution develops over a period of time may have been productive during the early stages but may have become dysfunctional or inadequate for its effectiveness and utility for a later point of time. Environment is changing and educational institutions must be responsive to the requirements of changed environment. The responsiveness can be infused through a process of self-renewal based on evaluation.

Internal evaluation symbolises the efforts made by an institution to examine its objectives, activities, ways of functioning, norms and values and other aspects of its process in the context of changing environment and changing profile of its members. On this basis the institution redefines its objectives and processes to maintain or improve the institution's vitality and effectiveness. Therefore, institutional self-evaluation is a stimuli to created responsiveness to change. Self-renewal process can be started with the discussion and deliberations of evaluation reports and acting upon their findings and recommendations.

Internal evaluation can also be seen to conform and correspond to the principles of organisational development. For, at the heart of organisational development, is the concern for the vitalising, energising, actualising, activating and renewing of organisation through technical and human resources. Evaluation helps to identify the deficiencies and show the scope to enable the institution to be set for organisational development.

Organisational development is a long-range effort to improve an organisation's problem-solving and renewal processes. It begins with the organisational diagnosis and works through organisational development interventions based on feedback. Self-evaluation has a similar aim of enhancing the institutional performance by diagnosing its present performance *vis-a-vis* set objectives, identifying deficiencies and bottlenecks through its feedback and facilitating institutional improvement through interventions to improve performance.

Hence, whether viewed from the point of view of self-renewal or improved performance and efficiency of the institution, with which the development and commitment for change are also bound up, internal self-evaluation seems to call for its institutionalisation as a regular and integral part of institutional life.

Institutional self-evaluation, thus, is bound up with the improvement in the management of the education system which the National Policy on Education, 1986, underlines as the critical factor for educational reorganisation and transformation toward national regeneration. Hence, the greatest contribution that heads of educational institutions/schools could make to the successful implementation of NPE, would seem to be through the instrumentality of institutional self-evaluation.

REFERENCES

Bhagia, N.M., 1983, "Research in Educational Administration: Retrospect and Prospect", NIEPA Occasional Paper 3, NIEPA, New Delhi.

Leaven, Carmel, "Evaluation and Education" in J.V.D. Cruz and P.J. Sheehan.

Ministry of Education, Government of India, 1966, Report of Education Commission, New Delhi.

Ministry of Education, Government of India, 1985, *Challenge of Education: A Policy Perspective*, New Delhi.

Ministry of Human Resources Development, Government of India, *National Policy on Education,* 1986, New Delhi.

Ministry of HRD, Government of India, 1986, *National Policy on Education, 1986: Programme of Action*, New Delhi.

Rao, Dr. T.V., "Process Evaluation for Institution Building and Programme Development in Education", Paper presented at High level Management Development Workshop on Evaluation of Educational Programmes and Institutions, Seoul, 20-30 October 1986.

Reynolds, David, ed., 1986, Studying School Effectiveness, London: The Falmer Press.

Smith, Dr. Kevin R., "Co-operative Management in Educational Management", paper presented at High Level Management Development Workshop, Seoul, 20-30 October, 1986.

Tyler, Ralph W., "Changing Concept of Education Evaluation", *International Journal of Educational Research*, 1986, Vol. 10, No.1, pp. 53-67.

Yow, Dr. Chew Tow, "The Organisation and Management of Evaluation for Organisational Development and Programme Improvement", Paper presented at High level Management Development Workshop, Seoul, 20-30 October 1986.

8

Citizenship Behaviour: An Indicator of a Civilised Society

*—A.B. Phatak**

Development of appropriate citizenship behaviour is the key to the development of a civilised society. There cannot be any better moment to discuss the issue today. People of India have witnessed the worst from a moral degradation in public life through the Tehelka tapes. Some people say it is only the tip of the iceberg. It appears that no segment of our society has remained unaffected by corruption. Either one is a victim of corruption or a party to the process of corruption. Let us be clear that this malice is not merely restricted to defence alone; it is visible in every walk of life, be it P.W.D., Police, Taxation, Housing business, Industry, Railways, Telecom Services or even Education. Justice Ranganath Mishra, former Chief Justice of Supreme Court, in his letter to the Chief Justice of Supreme Court expressed shock and horror regarding the dog raiding human behaviour in our society and expressed the need to take some immediate concrete steps to rectify the situation. The letter was treated as a writ petition and the outcome was the Verma Committee report. Let us hope it helps in creating a new climate in the country where we are able to witness a responsible citizenship behaviour. The Verma

**Ex-principal, Shah G.L. Kabra Teachers College, Jodhpur, India.*

Committee recommendation and outcomes of deliberations present in this seminar, would go a long way in changing the present scenario. Before discussing the steps which can help in developing responsible citizenship behaviour, let us devote some time to think about what we expect as a responsible citizenship behaviour.

What is Responsible Citizenship Behaviour?

Fundamental Duties

Through the 42nd amendment of the constitution article 51A on fundamental duties was added to our constitution. The ten fundamental duties listed in this article are well known. The list of fundamental duties provides a sound basis for responsible citizenship behaviour. The duties are in tune with the spirit of our Constitution which says "We the people of India solemnly pledge to abide by." These duties are also necessary for ensuring, sovereignty, unity and integrity of our nation and also for fostering natural integration, preservation of cultural heritage, protection of national property, protection of our environment and so on. In short, these are essential for a smooth functioning of our democracy and keeping it alive.

Other Behaviours

Though the duties listed above are quite comprehensive yet I would like to add a few more desirable behaviours to be expected of a responsible citizen. These have not been arranged in any heirarchical order.

These are:

1. *Respect for the laws of the land:* It should be a natural tendency on the part of every responsible citizen to respect rules whether anybody is watching or not. People say that in some countries breaking a rule is an exception, unfortunately in our country the rule is otherwise. If there is a rule of not walking on lawns we would invariably violate it. More examples could be quoted; we take pride in jumping a queue, plucking flowers from a public garden, parking vehicles in a 'no parking' zone, undertaking illegal constructions and encroachment on government land and so on. These need to be stopped.

2. *Protests in legal manner:* If any law or rule is unjust a responsible citizen has a right to protest, but there are legally approved civilised ways to register protests and these should be followed. What we are witnessing in parliament and assemblies is far from a responsible citizenship behaviour. The working of these highest democratic institution is paralysed for days together. If government is doing wrong, members should criticise it in parliament, so that people know the truth and at the time of the next elections they may take appropriate decisions about the party concerned. Not allowing parliament to function is anti-democratic and not a responsible behaviour.

3. Not becoming a party to a corrupt practice.

4. Exercising voting right judiciously without any fear or favour.

5. Protesting whenever your right is infringed or injustice is done. Many times, attitude of most of us is जाने भी दो यारो.

6. Not doing anything which will cause inconvenience to thers.
7. Checking wastage of national resources, light, water, etc,
8. Not being carried away by rumours.
9. Having tolerance for others' views.

What We can do to Inculcate Responsible Citizenship

I. Education

Education has to play a crucial role in developing responsible citizenship behaviour. Are we sensitising our students towards the problems of society? Do we ever discuss such problems, with students *vis a vis* their role in such situations?

There are a lot of things which need to be done in educational institutions. Justice R.N. Mishra also expressed the view that the key to save the society from the horrifying degradation lies with education. Kirit Joshi, an eminent educationist, says, "In a sense the teacher in respect of education for character development has no method and yet every method. Similarly, he has no specific content, yet every content."

Let us be clear that values cannot be taught, they are caught. Climate of the school, the behaviour of teachers and elders would go a long way in developing a responsible behaviour among students who would be citizens of tomorrow.

Again to quote Kirit Joshi, "All these (character development) need to be developed by three basic proceses: introspective observation, careful process of control and giving awareness of our self and of the world and their interrelationship by means of refinements of facilities and capacities." Such an introspective observation and self-control would help us in making our contribution towards the progress and unification of the society and the world at large.

Community

A community can exercise control over the behaviour of its members by exercising moral pressure. In olden times, people would hesitate doing wrong things for the fear of punitive action from their community. जात बाहर कर देंगे, रोटी-बेटी व्यवहार बन्द कर देंगे. This moral pressure of community has weakened now-a-days.

Leaders' Behaviour

There was an old saying: यथा राजा तथा प्रजा. We can now change it to: यथा नेता तथा प्रजा. The standards of moral behaviour are set by leaders. If they themselves have scant regard for values, they will be imitated by their followers. Let us genuinely march towards value-based politics and not tolerate leaders who do not behave like responsible citizens.

Charity Begins at Home

Everybody wants that society should be free from competition, but in his analysis he feels that everybody, other than himself, is corrupt. The better approach would be, instead of trying to reform others let us pledge today that we will not become a party to a corrupt practice and it is likely that a chain reaction in the positive direction may start; *small things go a long way in building character*. We may not be able to become a saint overnight but we can certainly inculcate small things in our life, e.g., observing punctuality, not violating any rules, not entering a platform without purchasing a platform ticket, not approaching a teacher for a favour for your son/daughter, not seeking any recommendation. These are small bricks for the formation of a strong character. I have practised most of these and it gives me great satisfaction when I introspect.

9

Institutional Planning: Why and How?

*—Radha Sexena**

Planning is an essential activity of national life. The function of institutional planning is to keep an institution occupied in the search for the best possible in the existing social environment. In the context of formulating a plan with clear objectives for any institution, it is necessary to reflect upon the existing circumstances. One cannot turn away from the realities of life and society. J.P. Naik wanted to emphasize the freedom of teachers to plan something new, to do something original and to face their problems creatively. Schools must have the freedom to plan their own programme of development and improvement. Such type of thinking has given birth to the concept of institutional planning.

Bhatnagar and Verma have said that the needs and requirements of every institution should be taken into consideration and that it should not only be associated with educational planning but also a 'planning atmosphere' be built up and maintained in each institution.

Institutional planning means that plans are initiated, formulated, and implemented by individual institutions to

**Reader in Education, Faculty of Education, Deemed University Banasthali Vidyapeeth, Jaipur (Rajasthan), India.*

achieve the predetermined objectives of educational development and qualitative improvement.

Planning by a school is not altogether a novel idea. A large number of schools in this country have a system of planning their yearly programme. A few schools have a procedure of having a seminar of the teachers for about a week in the beginning of the year and also a similar seminar towards the end of the academic year. In the first seminar, the teachers and the headmaster work together to plan programme for the entire academic year. These plans are based on the assessment of the experiences of the previous year. They conjoin the present needs and resources and fit well in the perspective plans in the seminar organised towards the end of the year, and an assessment of the work done in the course of the year is undertaken. Opinions and experiences are shared and exchanged, and decisions are made for improving the future programmes.

WHAT IS AN INSTITUTIONAL PLAN?

Dr. M.B. Buch (1969) defined: "An institutional plan is a set of programmes prepared by an educational institution on the basis of its felt needs and the knowledge of its resources—available and likely to be available—with a view to improve the school standards and practices and with a view to provide for the future development of the institution." The plan may be for a longer duration or a shorter duration; it is based on the principal of optimum utilisation of the resources available in the school and community.

The Education Commission (1964-66) has aptly said, "No comprehensive programme of educational development can ever put across unless it involves every educational institution and all the human factors connected with its teachers, students and the local community and unless it provides the necessary instruments to put in their best efforts."

S.P.Naik said that institutional planning is a unique answer to four problems, namely:

i) giving freedom to teachers;
ii) making teaching effective;
iii) involving every teacher in the formulation and implementation of planning, and
iv) effective work by monitoring resources.

Why an Institutional Plan

Planned work is always better than an unplanned one. An institution cannot be effective if does not organise its programme without giving them sufficient thought. An institution should have its long-term goals, priorities and targets which should be determined after serious and sustained thinking and about which there should be no vacillation unless there is detected something seriously wrong about them. In fact, what is required is goal-directed and need-based planning over a longer period of time. Institutional planning fulfils this need.

The main advantage of institutional planning lies in the fact that planned work is always more economical than unplanned one and that planned work ensures improvement and devolvement. It gives the right direction to educational planning in the country, i.e., the upward direction initiating flat bottom and going up to the top.

a) Institutional planning is realistic and need-based.
b) It is economic and cost effective.
c) Institutional planning gives scope for large participation. The persons who matter and those who are affected are consulted and involved from the very beginning.
d) It is related to various aspects of an institution--academic administrative, and financial, short term and long term

according to the nature of the programme. Hence, it becomes comprehensive, more practical and feasible.

e) Since it is at grassroots level planning, it gives psychological satisfaction of sharing and belongingness, which contribute to success in the implementation.

f) It is flexible, and dynamic changes can be done easily in response to local needs and demands.

g) It is freedom-oriented and initiative-based. Teachers, students and parents are at liberty to plan and implement the programmes which are useful and practicable. Nothing is imposed from above and their bureaucratic control.

Objectives of Institutional Planning

The objectives may be specific and the programmes need-based. Hence they may differ from one institution to another in order of priority and degree of importance given to particular programmes. The objectives may be given below:

i) Instruction or the teaching-learning is to be improved.

ii) Infrastructural facilities need to be developed.

iii) Resources of all kinds—material human and ideational—must be utilised to the optimum.

iv) Community and local resources must be utilised for improving the institutions.

v) Local talents and expertise need to be harnessed fully for developmental programmes.

vi) All kinds of co-curricular activities need to be organised with the community support and initiative and participation.

An institution is a growing organism responsive to the local needs and adaptive to the local conditions. The cultural values and ethos are to be properly realised and reflected through its programmes and practices. It gives the right direction to educational planning in the country, i.e., the upward direction initiating from bottom and going up to the top.

MAJOR CHARACTERISTICS OF AN INSTITUTIONAL PLAN

Need-Based

An institutional plan is prepared keeping in view the needs of the school as identified by the school staff. These needs may be the area of the overall organisation of the school, the internal school administration, the instructional programme, methods of teaching, environmental conditions which affect learning by pupils, etc.

Specificity

Every school is an entity of itself. It has its individuality. The plan for an institution in characterised by several factors like its own needs, the resources available to it, the needs of the community, the needs of the student population the ability and the potentiality of the staff, etc. Every school will, therefore, have its own specific plan.

Principle of Optimum Utilisation

The institutional plan is not expenditure-oriented. The institution, while planning, does not mainly aim at preparing its financial requirements for any programme of improvement and development. For planning, the major criterion is the maximum utilisation of the human as well as the material resources available within the school and the community. In fact, planning will begin with a question put up by the school staff to itself, "What can we do within the limited available resources in the school?" It can also have a supplementary question, "What additional resources could be raised by the school staff, students and the community for the improvement and development of programmes?" It will not aim at preparing a list of financial resources for a variety of programmes which could be implemented only when these resources are met by the state government.

Augmenting Human Efforts

As a corollary to the maximum utilisation of human resources special characteristics of the institutional plan will not only be the maximum utilisation of human resources but also a conscious attempt to augment the human efforts which are so essential for a large number of educational programmes which require imagination and thinking rather than finance and additional facilities. Programmes like deduction in wastage and stagnation, improved teaching methods, differentiated programmes for gifted and retarded students, enrichment programmes within the existing syllabus, improved competence of teachers are some programmes which can form the major contents of an institutional plan.

Goal-oriented

The entire planning at the institutional level is directed towards the national goal, namely, pursuit of excellence in every field. This national goal is the common feature of the plans of lakhs of institutions in the country. To achieve this goal, institutional plans will continuously fix higher and higher goals and thereby the plans will go on continuously improving and developing the institutions.

Cooperative in Nature

The institutional plan is the cooperative venture of the community school management, school staff and the students.

An ideal plan will be that which has been prepared through the close involvement of all these agencies. The principal of the school is, however, the kingpin in organising the preparation of the plan.

Reflects the State and the National Educational Policy

The institutional plan will reflect the educational policy at the state and the national levels. It will keep in view the guidelines issued by the State Education Department in the preparation of such plans. The institutional plan will be characterised by following the spirit of the state guidelines but will have the freedom to add, modify or reject the new programmes included in the state guidelines.

Two Aspects

Each institutional plan will have two major aspects: (i) improvement, and (ii) development. Whereas the improvement aspect will be mainly based on human efforts, the development aspect will require the support and the assistance of the management, community and the state department of education.

Long-term Plan

The plan for an institution will be of a long-term duration. The institutional plan may be for a duration of five years coinciding with the plan periods at the state and the national levels. This does not mean that every improvement project will have a duration of five years. Within the broad framework of the five-year plan prepared by an institution, there will be a number of programmes extending over shorter duration, and there might be programmes extending over a duration of two years, three years, four years, five years or even more.

Flexibility

This is a characteristic feature which differentiates the process of planning. The plans which have been prepared at the national and state levels for institutions have suffered from the element of rigidity. An institution plan is highly flexible, always open for modification as demanded by the circumstances. It grows and develops continuously. It attempts all changes, small or radical, based on experience. However, if properly formulated in the beginning, the changes can be carried out within the framework of the broad objectives.

Democratic Set-up

Institutional planning demands a democratic procedure within the school administration identification with the institutional plan on the part of the teachers which is possible only in a democratic organisation. Just as a democratic administration is an important requisite for institutional planning, a fairly successful implementation will again result into furtherance of the democratic process within the school.

Community Support

Support of the community through the community involvement is also a necessity for institutional planning. It is a truism that a good institutional plan will result in the establishment of a better support with the community.

Improved Motivation

An institutional plan, when successfully implemented, results into improved motivation on the part of the teachers, students community plan with proper implementation which will result into greater enthusiasm, keener awareness and a firm determination in all the involved agencies to improve education.

PREPARING A SCHOOL PLAN

Guidelines

There cannot be a given method which may be followed rigidly for preparing institutional plans of improvement and development as the schools in the country differ widely in size, strength, management, curriculum offerings, etc. There are government schools and private-aided schools. There are schools managed by local authorities and private management. There are schools run on public school lines not depending upon government for finance. Due to the multiple differences among schools, each school will have to formulate its own approach to prepare its own plan of improvement and development depending upon the local conditions, its own traditions and its own norms set up over a period of years.

This emphasis on the individuality of the school does not necessarily mean that there can be no systematic method of institutional planning which can be followed uniformly at all schools. What it means is that such matter can be evolved and prescribed but it should not be followed rigidly. Below are suggested some steps for preparing an improvement plan for a school.

A Peep into History

Before starting work on planning, it is essential to study the history of the growth of the institution over a period of last five to ten years. It is essential to be aware of the traditions of the school, to the role of community in establishing the school, the rate of teachers turnover, the knowledge of the instructional programmes, the level of the pupil performances, etc. This will give them the ideas of what approach will help to identify the traditions which have been set up in the school over a period of last five to ten years. Any plan for improvement and development of the school should take into consideration these traditions and the entire historical background of the school.

Philosophy

Has the school formulated its own philosophy and objective? If so, the school's philosophy and its objectives may be reviewed and modified as necessary. The institutional plan should keep the objectives of the school in mind. If the school has no philosophy, it is worth while to formulate one. It is also necessary to fix up certain goals for the school to achieve in the course of the next ten to twenty years.

Problem Census and Assessment of Needs

The basic requirement for planning is the awareness of the problems faced by the school and assessment of improvement and the developmental needs of the school. The school principal, teachers, students, management and the community should sit together and prepare a census of the needs/problems areas/of improvement and development of the school over a period of next few years. This problem census and needed assessment will be in the areas of school administration and organisation staff, space, utilisation, increased enrolment, improved curriculum, methods of instruction, in-service growth of teachers, wastage and stagnation and co-curricular programmes, etc.

This survey of improvement and developmental needs of the school should be undertaken with the close involvement of the school staff. If the students' involvement could be secured it will be an added advantage. If the school has established a close support with the community and can secure its involvement, it will be ideal. However, if the local community has not been involved over a period of years in the functioning of the school and the teachers feel diffident about the ways of involving the students, the work of surveying the improvement needs of the school should not stop. This, however, does not mean that the students and the community, should be kept away in the process of planning. This only means that proper conditions should be consciously created wherein gradually the participation of students and the community could be secured. It is very essential that the management, especially in the case of private-aided schools is not kept away in the process of identifying improvement and development needs.

Thus problem of census of the need survey of the school should be split up into two parts: (1) the improvement needs of the school, and (2) the development and expansion needs of the school. These two aspects of the survey should be tabulated in a suitable manner.

Survey of Resources

There are generally two categories of resources: (i) Human, viz., teachers, experts, artisans, artists, and (ii) Physical or material resources, viz. land building, equipment, teaching aids, etc. All these resources need to be properly utilised to the optimum. An institution can take the help of money, man and material from different teaching-learning proceses and for developing the physical infrastructure, industries, agricultural farms, commercial farms, etc., can be utilised for augmenting the resources.

Planning Improvement Programmes

Once the survey of the needs/problems/areas of improvement and also the survey of the resources are completed the next important step is to plan those areas of improvement which have been identified by the staff in the problems census/needs survey. In the initial stage, improvement programmes should be planned for those areas only which are feasible and for which there is readiness on the part of the staff. Care should be taken that all teachers who are interested in planning improvement programmes are involved in planning the programme. At the same time, one should not wait till all the teachers have decided different areas of improvement. They would require adequate help in devising appropriate programmes and preparing plans for the same.

The improvement programmes will take the form of a series of projects—individual or group. The same procedure that is followed in preparing a project should be followed here. For each project the outline should be prepared under the following heads:

1. Definition of the problem
2. The objectives (these should indicate the improvement aimed at)
3. Procedure (this should include the new instructional programmes, activities planned, etc.
4. Educational aids required
5. Method of evaluation of the project
6. The time target.

PLANNING FOR DEVELOPMENT

Planing for development implies planning educational facilities for the expanding population and for such type of socioeconomic growth as visualised in the community is not a distant future. Three basic studies are necessary planning for development:

1) The first study is an examination of the number and age group to be served over a period of the next 10 to 15 years.
2) The second study is in the area of programme organisation that the school should look to for a possible change in the educational structure.
3) The third study will be concerned with the type and kind of physical facilities that will be needed to serve the

number and age-groups likely to enter the school. This will include a study of the additional requirement in terms of space, furniture, equipment and teachers over a period of next five to 10 years.

One more aspect of developmental planning is to study the existing teaching staff and their utilisation. In many government schools, it is common experience to find that there are more teachers than required. Planning of development requires initiating such programmes in the schools where unutilised potentiality of teachers should be fully utilised, in private aided schools the experience is just the contrary, in such schools there is a shortage of teachers. A plan should be prepared whereby this shortage is gradually covered.

IMPLEMENTATION

It is one thing to have a blueprint or a plan of improvement prepared by a school. It is another thing to implement the same effectively. This is an important stage when a plan is translated into action, inputs lead to outputs. There will be a flowchart or a chain of activities to be performed in the course of executing the project. Different resources are coordinated and harnessed to bring about desired results or to realise the designed objectives. Monitoring is also necessary for effecting changes and taking up concerted efforts.

EVALUATION

The evaluation of a programme of improvement will be planned at different levels:

Level-I

There will be a periodical evaluation of the improvement

projects while they are in progress. Normally, this will be done by the teachers in charge of the project.

Level-II

There will be a detailed evaluation of the completion of a project undertaken by a teacher. This evaluation will normally be done by a committee of teachers involved in planning these projects.

Level-III

There will be evaluation of the school staff at the beginning of the year. This type of evaluation should be undertaken by the principal and a committee of senior teachers. The evaluation at this level is most important as it evaluates the school plan as a whole. For every improvement project, an improvement target has been fixed. If the improvement programme is really successful the school staff should feel that the instructional and other programmes of the school have improved. It is necessary that concrete evidence may be gathered as a convincing factor that improvement has taken place. Pupils opinion, teachers. judgement and the committee's finding should all be studied together to arrive at a definite conclusion about the effectiveness of the improvement plan.

PROCESS OF PLANNING

In some quarters a fear is expressed that institutional planning may result into a character of demands by the schools. This fear is justified if proper care is not taken in clarifying the concept and the scope of institutional planning to persons involved in the process. Further, such a fear may not have any place if emphasised that institutional planning is based on the principle of maximum utilisation of human and material resources available in the school and community and not finances coming from outside. It will be the responsibility of the principal to guard against this.

Another fear that is expressed amongst many quarters is that within the school the principal himself will prepare the plan without the involvement of the approval of teachers. This is happening in a large number of schools in this country. It is found here that a process for developing the school plan on behalf of the teachers is planned and pose it as the plan prepared by teachers. Even though teachers may approve the plan prepared by the principal it will be a plan institutional developed through a faulty process. In a programme of preparing institutional plans both the process as well as the preparing product are important. If, in the process of preparing the plan, various agencies concerned with schools are not involved the plan may not be implemented, howsoever excellent it might be on paper. Institutional planning requires a democratic approach. Properly planned staff meetings guarantee a sound procedure for preparing institutional plans.

The school staff should meet over a period of days and discuss various programmes–curricular as well as co-curricular academic as well as organisational and administrative. When teachers begin to discuss areas of improvement it is feared that they will come out with a large number of areas requiring improvement and also a list of additional resources which may not be available. It will be seen further that teachers are not in a position to specify their exact needs. But this is only a stage in the process of planning. The principal may list all needs, problems and areas of improvement as arrived at in the staff meeting. Some of the areas of improvement can be the school building, which might be overcrowded or congested, lack of teaching aids, lack of playgrounds, unwieldy curriculum and defective textbooks, etc. Quite a number of these areas of improvement may be beyond the scope of the staff like the change of curriculum or expansion of school building. One is the concern of the State Department of Education, whereas the other involve finances which may be the concern of the management. However, there is no harm in listing these as areas requiring improvement.

The next step is for the principal to take. He should ensure his staff for thinking to these areas of improvement which require additional efforts and not additional finance. The best procedure here is to have subject teacher groups where areas of improvement are identified very specifically. It is difficult for an individual teacher to identify specific problems demanding improvement. However, if groups of teachers of the same subject begin to discuss their problems, they can prepare a list of specific problems in a particular subject requiring attention. In the process of preparing such a list it may be found that some of the problems pertain to individual teachers in the same subject. The process of preparing the list of problems requires continuous discussion and self-introspection by teachers. If necessary, observing classrooms teachers may also help in identifying real problems.

One more aspect of the process of preparing institutional plans is to guard against taking up ambitious programmes for which the staff of the school may not be prepared. The process of planning and implementing requires that projects of a shorter duration are taken up first and brought to successful completion. It is only after the successful implementation of some projects that confidence will be developed amongst teachers to take up ambitious and difficult projects.

Bases of institutional Planning

1. Achievement of the best possible results in the given social and physical environment.
2. Reform and progress in technique, materials, resources, etc.
3. Making the best use of the talents of the students and teachers.
4. Generating a suitable atmosphere for the development of creativity.

5. Recognition of innate powers, their use, encouragement of efforts and leadership.
6. Encouraging mutual cooperation without injuring freedom of thought and action.
7. Achieving the maximum utilisation of building laboratories, libraries and other resources.
8. Practising self-service and self-achievement.

The Working Group of the Planning Commission has suggested the following means of bringing success to the plans of schools:

a) The State department of Education will 'have to begin to think a new plan in order to recognise or identify good schools and grant the greater aid as well as freedom to weaker schools towards improvement, and also to encourage competitiveness, creativity and experimentation amongst teachers and students. Instead of uniformity and rigidity, it will be necessary to adopt an approach which is dynamic and flexible.
b) The schools themselves should try to secure the means needed for their development. The best steps in this direction would be (i) the cooperation of local officials, guardians and the local community, (ii) a change in the method of giving grants in order to encourage superiority, and (iii) establishment of experimental and autonomous schools.
c) Transfers of teachers in government schools should be reduced to a minimum. Organising committees or boards of governors should be created, and in these the teachers should have an important voice, so that their commitment should be to the institution, and not merely to their cadre. Such a situation does not exist in private institutions and hence they should make efforts to attract the best teachers towards themselves.
d) Teachers have necessarily to shoulder the leadership in the formulation and implementation of institutional

plans. In single-teacher institutions within the radius of three to five miles will treat the higher secondary school as the centre, and function as a school complex and their institutional plan will also be a collective one.

e) A panel can consist of some selected teachers and principals who can give the benefit of their experience and knowledge to other institutions, apart from their own, by giving them extra time.

DRAFT OF INSTITUTIONAL PLAN

Session..........

Name of the school

Distt.

State

Distt. Education Officer

Coordinator

Head

Incharge of the Plan

Contents

Serial No.		*Page No.*
1.	For teachers	
2.	Introduction of school	
3.	Achievements of last session	
4.	List of activities	
	Academic	
	Co-curricular	
	Physical	
5.	Progress report of session	

No. of students

Class	Section	Boys	Girls	Total

Working days of a session . . .

Results . . .

a) Internal examination

Class	Section	Pass Percentage I, II, III, Fail

b) Board Exams result

Class	Faculty	Students	Pass Percentage Div. I., II, III, Fail
	Art		
	Science		
	Commerce		

Improvement Programmes

	Last session	*Present session*
1. Academic		
2. Co-curricular		
3. Physical		
4. Technical Improvement Programme		
5. From Deptts.		
6. Others		

FORMAT OF A PLAN

About the Schools

Name	
Type	Govt/Private/Aided/............
From	Primary/Middle/Secondary/Sr. Secondary
Nature	Unisex/Co-educational
Environment	Urban/Rural
Economic resources	Grants/Chanda etc.
Any other	

School Family

Head	Qualifications
Asstt. Head	Qualifications

Teachers	No.	Subject	Qualifications
1.			
2.			
3.			
4.			
Technical staff			
Clerical staff			
IV Class			

Physical Facilities

1. H.M. room
2. Office
3. Staff room
4. Hall

5. Laboratories
6. Library
7. Urinals
8. Drinking water place
9. Playgrounds
10. Audio-visual room
11. Others

Number of students	Section	Boys	Girls	Total
Working days of a session				

Results

Internal examination

Class	Section	Pass percentage	Div. I II III Fail

Board Exam's Results

Class	Faculty	Students	Pass percentage	Divi II III fail
	Arts			
	Sci.			
	Commerce			

Improvement Programmes

	Last Session	*Present session*
1. Academic		
2. Co-curricular		
3. Physical		
4. Teachers improvement programmes		
5. From Dept		
6. Others		

Planning for Improvement Programmes

1. Name of the programme
2. Incharge of the Programme
3. Coordinator
4. Required Expectations
5. Analysis of present situation
6. Targets of the programme and Time
7. Outline of execution plan
8. Facilities available
9. Evaluation procedure

   Progress Report

Signature of Plan Incharge

REFERENCES

Buch, M.B., 1969, *Institutional Planning for Educational Improvement and Development*. Regional College of Education, Bhopal.

Bhatnagar, R.P., Bhatnagar A.S., Aggarwal Vidya, 1992, *Educational Administration*: Lal Book Depot, Meerut.

Dash, M., 2000, *Education in India, Problems and Perspectives,* Atlantic Publication, New Delhi.

Mohantee, Jagganath, 2000, *Current Trends in Higher Education*, Deep & Deep Publication P. Ltd., Delhi.

Naik, J.P., 1969, *The Role of Teachers in Educational Planning and Development*, Regional College of Education, Bhopal.

Regional College of Education, 1968, *Report of the National Seminars on Institutional Planning,* Bhopal.

State Institute of Education 1968., *The Milky Way:* Bhuveneshwar.

Walia, J.S., *Foundations of Educational Administration,* Paul Publication, Punjab.

Bhatnagar, Suresh, Saxena, Ananica, 2000, *Modern Indian Education and its Problems*: R. Lal Book Depot, Meerut.

10

Evolving Management Strategies for Social Leadership in Secondary Schools

(A Study of the Total Literacy Campaign, Mumbai)

—*Sheila Tiwari**

INTRODUCTION

Education, as has been defined by the educational philosophers, means an all round development of mind, body and soul of an individual. Popular education in India, the provision of education for all, has achieved a lot during the half century since India gained independence. Many new schools have been opened and the government has tried to reach out to the remotest areas of the country, so that education is accessible to all irrespective of caste, creed and gender.

However, the reality is quite different. Various cultural, sociological and geographical factors have affected the progress of education in our country. While on one hand, there has been a rapid industrialisation and globalisation of the Indian economy and expansion of urban civilisation, the rural areas have not been able to enjoy the fruits of this industrialisation and globalisation extensively. Poverty and lack of economic activities in these remote areas have led to migration to urban

**Secretary, "SAHAS", Mumbai-India.*

and semi-urban areas. These migrants are mostly poor and illiterate. They belong to the working class who settle down in slums.

Illiteracy is a phenomenon which India can ill afford. In 1986 the National Literacy Mission was established to tackle the enormous problem of illiteracy in the country on a massive scale. Eradication of illiteracy in rural, semi-urban or urban area was set up as a mission. It set the target of achieving hundred per cent literacy by the 21st century. The method adopted for the purpose was the campaign mode which is time-bound and area- specific and envisages people's participation on a voluntary basis. In Mumbai, the Total Literacy Campaign was launched in 1993 initially in the nine municipal wards of the city. After a survey the target was set at making 84,000 people literate most of whom were women. However, at the onset of the programme it became evident that people's voluntary participation was not as forthcoming as had been expected. This was mainly due to the complex nature of the city—multilingual, multi-cultural population, predominance of slums and pressures of an urban lifestyle which left little time for people to participate in this programme on a sustained basis.

Based on the experiences in many of the campaigns in the districts, where school children had been involved in this programme, the school education department in Mumbai initiated secondary schools into the literacy programme on a massive scale. Fifty-six thousand school children, 3,000 school teachers and 300 schools were involved in this massive exercise. The teaching was usually on one-to-one basis—one child teaching one illiterate. The school teachers and the headmasters and the entire administrative staff of the school education department were deeply involved and committed to this programme, and at the end of the evaluation the target achieved was 61 per cent, which is a fair success rate in an urban area.

It was for the first time in the history of independent India that schools had changed their roles, albeit temporarily, and helped in community mobilisation on such a large-scale. The success of the literacy campaigns has created an urgent need to study the role of secondary schools in community mobilisation. The patterns adopted for the organisation of the literacy campaigns at the school level, and the various management and monitoring strategies were effective in solving problems and difficulties faced by schools in the campaign. The schools in Mumbai and elsewhere took up this programme as an additional task during the height of the literacy campaign. Additional staff was not allotted to them for this work; however, the school management, teachers and students did fit the programme into their already heavy work schedule, and managed to achieve the target.

PRESENT STATUS OF SCHOOLS

In the light of the above background we must analyse the role of the present school system in relation to children, the parents, the teachers and the surrounding community. A study of the system of formal schooling in India presents a scenario which is not very encouraging.

1 The schools only focuses on the academic performances of the students.
2. Schools are unable to give the child the experiences which will enable him to be competent and skilled to enter the work world and participate actively in decision making and in the cultural and political affairs of the community of which he is a part.
3. The parents in general are rarely taken into confidence in the conduct of the affairs of the school.
4. They are considered as unnecessary interference in the functioning of the school.
5. Teachers have had a very cavalier attitude towards anything other than academic.

6. They have also been timid about exerting any influence beyond the four walls of the school.
7. The schools have had no dialogue and no interaction with the surrounding community.
8. The cultures in the school and the surrounding community have been totally different.
9. Even though our society professes equality of opportunity, the child of parents of lower socioeconomic status who 'makes it' is a rarity (Podhoretz N. Makingit). Most do not attain an educational standard as high as those of comparable intelligence in other social classes. It is the talented exception who survive the inhibiting social and cultural influences and shine.
10. In the urban slums most schools lack the facilities, infrastructure, and, of course, the will to deliver the goods effectively.

Changed Indian Scenario

Since 1991 when the Indian market went global the economy has grown by leaps and bounds. However, in a free international market economy, there is stiff competition and only the best survive. Therefore, it is necessary that economic progress should be accompanied by social development. The problems of the mass of urban poor living in the slums of the different cities of the country need to be addressed on a priority level. They are generally living in deplorable conditions with lack of basic civic amenities and educational infrastructure. They have little knowledge about environmental issues, small family norms, health and nutrition and their own rights as citizens, and the resources available to them.

It is here that there is urgent need for schools, specially in the urban slums, to step in and play an active role as leaders of the society. To play a creative role in helping people to help themselves and make use of existing resources in a coordinated manner. The school should give supportive services through its faculty and student members for the non-participating members of the society frequently, 'newcomers' from a rural or non-urban background and make them feel involved in the community affairs.

Thus the faculty of the school should act as leaders of social change and endeavour to make children sensitive and aware to various social issues of major importance to the community, e.g., illiteracy, poverty, environment, education, gender quality, health and nutrition, sanitation. The school should have continuous interaction with the surrounding neighbourhood.

Objectives of the Study

1. This paper aims to study the impact of the literacy programmes on schools, teachers, students, illiterates and the surrounding community.
2. Based on the results of this study to design a project where secondary schools will play a social leader's role in the field of community development by initiating community mobilisation.

Scope of the Study

1) It is limited to the impact of literacy programmes on five schools of North Mumbai.
2) It aims to design programmes and projects only for schools located in the urban slums.
3) The leadership role of the schools will be limited to focusing on civic amenities, development of women and children, health and nutrition and functioning as community centre.
4) The thrust of the study is limited to the role of schools as community leaders.

Methodology

The impact study of the total literacy programmes on the schools, heads, teachers, students and illiterates was carried out with the help of the actual observation of the programme in progress through questionnaires (Refer to Annexures II to V) and interview.

During the conduct of the programme, actual field visits were made to the schools, and the community where these programmes were being carried out to assess and monitor the progress of the campaign.

Selection of Sample Population

After the completion of the campaign a questionnaire was distributed to all the heads of these schools, five teachers, 30 students and 30 adult learners from each schools. The schools of East Bhandup in the Northern suburbs of Mumbai were chosen because of the predominance of slums, close to these schools. A total of 25 teachers, 150 students and 150 adult learners were selected for the study.

In all, these schools 10 teachers with 20 students, each from classes VIII and IX had been selected for participating in the programme. Each student had to teach one illiterate, and one teacher supervised around 20 students. The teachers and students were selected randomly for the study. Every second teacher from the school and every fourth student of this teacher with his/her corresponding illiterates was chosen for the purpose of this study.

All the schools chosen for this study had worked for literacy campaign for at least two years.

They selected a community which was nearby to the school so that monitoring could be done on a continuous basis.

Majority of heads of the school accepted this work with enthusiasm and did not have a feeling that this was an additional workload assigned to them by the government.

Data Analysis Management Strategies Adopted by the Principals for Implementation of the Programme

1) All the teachers of the school were not assigned this work.
2) Teachers were selected on the basis of their eagerness to participate in the programme.
3) For both the years different sets of teachers were selected for the programme, so that the experience of community work was gained by a larger section of the staff.
4) Children from senior secondary school were selected for the task of working as volunteers, on account of their maturity and their eagerness to participate in the programme.
5) The learners were chosen in a way where the student volunteer would not have to spend too much time on commuting to teach them.
6) Timings for the teaching learning activity was adjusted mutually between the learner and the volunteer.
7) Proper training to the teachers and the student volunteers were given before the commencement of the activity —these included psychology of adult learner, methodology of teaching learning, how to evaluate the learner, how to monitor the progress of the learner.
8) The whole programme was monitored closely by the school head, the teachers, the students themselves and of course on an on-going basis by the staff of the school education department.

   The school education department monitored the programme fortnightly, the headmaster, weekly and the teachers twice a week. This included field visits to the community, actual observation of the teaching-learning process and discussions with the volunteers and the illiterates. The monitoring was done in an atmosphere of friendship and cooperation with mutual respect for each other.

9) Before starting of the programme in the community, a survey of the area was done and local leaders, youth groups, women's organisations and other social groups were taken into confidence which ensured maximum co-operation from the inhabitants and the learners.

10) Teachers and children also presented programmes in the form of street plays, rallies and group songs to create awareness about the need for literacy, environment protection, health and hygiene, communal harmony, small family norms, gender equity, etc.

11) The volunteers taught before or after schools hours. Heads and teachers visited the community after school hours or on weekends.

Response from Schools

1. The school ended its isolation and became part of the community.
2. The school's esteem and self-image improved.
3. Leadership was thrust upon the school but it was accepted willingly and the part was played effectively by the school.
4. The role of the school was expanded without infringing upon the main academic function of the school.

Response from Heads of the School

1. The school principals were happy to be given the role of leadership by the education department.
2. Each principal devised the programme in such a way that it did not disturb the normal working of the school.
3. The principals ensured that the teachers and students who were participating in this programme were not over burdened.
4. They opened up the school to the community.

5. They saw positive changes in the teachers and the students—in terms of development of leadership qualities, decision making, problem solving, coordination skills and expression of their creativity in the form of writing of plays, composing of songs and dances, using folk art and culture to spread the message of literacy.
6. They showed their willingness to expand the role of the school and to willingly accept any programme which would lead to the development of the community.

Table 10.1

Diagram showing role of headmasters in the programme

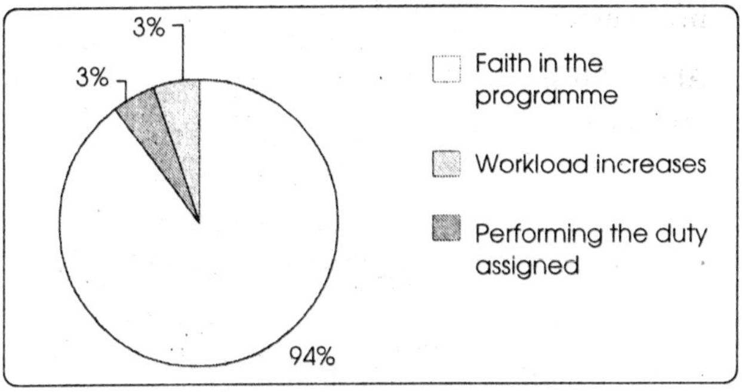

Table 10.2

Pie diagram showing co-operation received by the teachers from their principals

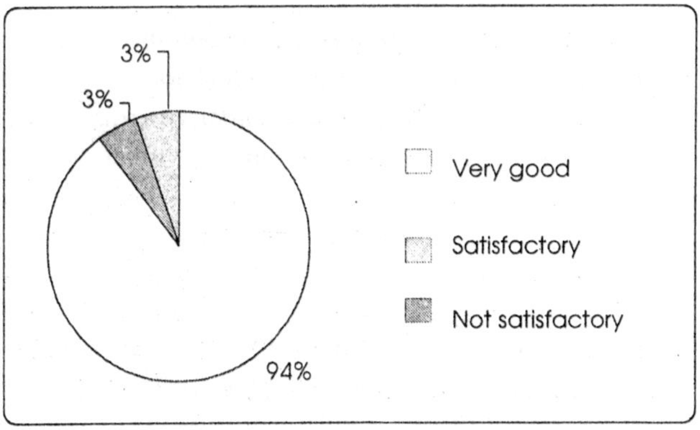

Response from Teaching Staff

1. Majority of the teachers selected for this work joined it enthusiastically after they understood the nature of the work.
2. Majority of the teachers faced some or the other problems while starting this programme.
3. Most of the teachers faced difficulties while trying to solve the problems.
4. Many teachers involved in this programme admitted that their schoolwork suffered to some extent due to their involvement in the programme.
5. About 90 per cent of the teachers admitted that their students, colleagues and the heads were very understanding, helpful and cooperative towards their work.
6. The family of the majority teachers involved in the programme were not very supportive and helpful.
7. Majority of the teachers feel that involvement in this work has given the students valuable life experiences which is not possible—otherwise in a normal school situation. They are of the firm belief that more such experiences should be given to the students and to the teachers as well.
8. Majority of the teachers interviewed have a positive attitude towards taking up such work. They are willing to accept such responsibilities in the future. This type of work will help in changing the role of the schools from producing mechanised human beings excellent in information and knowledge but weak in the life skills. It will also help in reducing the ratrace for marks and give the school and community a chance to work together for the betterment of the child who is a part of the community. (Refer to Tables 10.4, 10.5, 10.6).

Table 10.3

Pie diagram showing impact on teachers' work due to involvement in literacy programme

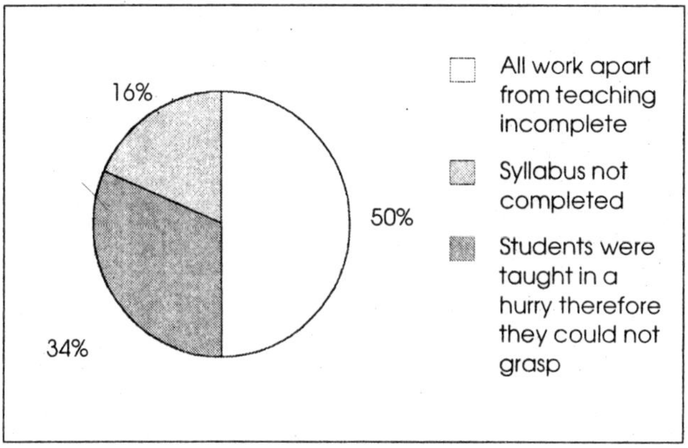

Table 10.4

Bar diagram showing problems faced by teachers while being involved in adult literacy programme

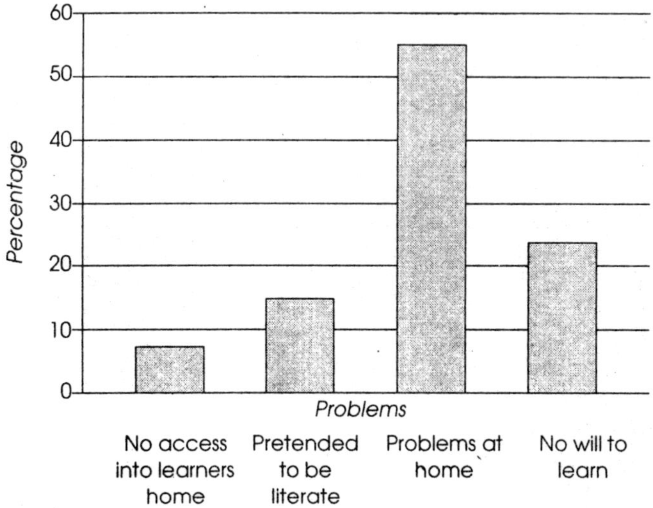

Table 10.5

Pie diagram showing attitude of the teacher's family towards his involvement in literacy programme

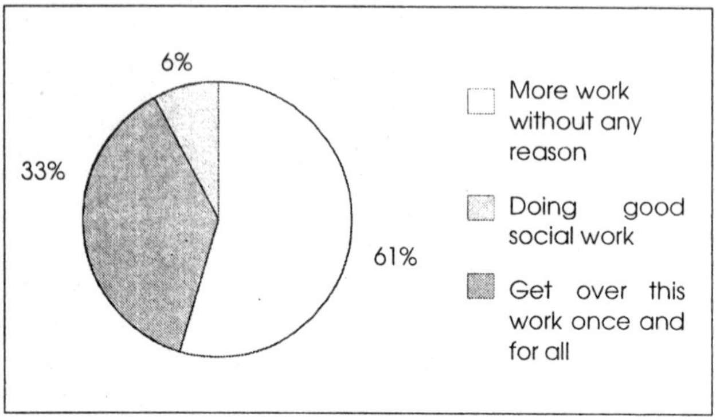

Students

1. Many of the student volunteers undertook the work of literacy voluntarily, some due to peer pressure. This was because an atmosphere had already been created about this programme due to media publicity, visits of officials, etc.
2. Majority of the students had to make a lot of effort to convince the adult learners for joining the literacy classes.
3. The students admitted that participating in the literacy programme affected their academic performance. Long hours were spent in the initial stages of this campaign.
4. Many of the students faced hurdles in the programme due to poor performance of their adult learners. Many times this led to a setback in the programme and also affected the volunteers' motivation. However the teachers and parents helped in boosting the morale of the children.
5. Majority of the student volunteers admitted that joining the literacy programme in no way affected their health.

6. Student volunteers got extra time to complete the backlog of the school work and their work was appreciated by their teachers.
7. Most of the children had a positive attitude towards this programme.
8. They admitted the fact that joining this programme was a great learning experience and would like to participate in any programme related to community development. (Refer to Tables 10.6, 10.7, 10.8, 10.9).

Table 10.6

Diagram showing the student volunteers' attitude towards the literacy programme

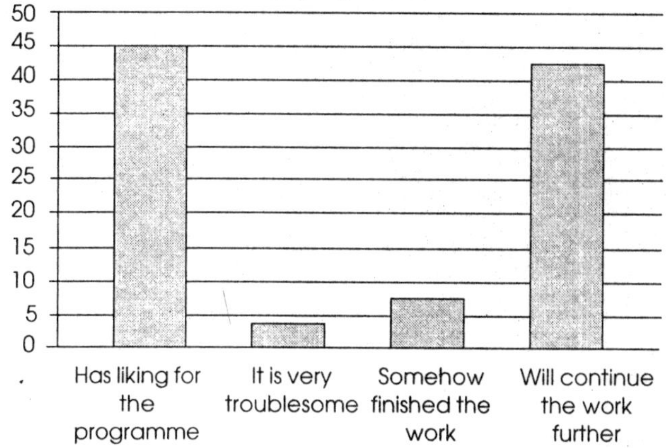

Table 10.7

Diagram showing impact on studies of student volunteers due to involvement in literacy programme

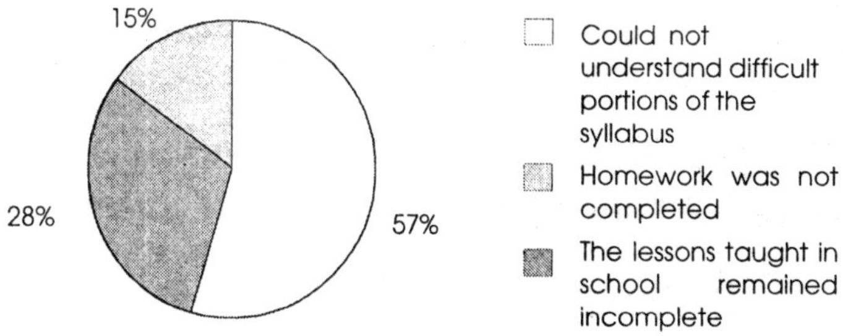

Table 10.8

Pie diagram showing impact on the students' volunteers' examination due to involvement in literacy

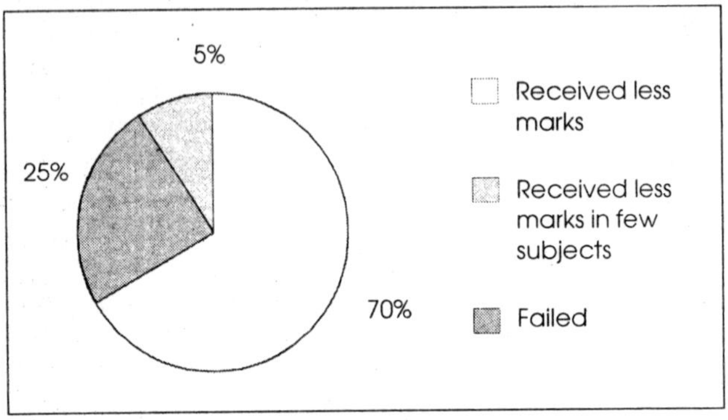

Table 10.9

Diagram showing efforts made by volunteers to initiate learners into the programme

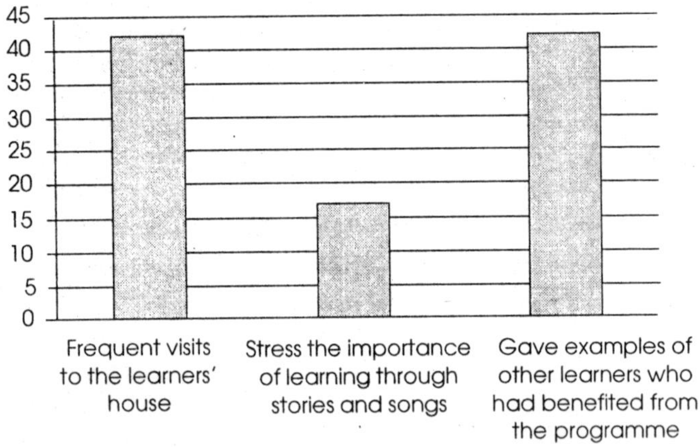

Response from the New Literates and the Community

1. Majority of the adult learners admitted to having hesitation in learning at the initial stage because of a many

reasons—(a) they felt it was too late to start. (b) public ridicule. (c) they would be unable to cope up with the programme. (d) pressure of domestic work.

2. The learners admitted that most of the young volunteers were very helpful and cooperative and this encouraged them to stick to the programme.
3. The guide teachers were also very helpful and encouraging.
4. Some learners faced resistance from their families but later on they were able to convince them of the utility of the programme.
5. The learners also acknowledged that the learning primers had made them aware about so many issues related to their communities, gender equity, environmental issues and various developmental schemes of government, about local self-government, health and nutrition, etc.
6. They were eager to participate in any improvement programme for the community, and agreed that schools were good institutions to initiate these programmes.
7. They also acknowledged to having gained a lot of confidence and boldness after participating in this programme especially. The fear of visiting their children's school and talking to the teacher had disappeared (Refer Table 10.10, 10.11).
8. They agreed that the community should play an important role in the school activities and the school should be opened up and function as a community centre for various activities.

Table 10.10

Bar diagram showing reasons for adults not willing to join the programme

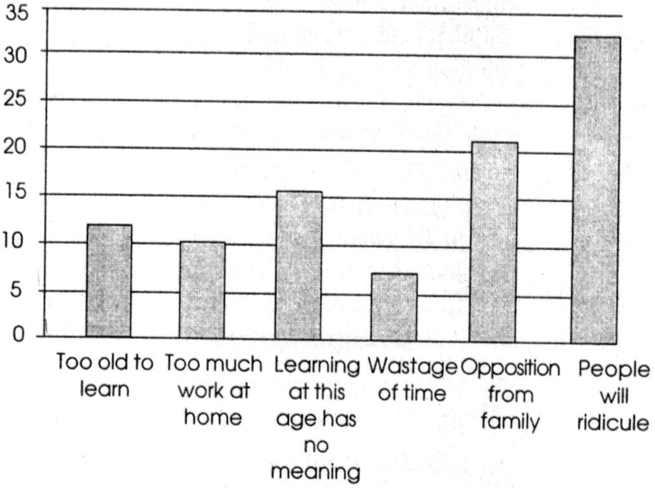

Table 10.11

Pie diagram showing reasons for objection by the adult learners family members

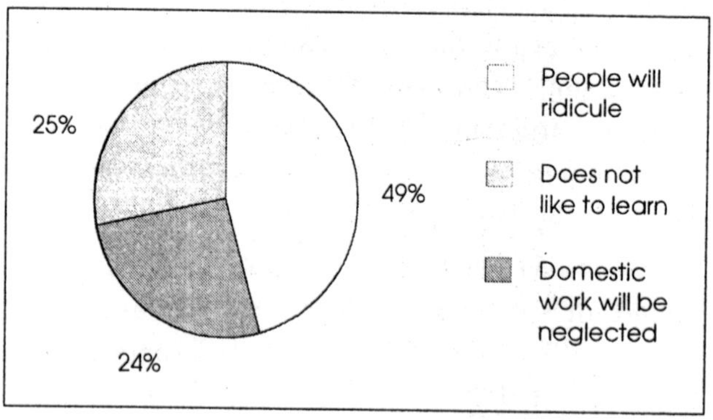

Outcomes and Conclusion

The involvement in the literacy programme has made it clear that the role of the school as an institution has changed. It has been expanded considerably, confined not to teaching and learning and academic pursuits but has reached out to the unity. As a fallout of this, there was a modification and extension of the principal's mainly teacher's professional role to make it more exacting than it had been. New skills were required for functions other than teaching, and greater time was spent to incorporate activities and programmes undertaken by the school due to its enlarged institutional function. At the end of the programme the teacher never complained about the hours and the extra effort they had to spare for the work. Their satisfaction was evident in the success of the adult learner which was in itself a great achievement.

The teachers also derived a sense of pride from the fact that the literacy programme undertaken by their schools gave them and their students ample scope for indulging in their creative skills—composing songs, writing poetry, performing street—plays giving speeches. It gave them a chance to interact with different municipal and government officials and speak on behalf of the community.

The students from these schools felt great pride in playing the role of a teacher. They learnt the skills of communicating with people from other sections of the society—this meant a widening of their horizon. Despite opposition from either their parents, peer groups, the adult learners, most of the student volunteers in these schools completed the programme—this reflected a commitment and determination to stick to a cause in which they had full faith. Even though sometimes they had to complete their backlog of school by giving extra time — which infringed on their leisure hours—the students did it willingly.

The set backs in the programme faced by the teachers and students did disappoint them but they learnt the skills of overcoming these setbacks by different ways and means. The opposition by the community to the programme was also tackled by gentle persuasion and constant visits by both the teachers and the students. These experiences gave the student volunteers training in the art of decision making and persuasion, and also gave them exposure to the hard facts of life. The teachers learnt about the different aspects of community life, other than their own. The students also learnt the art of team work and the teachers emerged as friends and ally in the community.

The positive outcomes and the responses has given these schools a rationale for reaching out to the community nearby. As David A. Goslin says, "Urban Schools ... have a special responsibility to train and motivate students to participate actively and intelligently in local governmental affairs and to accept their responsibilities as citizens for the welfare of the community in the absence of external sanctions for anti-social behaviour." In relation to this aspect of the urban school's function, it should be noted that the diversity of beliefs and cultural traditions characteristic of the city makes it of critical importance to put special emphasis on increasing student awareness, understanding and tolerance for the beliefs of groups other than their own. As Kelly opines, the birth of the technological age has outmoded most of our customary patterns of thinking. Many of our habits and institutions have become obsolete overnight. An era is born in which no mail is safe except through the goodwill of all his fellowmen. This calls for a brand of citizenship never before demanded of us. The urban schools have to play the role of attempting to teach children about maintaining relatively stable and meaningful relationships in order that as adults living in an increasingly complicated technological and urban environment, they will be able to participate in and have some measure of control over the different factors in the community.

The experiences gained through the literacy programme has given a fair insight in the field of community development.

It has been corroborated by various authorities who have had a long innings of working with the community.

What is Community Development

In this context I must quote from the experiences of G. Surya Rao who has worked extensively with the different communities in the slums of Hyderabad in Andhra Pradesh. He specifically states, "Community development is a process through which people undertake to improve the quality of life in their community through their own cooperative thought and actions." From the beginning the key concepts should be 'self-help' and felt needs. During the literacy programme some NGO's and schools working in the slums and community in the Bhandup and Chembur area organised groups of women and youths to address to the needs of the community, especially the need for drinking water and for establishing people's credit societies. This in fact encouraged the adult learners to participate in the programme more wholeheartedly because they could relate to the issues which were quite close to their basic needs.

Community Development Starting with People's Own Experiences and Participation

While organising the people in the community it was also observed that listening to the people and helping them to analyse their own experiences, and then providing them additional information on the various issues relevant to them proved more effective than thrusting information and schemes which the literacy volunteers and guides thought necessary. It was evident from the above experiences that community development helps them to go where they want to go. It is a process of personal and community growth and not simply one of target achievement. Community development will not take place until those needs are clearly perceived by the people themselves and put at the top of their agenda.

Development is Demand Driven

Since the initial stage the literacy programme in Mumbai encouraged participation of the community at all levels of the programme—planning, implementation, monitoring and evaluation. While doing this the women's groups, the youth groups and prominent citizens of the community were invited to create awareness among them about the programme. It therefore turned out to be a demand-driven programme rather than supply-oriented.

Community Development Leading to Empowerment

During the height of the literacy programme the communities were really empowered, especially in certain areas where schools and NGO's were working in collaboration with each other. Demands came to the teacher guide and the community workers, who were mostly from the teaching community, to organise meetings between the different governments, municipals and other agencies to get additional information for the services offered by the developmental programme of these agencies.

It is evident then that social mobilisation aims at transforming the passive recipient of the programme benefits into an active partner in the process of programme implementation. It engages a large number of people for achieving specific development goal through self-reliant efforts. It is a planned process that seeks to facilitate change and development and empowers the community for action. It is a process of education and growth towards a sense of competence and self-reliance.

Help can be given to a community to develop an approach and method for dealing with problems as they arise in a self-dependent manner. An example of the community, being empowered and seeking self-help for issues related to them has a relevance here. In the Dharavi area where Asia's largest slums are located, many small-scale industries (mostly chemical) are run by small investors, who employ labour who are actually migrants from Uttar Pradesh, a state in North India. When the literacy classes were started in the area there were a lot of protests from the entrepreneurs because they felt the labourers would become aware of the fact that they were being paid much less than the amount on which their thumb-impression was being taken. However, the labourers who were part of the programme insisted on continuing the classes. They had become aware of the fact that their employers had been cheating them all these years.

Community Volunteers as Educators Facilitator

Another important factor which drew the attention of the officials and the implementors of the programme was community development workers, be they teachers, from the NGO or the government, should be an educator, facilitator and not an organiser. They should belong to the community so that the community has a sense of affiliation with them. Here it is pertinent to state that the literacy programme tried to engage teachers belonging to the community, the volunteers (the school students) who were necessarily part of the community. It was this factor which aided the literacy programme in Mumbai.

Community Development of Strong Linkages between Community and Local Authorities

There was also a strong linkage between community and local authorities, the government and the municipal authorities. This linkage was vigorously pursued during the literacy programme. Since the municipal authorities were closely associated with the programme through the municipal school teachers and the school education department was involved through the schools, regular meetings and rapport sessions were arranged between the community residents, leaders, community volunteers and the school children. This was part of a process to monitor the programmes and also be in close communication about the developments at the grass roots levels. This helped in enhancing the effectiveness of the programme. In organising these meetings the school teachers from the municipal corporations who were the link between the community, school and the authorities, played a vital role.

School as Focus

A major development as a result of the literacy programme was that parents from the slum communities became interested in the education of their children. Those parents who were initially hesistant to reach out to the teachers and school authorities and discuss the academic progress of their wards, acquired confidence and courage to enter the portals of the school. Through their active participation the school authorities became more alert about the responsibility towards their students. The school authorities realised that they had to be more accountable to the parents and, in fact, they started encouraging the participation of parents into the school activities.

This drives home the point that school and community should complement each other. The community has a right to know, and should know, what is going on in the schools. Schools should be sensitive to changing needs, due to the rapid technical advancement leading to increasing complexity in the society. This would involve breaking down the barriers between school and community, and new relationships should be built. The literacy movement has already ensured this increasingly close cooperation between the community school and the other governmental and non-governmental agencies. In the present scenario it is also necessary that the children's work needs to be an integral part of the life of the community.

Aim of the Project

The Bhandup schools in North Bombay have learnt valuable lessons in community and school linkages which lead to overall development of the community and the schools. They have also realised their strengths and are ready to take on the social leadership for the empowerment and development of the community. They have interest in the close association between schools, community and government and non-governmental agencies. They are ready to play the role of catalyst, facilitators and agents of change.

1. Modalities-selection of the community

The first step is to select a community which is close to the school. It should be compact in area and a habitation which is feeder to the school, which means a large number of the school's students should be residing in the area. Since a number of students from the community would be studying in the school, it would be easier for the schools to access the community. The community leaders also would be more responsive to the role of schools as facilitators in the different programmes to be undertaken for development to the community.

2. Interface with community leaders and residents

The next step would be the meeting with the parents, the community leaders and the school staff to identify the areas where the school can help either in initiating the programmes, or solving difficulties faced in the programmes already under way.

The meeting between the schools and the community representatives have to be thorough and without any prejudices. The schools should endeavour to make the programme people friendly so that the community leaders and representatives feel identified with the school and feel that the programmes being undertaken is theirs and not being thrust upon them. Hence the school authorities have to play the part of listeners and give opportunity to the representatives to air their views about the general status of the things in the community, e.g., health, sanitation, education, women's issues, child labour, etc.

3. Identification of the areas where school can help

It is indeed not possible for the schools to play the role of development catalyst and intervene in all the issues related to the community. Schools are educational institutions and the teachers are there to impart education to the children. Therefore, it is necessary that the schools should make their roles absolutely clear to the representatives of the community. This will help in avoiding misunderstandings and define the role of the school.

Areas Where Schools Can Help

It has been agreed that schools can play a major role in creating awareness in the areas of health, sanitation, environment, hygiene, nutrition, women's issues, status of girl-child, inculcating creativity among the children of the community and other areas related to education. They can give valuable inputs towards promoting education of women and children by providing optimum use to the space of the school and its infrastructure. They can also help in bringing back dropout children to school, help in rehabilitation of child labour, provide shelter for street children.

4. Activities which can be undertaken by the schools

Educational

1) The children of the middle or junior secondary schools can take up project work and help in creating awareness about issues related to the community. They can undertake projects on:

a) The environmental status of the community.
b) Study of health, sanitation and educational facilities in the area.
c) Take up the issues of street children and child labour.

2) Teachers too can contribute by studying the issues related to women and those related to various developmental programmes of the government and their status.
3) Mass literacy programmes can be undertaken by the school and community volunteers.
4) Coaching classes for school dropouts and children can be started.
5) Scholastically backward children from the school can be helped by giving them extra coaching.
6) Balwadis, shelter for street—children, workshops on adolescents children, creative classes. Drawing painting, clay-modelling, music, drama, handicraft, etc., can be organised by the schools.
7) Programmes can be undertaken to increase the awareness on various government schemes. Under this programme periodical lectures and talks, film shows by qualified resource persons can be organised. Interface between the stake holders and service providers can be arranged frequently.
8) Study tours within, city, state, educational, religious and historical places can be arranged. Get-togethers can be arranged to celebrate important religious and national festivals.

Health

In the area of health and immunisation, teachers and community residents can be involved actively in ensuring that regular immunisation camps and health check-up camps are arranged. They should ensure that health delivery systems are improved and sanitation and hygiene are looked after by the municipal authorities.

Women's issues

There should be regular interaction with the women's groups. Income-generating schemes, literacy programmes, vocational training can be provided to the women. There should also be, cell in the school which will address the issues of harassment to women, which is especially common in the urban slums.

Parent-teacher association

Recently the Government of Maharashtra made it mandatory on every school to have a parent-teacher association (PTA). However, in most of the schools in the slum areas these organisations are not functional and if at all they are, then they are very weak. It is important that PTA in such schools should be strengthened and activated. The parents should voice their opinions and show concern about the school activities. This, of strengthening the PTA empowering the parents through the PTA falls on the school authorities because in the urban slums there is lack of awareness among the parents about their children's education and their school activities.

A very important role the school can play in helping the community is to make its premises and facilities available freely for the use of community activities. Care should be taken that these activities are conducted after school hours and does not infringe on the main functions of the schools. Increasingly the school premises can be made available for the community. It can function as a recreation centre for the children. Library facilities can be utilised by the community. Its sports facilities and its auditorium can be used for community functions. Lectures can be organised at the school, meetings can be arranged, festivals can be celebrated. In short, the school can be a hub of activities for the community. This is specially important for slum schools in urban areas, where community activities are restricted due to lack of space.

Selection of Teachers and Community Volunteers

The school should select committed teachers who are willing to devote extra time to these activities. Equally, the volunteers from the community should be devoted to the cause of community development wholeheartedly and willing to give spare time for activities related to these programmes. Care should be taken to assign each teacher with different work. It is necessary that teachers, leaders and coordinators from the community should be involved in the work together.

Training of the officials, coordinators and volunteers

Training is an important component for empowering the coordinators and volunteers to work effectively as facilitators and agents of change. The training should have the following components:

1. Defining community and community work and development.
2. Defining community development through community initiatives.
3. Defining the roles of the coordinators, volunteers, students, parents, youth groups, women's groups, government and municipal officials, and non-governmental organisations.
4. Capacity building to enable all parties to influence the development of the project. Capacity building is particularly meaningful and critical in helping marginalised groups such as women in slum communities to achieve meaningful participation. This involves orientation programmes, periodical meetings and building networks.
5. Monitoring should also be included as a part of the training programme.
6. Other components which are area specific and relevant to the needs of the particular areas.

Calendar of Events and Monitoring

Since the project undertaken will be on a pilot basis, it is necessary to chart a calendar of events and have periodical reviews and monitoring to maintain continuity and sustainability of the programme. In this process it is also important to involve the stakeholders, the coordinators, the volunteers, i.e., the community and the schools with their volunteers. The monitoring strategies can be worked out together by all the participants of the programme and the responsibilities can also be fixed.

Evaluation

The evaluation and impact study of the literacy programme has had a positive effect on the community and the participants. However, the model of the project outlined gives different dimensions to an educational institution which basically caters to the academic needs of the community. It is, therefore, important that the new programme should be evaluated periodically. This is necessary because many times a good programme suffers due to onset of fatigue in the participants and lack of response from either side. The evaluation will also help in deciding whether the project undertaken is sustainable, viable and can be implemented on an ongoing basis.

While implementing the project, if the following points are kept in mind, then it will definitely add to the success and sustainability of the project:

1. Volunteers should constantly reach out to the community and households.
2. There should be a continuous dialogue between the community and the coordinators and volunteers.

3. Motivational levels of all the stakeholders and beneficiaries should be constantly boosted.
4. There should be flexibility in the design of the project to adjust and accommodate differing local realities and use lessons learnt from experiences.
5. Finances and resources should be preferably raised from the stakeholders. Incentives and doles should be as far as possible avoided.
6. Empowering the schools and the community and transferring of control over decisions and resources will catalyse the process of empowerment and ensure improvement in service delivery by the different agencies.

Conclusion

The study of the impact of the literacy programme and the model outlined in the latter half of the paper have helped us to examine the different aspects of school which are relevant to its relationship with the community, showing how the school observes and responds to the social needs, and by approaching and even modifying its environment, is in its turn modified as a result of the experiences. Recognition of the school and its place in the community will have their effect on the curriculum, where social relevance is desirable, and on the responsibility and participation not only of parents and pupils but also of the wider public. In return for the services and facilities which the school is able to offer to the community, the school will benefit by sharing in community facilities. This will help in further integration with other fields of education, youth work and community work (adapted from the school and the community, C.D Poster, Mcmillian).

ANNEXURE I

List of Schools Involved in the Study

1. Shivai Vidya Mandir, Bhandup, Mumbai
2. Sahyadri Vidyalaya7
3. I.E.S. High School, Bhandup
4. Saraswati Vidya Mandir, Bhandup
5. Gyan Vikas Vidyalaya, Bhandup

ANNEXURE II

Evolving Management Strategies for Social Leadership in Secondary Schools

Impact study of literacy programmes carried out through schools and the fallout thereof

Questionnaire

1. What was the time period during which the school was involved in the literacy programme?
2. What was the area which was covered by your school'?
3. What was the demographic composition of the population in the area you chose?
    1) Maharashtrian
    2) North Indians
    3) Gujaratis and others
    4) Cosmopolitan

4. What was the reason you chose the particular area ?
   a) Close to your school
   b) More children
   c) More illiterates in the community
   a) The education department assigned the area to you.
5. What was your initial reaction to the project?
   a) Just another work assigned to you by the department
   b) Enthusiastic
   c) Negative attitude.
6. How many students were involved in the work and of which class?
7. How many teachers were involved in the programme?
8. What was the reaction of the students and teachers to the programme?
9. What was the response of the community to the programme?
10. Did the programme affect the studies of the students?
11. Did it affect the teachers' work?
12. How did you manage and organise and monitor the whole programme, so that it did not affect your work schedule of the school?
13. On the basis of your experiences, while conducting the literacy programme, would you like to be adopt a community and act as a nodal agency for the overall and total development of the community—health, nutrition, environment, education, sanitation?
14. Describe in brief the strategies you would devise for conducting the programme.
15. Apart from literacy, what other programmes did you organise for the community, and how was the response?

ANNEXURE III

Questionnaire for Teachers

Name Age Sex Sub.

1) What was your initial reaction to the literacy programme?
2) How many students were working with you on this project?
3) What was their reaction to this programme?
4) What was the response of the community to the programme?
5) How did you organise the whole programme, in consultation with the headmaster on your own?
6) What were the monitoring strategies evolved by you?
7) Did the programme affect your routine work, at school and at office? How did you balance both?
8) What were the other supportive programmes organized by you at the community level?
9) Do you think schools can and should play a more active and positive role in the community development ? In what areas will you support the programme if it is adopted by your school?
10) Do you think that there is a positive effect on the students participating in this programme and that it is a good learning experience?

ANNEXURE IV

Questionnaire for Students

Name Age Sex Class

1) What was your initial reaction to the literacy programme?
2) What was the response of the community to the programme?
3) How many times did you visit the community for this programme?
4) Did involvement in this programme affect your studies? How did your parents react to your participation in this programme? Has participation in the programme helped you? if so, in what way?
5) If any such community work is undertaken in future, will you be willing to participate in it?

ANNEXURE V

Questionnaire for Neo-Literates

1) Did you like the programme?
2) Do you think you and the community have benefited from the programme? In what way?
3) Would you like your children to participate in future programmes of community development through schools?
4) What are the areas where you think your community needs help?
5) Do you think schools should participate and play a major role in this context?

REFERENCES

Survey of the Adult Education work carried out by SAHAS in Bhandup (East) —its problems and solutions. Dixit Vandana, Dissertation submitted for part completion of M.Ed Degree by Yashwant Rao Chavan Open University Nasik.

Poster C.D., *The School and the Community,* Macmillan.

Claydon Edita, L.F., *The Urban School*, Pitman Pacific Books.

Rao G., Surya, *Urban Development through Community Initiative*, Retrospect & Prospect, New Delhi, Atlantic Publishers.

DPEP Calling—May '98 Journal published by DPEP Bureau.

Gill, Kirrin, If We Walk Togethe1—Communities, NGO's and Government in Partnership for Health—The Hyderabad Experience, The World Bank.

Tiwari, Sheila, *Total Literacy Campaigns—An urban experience. Some observations*. Paper read at M.S.University Baroda, July 1994.

11

Effective Planning and Management

*—Madhu Mathur**

INTRODUCTION

The thrust of the National Policy on Education and the Eighth Five Year Plan identifies the following components: modernisation and upgradation of infrastructure facilities; quality improvement in technical and management education; concerted response to new industrial policy and industry-institution research and development laboratories interaction; resource mobilisation; and institutional thrusts.

An analysis of the issues facing the less developed countries can be made within a broad perspective, taking into consideration the major objective of education policies and the critical factors determining the development and functioning of education systems. In this framework, the focal points of discussion will be (1) Formation of skills; (2) Participation; (3) Equity; (4) Efficiency; and (5) Planning and management.

Educational planning is the exercise of foresight in determining the policies, priorities and costs of an educational system having due regard to the economic and political realities concerning the system and the needs of a country and its people. It is the process of preparing a set of decisions directed at

**Reader, Faculty of Education, Deemed University, Banasthali Vidyapith (Rajasthan), India.*

achieving predetermined goals. UNESCO has examined this concept and defined educational planning as the application of education itself to instil in students a national and scientific approach to problems. Educational planning is a natural process (thinking) of setting clear objectives and choosing the most efficient and effective means of perceiving them through practical action.

INSTITUTIONAL PLANNING

If we go by Lincoln's definition of democracy and apply it to institutional planning, we can say that institutional planning means the preparation and implementation of plans of the institution, by the institution and for the institution. It aims at involving thousands of teachers in the process of planning. The main idea behind institutional planning is that every educational institution will identify its own problems with a view to finding out solutions to the problems to assist in its own needs of development and improvement, and mobilise resources and develop appropriate programmes to meet the needs by itself.

Prof. M.B. Buch has defined institutional planning as a programme of developmental improvement prepared by an educational institute on the basis of its felt needs, and the resources available or likely to be available with a view to improving the school programmes and school practices, and constitutes plans for the institution. It is based on the principle of optimum utilisation of the available resources in the school and the community. The plan may be for a long or short duration.

The Education Commission (1964-66) observed, in view of the great need to improve the standards of education at school stage, "We recommend that a nationwide programme of school improvement should be developed such that a condition will be created for each school to achieve continuously and also achieve the best results of which it is capable." No comprehensive programme of educational development can be put across unless it involves every educational institution and all the human factors connected with it (teachers, students and the community). It must provide necessary inducement to make them put in their best efforts. For various reasons, this involvement does not take place and the motivation is not created at present.

The main aim of the programme is to motivate these human factors which have a large share in determining standards. The Education Commission further said that even within its existing resources, however limited they may be, every educational institution can do a great deal more through better planning and hard work to improve the quality of education it provides. The emphasis in this movement should be not so much on physical resources as on motivating the human agencies concerned to make their best efforts in a coordinated manner for the improvement of education. Thereby we can reduce the shortcomings of the physical resources. These include reduction in stagnation and wastage, improvement of teaching methods, assistance to retarded students, special attention to gifted students, enrichment of its curricula, trying out new techniques, improving methods of organising institutional competence of teachers through self-study programmes. It is the planning and implementation of programmes that should be emphasised.

OBJECTIVES OF INSTITUTIONAL PLANNING

a) Improvement of instruction.

b) Improvement of library, laboratory equipment and other facilities in the school.

c) Optimum utilisation of existing resources.

d) Harnessing community resources and goodwill to improve and develop the school.

e) Providing an opportunity to the staff and the students to join hands and improve the school.

f) Developing co-curricular programmes in the school like work experience, social service, adult education programme, youth service, etc., which will make the school community-centred.

g) Imparting realism and concreteness to educational programme.

CHARACTERISTICS OF INSTITUTIONAL PLANNING

1. The plan is prepared on the needs of the school and identified by the school staff.
2. It is based on the principle of optimum utilisation of the resources available within the school and the community.
3. It is a cooperative venture of the school management, school staff and students.
4. It is goal-oriented.
5. It is specific for an institution and there cannot be a sample plan for all the institutions.
6. It aims at school improvement.
7. It is continuously developing and cannot be rigid.
8. It forms the basis for the distinct plan for development and improvement.

RELATIONSHIP BETWEEN POLICY MAKING AND PLANNING

Planning and policy making are interrelated. Policy determines the principle for action and planning provides the instrument for the application of policy and review. Policy decisions are needed in the planning process and in defining its goals and limitations. Koontz and Donnell has rightly said that "the more strategies and policies are carefully developed and clearly understood, the consistent and effective will be the framework of plans." Therefore, planners who ignore policy only jeopardise the good results of their endeavours. On the other hand, planning process has various possible feedback effects of policy.

The following flowchart shows the relationships between policy and plan.

Relationships between policy and plan

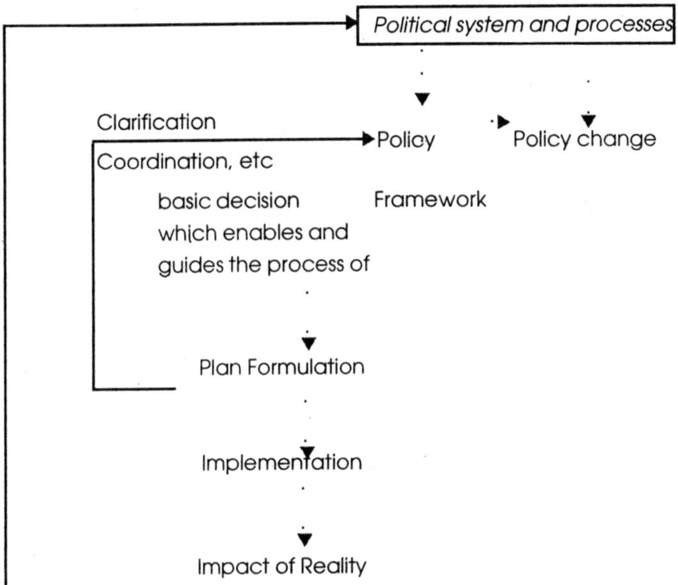

Source: Who Chronicle, Vol. 31, No. 11.

IDENTIFICATION AND QUANTIFICATION OF NEEDS

J.P. Naik defines institutional planning "as taking decisions for further actions with a view to achieving predetermined objectives through the optimum use of scarce resources."

The scare resources are time, talent and money. Planning needs to begin from the bottom, that is, from the institution proper. The quantity and quality of educational needs play a very important role in institutional planning.

Let us see the necessities of institutional planning which require quantification:

1. A felt need for planning on the part of the head of the institution.
2. Understanding the main problems and trying to guess the solution.
3. Cooperation, goodwill and mutual trust among faculty members.
4. Emphasis on human efforts rather than material resources.
5. Continuity of efforts, even if there are difficulties.
6. Formulation of easily attainable goals rather than overall ambitious schemes.
7. Catering to the exact needs, interests and attitudes of the pupils.
8. Intensive utilisation of existing resources, rather than searching for need resources.
9. Active leadership.
10. Completion of task within the working hours.

MATERIAL RESOURCES AND IDENTIFICATION OF NEEDS

Buildings, playgrounds, sanitary facilities, library, laboratory equipment, furniture, etc., can come under this category.

1. The institution should have a suitable accommodation and extensive playground which is accessible to all communities, irrespective of nationality, religion or caste.
2. The premises of the institution or the subsidiary buildings should offer training, etc., for all. A playground or a vacant site sometimes can be used for conducting functions, and it can also serve as classrooms.
3. For the campus of the school nearly ten acres will be needed except in urban areas. At least five acres with provision for a playground should be provided in the urban areas.
4. If outstation students are admitted there should be hostel facilities.

5. The building for the institution may be of two or three-storeyed one, if the required space is not allowed.
6. Quarters for the staff may not be possible in urban areas but it is desirable that the head of the institution and the warden of the hostel are provided with quarters.
7. Sanitary facilities should be adequately provided for the staff and separately for men and women students.
8. It should have suitable equipment and furniture.
9. It should provide suitable and adequate apparatus and equipment in the science laboratories.
10. If an institution is started in a temporary building, a plan for constructing permanent building should be made.

STAFF

Teaching staff on such scale as may be fixed by the department should be appointed with qualification fixed for them. The number of teachers and other employees should not exceed the number of posts fixed by the Director of School Education.

ENDOWMENT, LOCAL AND PUBLIC CONTRIBUTIONS

The school should collect enough funds to strengthen the financial resources of the school and thereby promote the school's prosperity. The entire annual income derived by way of interest from the endowment fund should also contribute towards the upliftment of the school.

FEES AND ACCOUNTS

The fee collected should be moderate and a separate account should be maintained for such special fees. The unutilised amount at the end of the year should be carried over to the next year's account under the same head. The staff of the institution should be engaged as full-time employees except for some special subjects, particularly for vocational courses. The funds of the institution shall be utilised for *bona fide* purposes connected with the institutions.

It is noted that even within the limited resources, every educational institution can do more through better planning and hard work to improve the quality of education. The emphasis should be not so much on physical resources but on motivating the human agencies concerned to make their effort in a consolidated manner for improvement of education. There are a large number of programmes which an educational institution can undertake on the basis of human effort, i.e., the effort of teachers, pupils, principal and the community in spite of limited resources. The initial effort should be made to improve the facilities provided in the school through the cooperation of the community. Success in such a programme will depend upon intelligence, planning and continued effort. It is essential that all officers of educational departments and headmasters of schools make an effort to improve the school.

Institutional planning should emphasise the following:

1. Its emphasis should be on physical resources to undertake a number of programmes on the basis of human effort, in spite of scarcity of physical resources.
2. It is operative in nature and based on micro-approach.
3. Results in overall change of the institution.
4. It is more practical and realistic.
5. Teachers are also involved in the formulation and implementation.
6. It shifts the emphasis from expenditure to utilisation of resources.
7. It involves the community and the students.
8. It is need-based. There are specific aims, methods and procedures.
9. It is a cooperative venture mainly based on democratic procedure.
10. It is developmental and is formed on the basis of the distant plans. It must continuously develop according to the changes in the environment.

ROLE OF THE HEADMASTER, TEACHERS, PUPILS AND COMMUNITY IN INSTITUTIONAL PLANNING

The success of institutional planning depends upon the dynamism and interest of the head of the institution. He has to identify the needs, the scarce resources, like interests, abilities and capabilities of the teachers, and make them work enthusiastically for the welfare of the institution.

The manpower in an institution is so important that the teachers, the students and the members of the community can jointly work towards the progress of any institution.

SCHOOL IMPROVEMENT CONFERENCES

The director or headmaster had arranged for school improvement conferences where the articles contributed by local people regarding the needs of any institution were displayed and the public were invited to have a look at them. This motivated the people to contribute on a competitive basis. Thus the local resources from the members of the community could be harnessed for the benefit of the institution.

PARENT-TEACHER ASSOCIATIONS

Every school as per the orders of the government should establish a Parent-Teacher Association (PTA) and register it, though it is customary for many schools to make use of the PTA only to raise funds for building projects, furniture, etc. This could be utilised to keep in touch with the parents regarding the academic progress of the students.

CONSTRAINTS UPON PLANNING

The greatest constraint upon educational planning is the inevitability of starting from where you are. Virtue in educational planning consists partly in acquiring and making use of a profound understanding of the existing system and partly in accepting realistically that most change, however carefully planned, will be gradual and unspectacular. This should not obscure the fact that from time to time the various dynamics already mentioned lead to a situation where planning and planned change must be so urgent and immediate that their effects are sudden and disturbing. Nevertheless, it is true that plans should never be based on any starting point other than present realities. They should provide for the evolution of the existing system so that it has some new, desired capacity. For this reason it seems likely that 'the planning function' in an education service should never be too a divorced from the experience and understanding which comes from taking responsibility for day-to-day administration.

Existing Policies

The authorities will probably already have a policy upon the matter which the planner is about to tackle. It may be a policy to have no policy, or it may be a policy which needs changing; but in either case it will have collected around itself a set of public expectations, political implications and assumptions in the clerical and administrative staff which together constitute a formidable inertia. These factors need consideration early in the planning process, for they exercise a powerful influence on the preparation, presentation and implementation of plans.

Existing Procedures

The explicit or implied policies which have just been mentioned will be enshrined in clerical and administrative procedures ingrained in the staff of the authority. It is of vital importance to the administrator, therefore, that staff at all levels should be adequately trained and alert to the need constantly to ensure that procedures are the most efficient instruments for affecting policies and that they do not degenerate into rigid constrictions of desirable improvements.

Existing Staff

Planning, which is an instrument for improving a service for people, should always provide for the human elements, although there is an understandable tendency for the concrete issue of providing building, equipment and transport to assume an undue prominence.

The education authorities of this country have experienced over the last 50 years an unprecedented amount of change. Curricula, school and college organisation, teaching methods and forms of administration and political authority have all been radically realigned. As we seek evidence of the effectiveness of much that has been attempted, the importance of understanding how the 'critical unit of works' really works (the teacher in his classroom, the head with his staff and adviser in his team, the education officer in his hierarchy) is being driven home to us more and more.

Existing Building

The procrustean bed is never more starkly revealed than when the existing stock of buildings seem inappropriate for its future use. Fifteen per cent of the country's primary schools still date from before 1903; many secondary schools are on split sites; colleges of further education are working in annexes and make-shift accommodation. The qualitative problems, are however, greater than those of quantity. The planner must judge what it is reasonable to expect the staff to achieve against the odds: get it right and you raise people above themselves; miscalculate and you destroy their morale.

FINANCE AND BUDGET FORECASTS

The planning process requires some realistic estimate of the future flow of resources into the sector of the service under consideration. This is often the most difficult to assess all the variables. Buildings, number of staff, their state of training, the theoretical objectives can all be researched and known fairly accurately.

CONCLUSION

Effective schools require programmed planning and development of resources to ensure future improvement of services. This emphasis calls for the transformation of the planning process into the technological age through Computer Aided Design (CAD) of school plants. In so doing, the planner is guided by the wider demands of society on school facilities, hence contemporary design would increasingly be amenable to adaptation and flexibility, whenever the need arises. The school can no longer be regarded as a parochial institution, ministering only to the needs of its pupils and teachers. It must now, in addition, cater for community and custodian services, whenever occasions permit this. More intensive use of school facilities is therefore inevitable in these days of economic hardship.

Through this approach, it is expected that we can overcome the challenges of enrolment growth, without denying children the right to education, especially at the first two levels.

REFERENCES

Chandrsekaran P., 1994, *Educational Planning and Management,* Sterling Publishers (P) Ltd., New Delhi.

Goel, S.L., Goel, A., 1994, *Education Policy and Administration,* Deep and Deep Publications, New Delhi.

Mukhopadhyay, B., 1994, *Motivation in Education Management, Issues and Strategies*, Sterling Publishers Pvt. Ltd., New Delhi.

Ochp, L.O., 1978. "*A Model for Participative Decision-Making in Secondary Schools*", Unpublished Ph.D. Thesis, Cordiff: University of Wales.

Singh, Rajendra Prasad, 1997, *Educational Finance and the Planning Challenge*, Kanishka Publishers, New Delhi.

12

Strategic Considerations for Promoting Micro-Enterprises in Developing Countries: A Role for Higher Education Institutions

—Harry G. Miller*, Fred Kirschstein**

Revolutionary changes are occurring in the field of Third World development (Page and Steel, 1984). Government-supported universities, international private voluntary organi-sations (PVOs), government agency-sponsored development assistance programmes and business associations have dis-covered a bustling underground economy which has been labeled the 'information sector" in contrast to the 'formal sector' (Bear, Jackelen and Tiller, 1982; Grindle, Shipton and Mann, 1986). Estimates of the informal sector's impact on the economics of some countries range as high as 70 per cent of all economic activity (Miller 1987). Other estimates suggest that the informal sector may be the source of at least 50 per cent of the labour force and production (Vaughn, 1981). Typically existing outside the legal structures of national bureaucracies, micro-enterprises found within the informal sector may be the true representatives of a free market economy and the internal

**Dean / Professor, School of Technical Careers, Southern Illinois University, Carbondale, Illinois.*

***Director of Programme Development, Foster Parents Plan, Warwick, Rhode Island.*

'engines' that development economists have long sought to enhance development.

The informal sector's ubiquitous presence in the economies of Third World countries has been invisible to economists who for years have been frustrated in their attempt to explain the stubborn intractability of poverty. Taking place outside of the more formal economic structure of a country, micro-enterprises include a broad range of vending, services and manufacturing such as fruit and vegetable vending, tailoring, dressmaking, wood and metal working, mechanical and electrical repair, clothmaking and small food services (Bear, Jackelen and Tiller, 1987; Allal and Chuta, 1982). Frequently, such micro-enterprise operations are neither "...taxed, licensed, safety inspected nor registered in the national accounts" (Sasono, 1986). Micro-enterprises provide an opportunity for low-income individuals "...who lack land, education, or any likely prospect of formal sector employment, and they do so at a relatively low cost" (Bear, Jackelen and Tiller, 1982, p. 11).

Although almost every country has some form of micro-enterprise activity, each country seems to have its own definition of the phenomenon. In some instances, micro-enterprises are defined by the number of employees, the value of fixed assets and/or the level of capital costs per workplace. Such numerical characterisation may have relevance to particular economic settings and activities of a country, but is difficult for generalisations among countries. What constitutes small, medium and large micro-enterprises is best described in qualitative terms within specific settings (Vaughn, 1981).

Despite size and variation, micro-enterprises within the informal sector are typically characterised as family owned and operated (owned by nationals), labour intensive, and dependent on local domestic capital for start-up and expansion; they adapt technology to indigenous resources with low-cost goods and repair services which fulfil the basic needs of middle and low-income segments of the local population (Page and Steel, 1984). In addition to complementing modern sector production and services, micro-enterprises possess the potential to shift and improve their goods and services to compete for higher income consumers (Page and Steel, 1984). Such small-scale informal economic endeavours are relatively easy to establish and thus "... provide more managerial and job opportunities, especially for the less skilled than other forms of enterprises .... With their impact on the distribution of skills and opportunities, they may be seen as forces that increase the possibility for stable and democratic change" (Hunt, 1985, p. 6).

The potential importance of the informal sector through micro-enterprises has led to major changes in direction for development-oriented institutions. Institutions of higher education, international donor agencies, private voluntary organisations and finance institutions are all searching for more effective ways by which they can contribute to the development needs of the informal sector. To date, such assistance strategies as technical training, non-formal education programmes, specific skills training and credit services have not been especially effective in developing models for implementation in a variety of local settings. This article analyses the impediments to effective assistance for the development of micro-enterprises and suggests that a developing country's higher education institutions can play an effective role in promoting private sector economies. Recognising that each country needs to evolve its own unique strategies to fulfil specific development needs and that the promotion of micro-enterprises is a relatively new focus for macro- and micro-government interventions, the purpose of this article is to examine some of the primary issues in the development of micro-enterprises and to offer considerations for implementation by higher education.

CREDIT MECHANISMS FOR MICRO-ENTERPRISES

Whereas larger enterprises typically have collateral, credit experience and, frequently, government incentive schemes tax rebates for development, a major constraint for micro-entrepreneurs in the informal sector is the availability of capital through established credit lending institutions (Page and Steel, 1984). Commercial banks in developing countries typically cite high transaction costs, lack of collateral to support loan applications, absence of formal education or technical know how, as well as the highly mobile nature of informal sector businesses to support their refusal to lend to such high risk investments (Allal and Chuta, 1982). And in truth these factors often result in a large number of macro-enterprise failures and bankruptcies. In other words, micro- entrepreneurs are forced to rely on personal and family savings, supplier credit and/or informal sector moneylenders (who are frequently landlords) for their capital development needs.

For most micro-entrepreneurs, profits are rarely used in developing a working capital fund and they are rarely reinvested as a means to sustain or increase their business activity. For most, "...an immediate family need almost always take precedence and, rather than being reinvested, profits are consumed in the form of better nutrition, medicines, schooling for children and improved housing or on such family events as births, deaths and marriages" (Bear, Jackelen and Tiller, 1982, p. 10).

Most development organisations have assumed that since informal sector entrepreneurs are poor, they would need access to credit for their business operations. The dilemma was how to deliver a large number of small loans in such a way that administrative costs would not make the lending process financially insolvent. Credit unions, credit cooperatives, and various plans to link the poor to the formal banking structure have experienced limited success at best. Some unique concepts have worked. Boston's ACCION International which pioneered the solidarity group-lending concept in which small groups of micro-entrepreneurs are formed to qualify for loans is a case in point. A basic feature of solidarity groups is that each member of a group must co-sign other members loans to insure loan repayment. Replicability, however, may be constrained by cultural factors and a predominant focus on the urban trading market. In Nepal, Foster Parents Plan has succeeded in linking poor entrepreneurs to the formal banking system primarily because of government banking policy requiring a capital loan fund set aside.

Many of the problems are attributed to the failure of development organisations to separate social purposes from needed business practices. Policy decisions that have been attempted, but with only limited success, include: interest rates set below market value; loans set aside for members before second loans could be made to creditworthy clients who had repaid their first loans; volunteer or low-paid management assistance; elimination of collateral for loans; and no-fault penalties for non-repayment of loans.

Given the current state of micro-enterprise assistance, it is apparent that development is dependent on such variables as local business conditions, past development experiences, availability of needed resources and capabilities of existing assistance organisations. That is, different types of organisations within varied economic settings with differing capabilities to reach and meet the needs of specific micro-entrepreneurs need to be identified and classified to determine appropriate intervention assistance. Different types of assistance must be provided to meet the specific needs of diverse types of small micro-entrepreneurs. Grindle, Shipton and Mann (1986) imply that importance for determining the level and type of intervention assistance is based on organisational capabilities and micro-enterprise needs. A comparison of cost, beneficiary services, skills required of programme staff, appropriateness for micro-enterprises and types of financial and human resources available for micro-enterprise enhancement are some of the components for interfacing services with needs.

Most developing countries have regionally based, publicly supported higher education institutions that can be more fully used by both internal and external assistance agencies for micro-enterprise development. Although loan and credit needs vary, higher education institutions can provide through their resources, both in terms of physical plant facilities (including instructional laboratories and maintenance shops) as well as the manufacture and repair of basic tools and other equipment needed by micro-entrepreneurs for their business operations. Since most micro-enterprises are relatively small operations, the making of pushcarts, measuring scales, bicycle repair tools and portable vending stands and even certain parts for small gasoline engines can be undertaken without the need for commercial loans. In addition, higher education institutions can provide an 'incubator' environment including the use of facilities and equipment for start-up enterprises with a rent index based upon profits for facility and equipment use.

MACRO-POLICY IMPEDIMENTS

Given the size and relative importance of the informal sector to the economies of the Third World countries, it is important to examine government policies which enhance or inhibit their success. Although it is widely assumed that extensive government control and regulation inhibits 'informal development,' little evidence is available as to direct impact or causal relationships (Grindle, Shipton and Mann, 1986). For example, a flourishing informal sector may be the result of several macro-policies or of an implementation of a single policy at the municipal level. Further, the need is eventually for formal sector matriculation rather than perpetuating their informal status.

Macro policies or the national policy environment which affect the informal sector range from macro-economic aggregates such as interest rates, inflation and public expenditures to registration procedures, taxes, technical services and the availability of credit. Haggblade, Liedholm and Mead (1986) identify six macro-areas of policy that could directly affect micro-enterprise development. These policies include: trade, monetary, fiscal, labour, output and regulatory control. Ironically, there is no way to ensure that drawing the attention of government to the needs of the informal sector will not in and of itself create further bureaucracies which would limit micro-enterprise initiatives. "Registration and tax laws that apply to enterprises too small to be able to comply readily force them to remain clandestine. On the other hand, exemption of SSEs (small scale enterprises) would sharpen the line between formal and informal sectors and discourage firms from expanding to the size covered by the laws" (Page and Steel, 1984, p. 36).

While each country will be different on the specific set of legal constraints, it is clear that a primary set of recommendations to facilitate the informal sector would include some or all of the following:

1. Business licensing procedures which are simple, inexpensive and include incentives for registration.
2. A 'no questions asked' amnesty on past business activities and practices.
3. Incentives for credit and financial mechanisms specifically targeted at the informal sector.
4. The creation of urban business exten..ion services.
5. A business insurance scheme designed to protect micro-enterprises from infrastructure breakdown and cash flow crisis.

For the immediate and medium range future, most development efforts must work within a developing country's economic policy environment. Recognising that each country and, more than likely, regions within a country will differ economically with different needs for micro-enterprise assistance, a more precise description and understanding of the macro-policy impact on micro-enterprises is needed. A major role for regionally-based government-supported colleges and universities exists in delineating and measuring the impact of government policies and 'bottlenecks' which may exist and directly limit micro-enterprise development. Further, more specific research needs to be undertaken to determine as directly as possible causal relationships for the support of growth and non-growth. For example, to what extent is a developing country's foreign currency exchange rate related to the development of micro-enterprise in the informal sector? Are the abilities of microenterprises to produce dependent on the need for foreign capital to obtain spare parts and tools from international markets? It is through field-based research that development impediments can be identified, defined and refined for appropriate recommendations for further enhancement. It is from these that specific policy modifications, special compensations and assistance programmes can be more directly applied to the needs of micro-entrepreneurs. Development efforts at the 'grassroots level' must go 'hand in hand' with the need for broader macro level-changes.

TECHNICAL SUPPORT ASSISTANCE

A major need in developing micro-enterprises is providing for assistance at the technical and managerial levels (Vaughan, 1981). Typically, micro-entrepreneurs are either craftsmen who have technical experience but lack management skills, or are trade merchants who have commercial backgrounds, but lack specific technical experience (Page and Steel, 1984). For the most part, micro-enterprise development is based on personal experiences and relationships and, more often than not, entrepreneurs have some technical background but lack appropriate experience in such areas as marketing and bookkeeping (Bear, Jackelen and Tiller, 1982). As Hunt (1985) notes, "Some believe that these inputs are more important than credit particularly for firms that have survived the early start-up crises" (p. 21).

It is frequently assumed that the private sector could provide the technical and support assistance needs for developing micro-enterprises, but there are countries such as Somalia where governmental policies and level of economic development have constrained private sector development. That is, there is no viable private sector capability to provide micro-enterprise assistance for managerial and technical training. The effectiveness of assistance may be a function of public and private institutional collaboration. Regionally-based colleges and universities offer a public sector presence for providing micro-enterprise assistance through adapting expertise in the form of outreach/extension services to meet specific needs.

Through faculty and facilities, higher education institutions can provide some of the needed support for the development of micro-enterprises. Outreach programmes, consultant services, applied research, use of laboratory equipment, dissemination of information, and knowledge of and presence within the region can be used to facilitate assistance and development. As Miller and Reeder (1987) state, "Higher education as an institutional linkage can provide unique and essential support mechanisms for economic growth in developing countries role as a depository of knowledge and expertise and its basic mission of teaching, research and service can be related either directly or indirectly to assisting private initiatives for small business development" (p. 53). The adaptation of needed knowledge and basic services necessitates a role of both generalists and specialists based on fulfilling practical and immediate needs of micro-enterprises.

Five strategies in developing effective outreach /extension programmes by institutions of higher education are to:

1. Provide knowledge and skills that fulfil precise information/skill needs of micro-entrepreneurs.
2. Design instructional programmes and learning situations in which micro-enterprise participants can at least

partially practise and become actively involved in what is to be learned.

3. Emphasise personal development opportunities by fostering a positive view of capabilities and potentialities as a means for improving the level of performance.
4. Develop strategies for acknowledging successful participation and achievement in an outreach programme.
5. Provide continuous field-based follow-up programmes to specific intervention programmes.

Prerequisites for an effective educational outreach/extension programme are knowing what is needed, developing appropriate learning strategies and assessing performance and/or results. Being able to choose among technical options, to adapt technology to existing conditions, to inform and train area users in small business practices and to provide training in maintenance and repair is a role uniquely suited to the capabilities of higher education institutions and their faculties.

Recognising that macro-policy changes and reform are needed and directly affect micro-enterprise development, it is also important to recognise that the type of micro-enterprise and the type of assistance provided by higher education institutions, PVOs and donor agencies need further clarification and delineation. Each organisation provides a special capability and potential. The development stages of micro-enterprises ranging from the identification of potential micro-entrepreneurs to business start-ups to market expansion, is a critical factor in determining what type of assistance and what type of organisation would facilitate the development process in a more cost-effective manner.

However, informal sector businesses are primarily the province of the poor. To work with the poor one must first reach the poor. Private voluntary agencies have special capabilities of working at the grassroots level and are uniquely qualified to undertake the identification and organisation of micro-entrepreneurs. PVOs can apply the social organising techniques necessary for the successful implementation of many types of assistance which universities and government agencies have to offer small businesses. Working primarily with the uneducated poor, PVOs have successfully utilised non-formal education techniques to introduce complicated subjects to the poor, i.e., preventive health practices, new agricultural techniques, and forms of appropriate technology.

Given the importance of the informal sector there is a special and compelling need for collaboration among the groups attempting to assist micro-enterprises. If the potential for true development is as great as some believe, then government, business, universities, and PVOs must set aside parts of their own self-interests for the collaborative efforts necessary to assist the informal sector.

Poverty in developing countries is the result of a mixture of conditions and practices. Land, labour, and capital, both physical and financial, are the resources available to an economy, and their use determines the extent of prosperity. The promotion of the private sector, and in particular micro-enterprises, provides an economic development opportunity to build aagencies such as PVOs in Third World countries provide important human development services for self-help programmes. Small is not only beautiful, but fecund.

REFERENCES

Allal, M., and Chuta, E., 1982, *College Industries and Handicrafts: Some Guidelines for Employment Promotion.* Geneva: International Labour Organisation.

Bear, M., Jackelen, H., and Tiller, M., 1982, *Micro-enterprise Development in the Urban Informal Sector*, Washington, DC: A.T. International.

Grindle, M.S., Shipton, P.M., and Mann, C. K., 1986, *Capacity Building for Resource Institutions for Small and Micro Enterprises: A Strategic Overview Paper.* Washington, D.C.: United States Agency for International Development and Harvard Institute for International Development.

Haggablad, S., Liedholm, C., and Mead, D., 1986, *The Effect of Policy and Policy Reform on Non-Agricultural Enterprises and Employment in Developing Countries: A Review of Past Experiences.* Washington, DC.: Employment and Enterprise Policy Analysis Discussion Papers, Office for Rural and Institutional Development, Bureau of Science and Technology, United States Agency for International Development.

Hunt, R.W., 1985, *Private Voluntary Organisations and the Promotion of Small-scale Enterprise.* Washington, DC.: United States Agency for International Development.

Miller, H.G., and Reeder, R.C., 1987, 'Promoting the Indigenous Private Sector in Developing Countries: The Role of Higher education", *Journal of Studies in Technical Careers*, IX, 51-59.

Page, J.M., and Steel, W.F., 1984, *Small Enterprise Development: Economic Issues from African Experience.* Washington, DC.: The World Bank.

Sasono, A., (1986), "People's Economy", *Journal of the Society for International Developments*, 3, 69-72.

Vaughn, G.L., 1981, *Guidelines for Management Consulting Programs for Small-Scale Enterprises,* Peace Corps: Information Collection and Exchange.

13

The Anatomy of Schools Improvement Programme: The Plantation Schools Education Development Project in Sri Lanka

*—Ritchie Stevenson**

During the British colonial period, Tamil workers were brought from South India to work in the tea estates in the hill country of Sri Lanka. Large numbers of these workers were deployed in the provinces and districts immediately to the east of Colombo.

Due to the nature of plantation agriculture, these workers were largely confined to the plantations and were isolated from much of the community. The social welfare measures initiated by the government at the national level did not reach into the plantation communities.

During the colonial administration, few plantation managements provided even basic education facilities and few children from the plantations attended schools.

Education in the plantation area in Sri Lanka has a long history of neglect and discrimination. The effects of educational reforms brought about in the forties by way of introducing free education and central schools in rural areas never trickled

**Education Consultant, Plantation Schools Education Development, Sri Lanka.*

down to the plantation communities. Plantation children had to be content with an inferior type of education imparted to them in places that were poor apologies for schools. By the sixties almost all missionary and private schools had been taken over by the government and were, in effect, state schools. However, the plantation schools were not taken over at that time. Whilst the state schools followed the national curriculum, estate schools were following a different and simpler curriculum consisting of basic reading, writing and arithmetic.

The process of taking over the plantation schools did not really commence until 1977. In the two years that followed, over 700 schools were taken over by the state. When this occurred it became clear that the schools were inadequate in terms of physical facilities and teacher supply. Even after the takeover for many years the estate schools remained under-resourced.

Studies conducted at the time identified the following problems:

a) Poor infrastructure

b) Majority of teachers unqualified and with poor skills

c) Teachers lacked an abiding interest in the plantation sector

d) Unavailability of facilities for secondary education

e) High dropout rates

f) Inadequate number of supervision visits by circuit education officers

g) Unavailability of education officers at the regional level with responsibility for plantation schools

h) Inadequate support for curriculum development and implementation

i) Insufficient number of teachers

j) Large proportion of single-teacher schools

k) Amalgamation of schools had reduced the resources available to smaller schools

The plantation community has the lowest literacy rate in Sri Lanka when compared to their urban and rural counter-parts. This sector has been caught in the deprivation trap of poverty, illiteracy, ill-health, isolation and powerlessness. Achieving universal primary education in the plantation sector is held as a prerequisite for achieving equity in Sri Lanka.

In order to raise educational participation and quality in the plantation area through positive discrimination, the Plantation Schools Education Development Programme (PSEDP) was launched in the mid-eighties to cover a period of 12 years with financial assistance from the Swedish International Development Authority (SIDA).

The foci of the PSEDP were:

a) Enhancement of the learning environment

b) Improvement in the preparation and motivation of teachers

c) Strengthening of educational management

THE PROJECT

In 1986, an agreement was reached with SIDA for a 12-year, three-phase programme to develop the plantation schools. Initially, the project was to consist of three four-year phases. However, the civil disturbances in the country in 1988-89 caused the first phase to be extended from four years to six years. Expenditure during these periods was disbursed as follows:

Table 13.1

Expenditure on and scope of the three project phases

Phase	*Period*	*Expenditure in millions of Australian dollars*	*Number of schools covered*
Phase one	July 1986 to June 1992	6.7	204
Phase two	July 1992 to June 1994	4.8	129
Phase three	July 1994 to December 1998	16.4	317
	Total	17.9	

Although the overall goal throughout the project was to develop education in estate schools in quantitative and qualitative terms in order to integrate these schools into the national system on an equitable basis, more specific goals were defined for each phase. These also varied for each phase as evaluations were completed and increasing emphasis was placed on quantmifiable indicators:

Phase 1

a) The improvement and expansion of all elementary schools located on the plantations.

b) The improvement and expansion of education at the secondary level for children attending plantation schools at the elementary level.

Phase 2

a) Increasing primary school participation in terms of enrolment of eligible age groups and enhancing the level of completion of the primary cycle by students enrolled from amongst the Tamil-speaking plantation people.

b) Expansion of participation in the secondary cycle by those completing the primary cycle.

c) Elevation of student achievement levels, particularly in mathematics and Tamil in the primary cycle.

Phase 3

a) Enrolling at least 90 per cent of boys and girls of school age in the primary cycle in the catchment area of each target school by the end of the third year of this phase of the project.

c) Increasing retention in the primary cycle to 80 per cent, and ensuring a completion rate of 60 per cent of all students enrolled by the end of the third year of the programme.

d) Increasing the transition rate of students from the primary cycle to the secondary cycle to at least 60 per cent by the end of the third year of the programme.

e) Ensuring at least 80 per cent of boys and girls completing year three are able to read, write and use basic computing skills.

f) Ensuring at least 60 per cent of the boys and girls completing year four have attained the minimum achievement level in mathematics and Tamil as measured by the test instruments available.

THE PROJECT MODEL

The overall objective of PSEDP was to enhance the learning environment in the primary schools and thereby help children to achieve the level required by the national goals of primary education. This objective was to be achieved through the participation and coordinated efforts of principals, teachers, students, parents, community and the education authorities. The target group was the Tamil-speaking children of school-going age in the plantation area.

A set of activities, within the context of programme development, was identified to achieve the objectives of the PSEDP. The following diagram illustrates the strategies used to enhance the classroom learning of the children:

Figure 13.1

Strategies to Enhance Student Classroom Learning

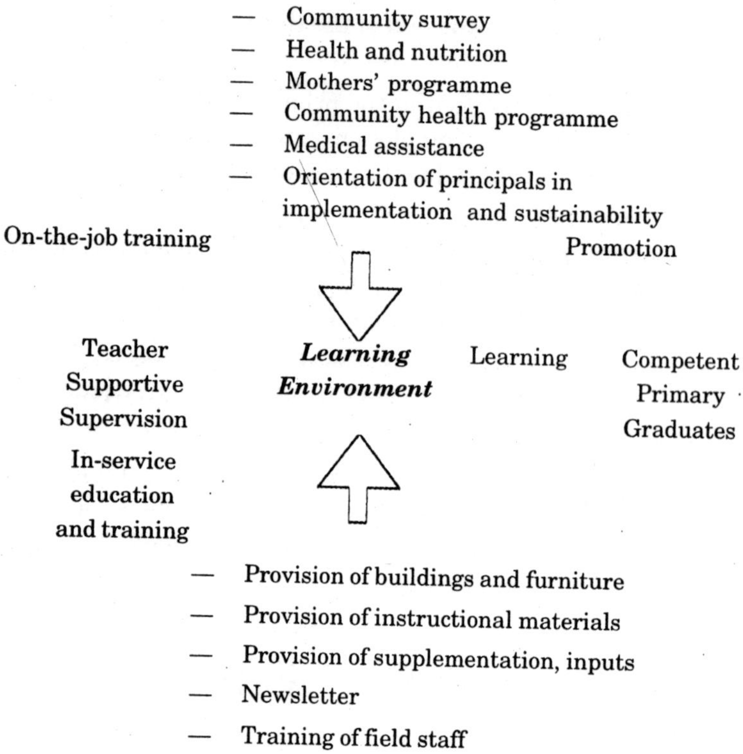

MONITORING AND EVALUATION PROCESS

Project activities were monitored from the beginning.

Monthly, quarterly, and annual meetings were held with the Swedish provider represented. These meetings considered financial projections for programmes as well as results from the previous period. In addition, monthly technical meetings were held with district and provincial officers to overcome any obstacles relating to civil works and provision of furniture.

A full-time expatriate consultant worked on evaluation and monitoring from 1987 to 1991. In addition, from time to time, the project obtained the services of an international consultant to improve the planning, monitoring and evaluation components of the project.

The monitoring and evaluation design was fine-tuned at the beginning of the second phase when a number of carefully selected quantifiable indicators were developed. These measured:

a) Net enrolment ratio
b) Retention rate
c) Transition rate
d) Repetition rate
e) Dropout rate
f) Admission pattern
g) Completion rate
h) Enrolment pattern
i) Promotional rate
j) Achievement test score
k) Reading, writing and computing skills score

At this time an Educational Management Information System (EMIS) was also established in order to measure and more accurately record improvement. This system resulted in a number of important developments in project schools:

a) Establishment of a school-based database with historic data as well as provision for regular updating.

b) The providers of this information began to use the data for their own institutional improvement.

c) School heads became trained in data analysis.

PROVISION OF BUILDINGS

Most of the estate schools were small, and poorly constructed of inferior materials. These schools had not been of high priority when built by plantation management. Grounds, too, were also small and inadequate. Development of this infrastructure was a high priority in the early phase of the project.

Unfortunately, during the first phase, a number of problems prevented building targets from being achieved:

a) The School Works Department was unable to cope with the additional work required by the project

b) This Department also did not have adequate numbers of technical staff to supervise outside contractors when they were employed.

c) There was a shortage of suitable contractors to construct school buildings in the districts.

d) The civil disturbances in the country during 1988 and 1989.

Furthermore, problems arose with the acquisition of land on which to build schools. In spite of a firm government policy, some estate managements were very reluctant to release the two acres required as this was often high value tea-producing land. Even after the takeover of land by the school, some of this land was again encroached upon by outsiders.

Construction of the target number of schools inevitably became delayed. Some schools were phased out of the quality part of the programme earlier than intended until the necessary buildings were provided in the more impoverished areas. A full-time expatriate engineer was employed to supervise work from 1988 until 1992. He was followed from 1992 until 1999 by a local consultant engineer who provided detailed quarterly reports on progress and was responsible for quality control.

Part of the project emphasised the importance of proper maintenance of school buildings. A maintenance manual was published and distributed to all project schools. Workshops and seminars were also organised to train principals and other staff in maintenance procedures. Toolboxes were issued to 400 schools and modifications made to buildings to reduce the cost of maintenance.

The project has now provided 51 per cent of plantation schools with the necessary buildings.

Table 13.2

Magnitude of the building programme to date

Type of facility	*Number*	*Type of facility*	*Number*
Classroom 20' x 20'	2624	Home science units	6
Office/store 20' x 20'	289	Commerce units	6
Office/store 40' x 20'	28	Workshop/Agric units	7
Science rooms	27	Principals' quarters	167
Science labs (O/L)	62	Teachers' quarters	367
Science labs (A/L)	5	Latrines	1436

In total the equivalent of $2.3 million Australian dollars has been expended on the building component of the project.

INSUFFICIENT AND UNQUALIFIED TEACHING STAFF

At the commencement of the project in 1984 there were 558 plantation schools with 1,148 permanent teaching staff. Additional teachers required to provide for all students under the compulsory education remit was 3,271.

Since that time a further 4,552 teachers have been trained and appointed under the plantation sector teacher programme. The majority of these teachers have been drawn from the plantation sector and trained in these areas. One of this the issue of non-abiding interest in the plantation sector is no longer such a difficult problem. Over 80 per cent of the supply of fully trained teachers to the plantation schools has now been met.

Furthermore, as part of a deliberate policy all amalgamated schools were deamalgamated. As a result each school now has at least two teachers. There are no single teacher schools remaining in the plantation sector. This retains ease of access to the schools by students and ensures teachers have some peer support in their workplace.

Most of the incumbent teachers in the plantation schools were untrained when the project was started in 1986. The project organised a comprehensive training programme, and conducted intensive workshops and seminars for teachers to improve their skills.

Table 13.3: Teacher participation in the training programme

Seminar / Workshop	*Phase one*	*Phase two*	*Phase three*
General primary	1320	494	3624
Primary science	368	—	660
Primary maths	27	—	889
Primary english	322	—	—
Principals' orientation	401	211	1038
Sustainability	—	—	242
Training of field staff	—	88	128

In recent years a number of teachers' centres with attached residential accommodation have been constructed to act as a focus for professional development activities.

HIGH STUDENT DROPOUT RATE

Throughout the project a number of key issues were established by the planners as target indicators of success. These were:

a) Enrolmesnt of all school-age children
b) Retaining all students to completion of the primary cycle
c) Reduction the repetition rate
d) Increase of the promotion rate
e) Increase of the transit rate to the secondary cycle.

Table 13.4: Results achieved in the primary sector by 1998

Objectives	*Target set in 1994*	*Results*		
		Male	*Female*	*Overall*
1. Enhancement of enrolment	Net enrolment of 90%	95.9	96.4	96.1
2. Retention and completion of primary cycle	Retention rate of 80%	82.9	85.1	83.6
	Completion rate of 60%	75.7	78.6	76.8
3. Transition from primary to secondary	Transition rate of 60%	79.9	82.4	81.2

Whilst these are average figures and the results vary from district to district, the targets set have, in the main, been exceeded.

SECONDARY EDUCATION

When the project commenced there were 741 primary schools and 92 secondary schools in the plantation sector. By the end of 1998 the number of secondary schools had increased to 212.

This was partly an outcome of strategies which increased the transition rate of students from primary school to secondary school to more than 70 per cent—even though the original target was to increase the transition rate to 60 per cent.

The secondary enrolment has increased sharply in the last six years of the programme from 16,157 in 1992 to 26,275 in 1998. Furthermore the proportion of girls moving on to secondary school rose from 46 per cent to over 50 per cent.

It was clear also that in a number of neighbouring non-project schools similar trends could be observed, indicating that the project had created a culture which caused similar effects in these schools as well.

SCHOOL SUPERVISION

The project established an external pedagogical support system for improving teaching effectiveness. A well-focused supervision format was designed for use by supervisors. The visits which took place were intended to be supportive in nature and helpful to the teachers in project schools. Teachers were observed at work and given guidance to improve their pedagogical skills.

During phase one of the project the following number of supervision visits were carried out:

a) Classroom supervision 703
b) Team supervision 31
c) General supervision 261

In the second and third phases of the project the supervision format was revised and greater emphasis given to classroom supervision. There were 2,398 and 5,250 classroom supportive visits, respectively.

These visits were also used to identify the training needs of teachers and, therefore, to design the workshops and seminars which became part of the project.

In the period 1990 to 1994, 31 additional permanent education administrative service officers were appointed. These officers had responsibility for oversight of the plantation sector development at the local level and they provided much of the external pedagogical support for these schools. However, some districts still face the problem of having inadequate numbers of Tamil-speaking officers.

CURRICULUM DEVELOPMENT

The project produced a range of purpose-written resource material for plantation schools. This included supplementary readers for primary classes during the first phase and quantities of self-learning units and booklets during the second and third phases.

These materials had the following salient features:

a) A non-graded, multi-level approach
b) A concept and competency-based approach
c) They were sustainable for a longer period and were not text book based

SCHOOL-COMMUNITY RELATIONSHIPS

The project conducted a variety of activities to establish greater rapport between the schools and their communities.

During phase one parents' days were encouraged and shramadana (*voluntary*) activities were carried out. In phase two and three mothers' programmes were added to the activities.

These activities targeted all the parents in the school catchment area. Principals were encouraged to invite parents to gather on regular occasions to observe cultural items displaying the importance of good health habits, to take part in discussions with estate medical officers or for discussions about the importance of sending their children to school and obtaining a good education.

Since most children on plantations live under more adverse health conditions and are subject to malnutrition, the project incorporated a health component and a number of strategies were implemented to improve health conditions in the sector:

a) Health charts were maintained in all primary classes.

b) Health competitions were held amongst students to highlight good health habits.

c) Screening visits were used to identify eye defects and supply spectacles.

d) Health and nutrition seminars were held for teachers to assist them in identifying defects and disease amongst children in order that referral and corrective action could be taken.

As a consequence of these activities, the health habits amongst school children improved, a good rapport developed between the school and the community and children began to be enrolled at school at the correct age. Furthermore the dropout rate among primary children fell significantly.

CONCLUDING COMMENT

Programme activities were planned carefully, particularly in the second and third phases, to ensure they could be sustained in the future after the project was finalised. Sustainability was emphasised in a number of ways:

a) The Compulsory Education Act was passed in 1996. This mandated that all children aged five to 14 must be enrolled at a school. This strengthened and sustained the first project objective which was to ensure all school-aged children attended a school.

b) Some of the project activities, such as the community survey, on-the-job training and the mothers' programme were incorporated in the Education Reforms that were introduced in 1997.

c) From year 2000 there is a separate programme for primary education in the national budget. This will bring the following benefits to primary schools.

   a) Primary schools will receive funding based on the number of pupils on their roll.

   b) Two per cent of the recurrent education budget will be allocated for procurement of consumables under quality, inputs.

   c) Each school will receive a cash advance at the beginning of each year for quality inputs, thus removing thes spend-first system.

   d) Under the General Education Project 2 all principals will be trained in management. One of the training modules will be on maintenance of buildings.

These ongoing strategies will assist in sustaining the gains made during the course of the plantation sector education development project and will ensure the funds made available have maximum effectiveness.

REFERENCES

Plantation Schools Education Development Project, 1999, Project Completion Report 1986-1998, Special Implementation Unit, Ministry of Education and Higher Education, Battaramulla.

Plantation Schools Education Development Programme: Implementation in Central Province, Provincial Ministry of Education, Gattembe, Peradeniya.

Objectively Quantifiable Indicators 1998: PSEDP Schools in Nuware Eliya District, Information System Unit (ISU), PSEDP Project Cell, Hatton, December.

Learning Achievement of Grade 3 Students in Essential Learning Competencies Published by the Information System Unit (ISU), PSEDP Project Cell, Hatton, November, 1998

Discussions with Uno Jonsson, Senior Education Adviser, Swedish Institute for Public Administration, Ministry of Education and Higher Education, Battaramulia, Sri Lanka, 1999.

Visitation with Sisira Liyanage, Deputy Director-General, National Institute of Education, Maharagama, Sri Lanka, 1999.

14

Management of Universities

—*Gur Pyari Satsangi**

Universities are the apex institutions of learning. The whole administrative and academic set-up of a university demands a high level of administrative acumen and effective management to function satisfactory. In fact, the management of any university can be portioned into three component organisations: academic management, management of departments and management of Students. Each of these three components have their our peculiarities which need to be considered independently.

ACADEMIC MANAGEMENT

The Academic Council is the principal academic authority and is responsible for the maintenance of the standards of teaching, research and examinations. The Executive Council/Syndicate as the principal executive authority at times transacts academic business on the pretext of urgency. It is not uncommon for the Executive Council to approve academic matters forwarded by the faculties and board of studies and reporting its action to Academic Council. Such actions may be legally correct but are democratically corrupt. The Executive Council defends its action on the ground of urgency since the Academic Council meets twice a year. Further, University Acts

**Lecturer, Faculty of Education, D.E.I. (Deemed University), Dayalbagh, Agra, India.*

empower the Executive Council to dispose of academic matters such as appointment of members of Board of Studies, examiners, moderators, publication of results, including Ph.D theses, approving the academic decisions made by the Vice-Chancellor, etc. Strictly speaking, all academic matters should be under the purview of the Academic Council. The report on the Standards of University Education has aptly remarked, "Bodies like the Senate and the Syndicate are concerned with administration in the narrow sense of the word and should not concern themselves much with academic matters or trespass into areas with which they cannot deal competently." The major build-in defect of the Academic Council is that it meets only twice in a year. The Executive Council defends its action on the basis of urgency and justified decisions since it is the executive authority of highest order.

The Kothari Commission had suggested that the Standing Committee of the Academic Council may be constituted for the purpose of disposing of urgent academic matters. When the Executive Council makes academic decisions it has no sanctity because the Academic Council is the principal academic authority with a responsibility for the maintenance of the standards of teaching, research, extension and examinations in the university. Therefore, it is necessary to create an executive authority of the Academic Council known as 'Academy' which can take all academic decisions. The prerogative of the Executive Council by which it is currently empowered to make decisions on academic matters should be transferred to the 'Academy'. If there are any operational constraints in the implementation of the 'Academy' decisions such as finance/ administrative difficulties, the matter may be referred to the Executive Council/Syndicate for its concurrence. All the actions/decisions of the 'Academy' should be placed before the Academic Council for rectification. As far as possible the Academy should take routine and emergency decisions and new decisions/breakthrough decisions should be taken at the Academic Council session only. The Model Act Committee has suggested that the Academic Council should remain sovereign in its field and assume responsibility for academic standards. It observes, "If it makes a mistake and lowers the standards of the university it assumes the responsibility for the poor estimate in which the degrees of that university will be held." This statement equally applies to the Academy which is the executive committee of the Academic Council.

MANAGEMENT OF DEPARTMENTS

An important function of the Executive Council is the management of teaching-cum-research departments. The department is the primary task centre of the university. It is a group of scholars brought together with a common subject matter interest. The university organises several service departments such as library, workshops, instrumentation centre, computer centre press and publications to provide support to teaching departments. The university also provides multiple and complex of services for all the above units such as power, water, transport, communications, maintenance, etc. The university has a statutory obligation to establish, maintain and manage university extension boards, information bureaus, employment guidance bureaus, medical and health services, etc.

The heads of study departments in many universities are in conflict with the administrative hierarchical structure of the university. Many academicians waste their time and energy at the cost of scholarship and research for the maintenance and development of the department. On the basis of academic assessment, the UGC and other funding agencies give grants for the development of department but utilisation of these grants is a hard task. The reason is that the administrative structure of university adopts bureaucratic procedures, rules, and regulations in administering the research grants. Some of the rules and procedures are inescapable but others could certainly be simplified and reduced to the absolute minimum. Administrative heads override the academic heads and very often they treat academic heads as subordinates. The superfluous rules and regulations obstruct the utilisation of grants for the purchase of furniture, equipment, apparatus, etc. Many universities have not repaired creaking and cumbersome administrative machinery. Perhaps keeping this in view, Dr. Kothari Commission suggested, "The departments of a university are its main operational units on the academic side. We are of the view that wider administrative and financial powers should be delegated to them."

The UGC is repeatedly requesting universities to confer autonomous status on academic departments and colleges, etc. As per the Andhra Pradesh Universities Act 1991 the Board of Management has power to confer in consultation with the Academic Senate either *suo motu* or on a representation received in this behalf from a college, autonomy on any college in the university area and to likewise withdraw such autonomy. But there is no provision to confer autonomous status on university departments. In Maharashtra universities, the Executive Council has power to confer autonomous status on university departments, colleges and recognised institutions on the recommendations of the Academic Council and the Senate.

One of the duties of the Executive Council is to accept donations, grants, etc., on behalf of the university. Whenever the UGC or any other funding agency gives grants to a particular academic department for doing research/teaching, only then, members of the Executive Council become aware of the working of the particular academic department post-graduate centre, etc. Generally the Executive Council is ignorant of the working of the academic department. The Bombay University Act has made a provision under powers and duties of the Executive Council to arrange for inspection of university departments and postgraduate departments in colleges with a view to assessing their academic performance and needs. Such provision should be there under the power and duties of the Executive Council in every University Act.

It is also the duty of the Executive Council to provide necessary infrastructure with utilities, etc., for the proper working of the university departments. Science and technology and engineering departments are dependent on technical staff to carry teaching, research and extension. Of late many non-teaching professionals who support academic staff are closely associated with faculty members in the performance of their functions. But at the same time they do not enjoy the rights, privileges and status the faculty members are entitled to. Many universities are facing problems in assigning appropriate status to the new categories of professionals.

Similarly, the university is also dependent on professional/technical staff for the successful maintenance of medical and health services, electrical, civil and mechanical services, press and publication, etc. Thus the university has to maintain coordination and balance between various segments of employees: teaching, non-teaching professionals, technical and administrative staff. It is quite unfortunate that no one thinks that they are all working in one institution with a common mission and objectives.

MANAGEMENT OF STUDENTS

The new mission of the university is achieving an ideal democratic community within the institution. The major segments of university community are faculty and students. Both faculty and students as members of the university community should participate in the decisions that affect them. The participation of students and teachers in the management of a university is consistent with democratic values of a university community.

Kothari Commission has observed, "As one positive step to encourage students to take part in the university government and to make them realise their responsibilities in the day-to-day functioning of the university, we recommend that representatives of the students' community (including under-graduate students) should be associated with the Academic Councils and Courts of the Universities." Thus the Commission was in favour of student participation in the two highest authorities, i.e., Senate and Academic Council. The subsidiary authorities of the Academic Council are Faculty Council and

Boards of Studies. The students should participate in the Boards of Studies at the department level and Faculty Council at the faculty level. But the CMU is not in favour of student participation in the Academic Council and Board of Studies. The CMU says, "Students should be given opportunity for participation in the Senate/Court but not in the other bodies like Syndicate, Academic Council and Board of Studies." Perhaps the CMU thought, the students are transitory, young, immature and inexperienced and their competency is questionable in the academic decisions.

"No person has the right to make a decision that affects the lives of others," is a popular democratic slogan. Today, students are seeking admissions into higher education as a right rather than a privilege. They are entering higher education with different socioeconomic backgrounds unlike traditional students of affluent background and also with the twin objectives of upward social mobility and gainful employment. The teachers are not making efforts to understand the behaviour pattern of modern students and develop an alien nature towards student community. The mutual confidence and trust has been shattering and a crisis of confidence has been developing. Whenever the Board of Studies makes a change in the curriculum, the student is suspicious about the motives behind change. He knows today's teacher is more concerned with his growth and advancement rather than student advancement. What is good for the teacher may not necessarily be good for the student. It is not uncommon that obsolete specialisation subjects are forced on students for the survival of teachers. Certain specialisation/subjects have neither academic viability nor employment potential, still the university offers them on the advice of academicians.

In the words of James A. Perkins, "The academic process is now viewed as one in which teacher and learner are equally involved, both in the selection of topics and in the manner in which these can be taught. As students insist on the right to participate at the point where decisions are made about the content of their instruction they are focusing on the department." The academic autocracy should be changed into academic democracy through participation of students in the Board. One need not question the academic competency of a student or the effectiveness of student participation in the Board. What is important, however, is that the students have all opportunity to influence the university affairs. The mere presence of students in various authorities has affected decisions in some universities as some professors have been reluctant (or even afraid) to take positions publicly that are unpopular with the students.

One of the major functions of the Executive Council is to promote the health and welfare of students. The major cause of student unrest on the campus is the inadequate student services, which constitutes an integral part of education. The students are demanding a greater voice in the management of student services. The important student services are living facilities, counselling and guidance, services student activities, health services, financial aid, etc. The CMU has opined that the student participation should be necessary in the following forums: (1) Committees concerned with the corporate life of students and extra-curricular and co-curricular activities; (2) Advisory committee for halls of residence/hostels, etc. and (3) Committee for games, social services and cultural activities. Many universities have been participating in them but the anticipated results are not forthcoming. There is no central agency to coordinate all these activities and to estimate inputs that are necessary in the performance of various activities. The Maharashtra state had made a provision in the Universities Acts for the creation of a Student Council and identified it as one of the authorities of the university. The Act prescribed the composition and size and the Council. The Vice-Chancellor is ex-officio President and the Director of Student Welfare is ex-officio Treasurer of the Council. There is a Students, Executive Union, which shall implement the policy decisions taken by the Student Council. The functions of the Council are to:

1) Supervise and coordinate the activities of different students' association societies and other organisations;

2) Recommend the Executive Council for the financial allocation to be made for the activities to be undertaken under the relevant budgetary heads;
3) Allocate funds for different activities of students' associations, societies and other organisation, as sanctioned by the Executive Council;
4) Submit an annual report of its work together with a statement of its accounts to the Executive Council, within a date to be fixed by it;
5) Make recommendations to the Executive Council regarding any matter affecting the corporate life or welfare of the students; and
6) Make recommendations to the Executive Council regarding the facilities existing for instruction.

The CMU also recommended that such a Council should be constituted in every university.

The complex activities of a university are difficult enough to be managed by the single authority, i.e., Executive Council. The high concentration of power under one authority is not desirable, and the authority of the Executive Council should be distributed by creation of new authorities. Further, the traditional authorities are not able to cope with the changing environment of a university. The traditional authorities should be redesigned/restructured and new authorities should be created, wherever necessary, in the management of university.

REFERENCES

CMU Recommendation, No. 79.

Report on Standards of University Education, New Delhi, UGC, 1965. p.95.

Model Act Committee Report, p.22.

The Education Commission Report (1964-66), Chapter XIII, The Government of University, p.327.

Education Commission Report, Chapter—XIII, The Government of University, p.328.

CMU Recommendation, No. 129.

James A. Perkin, (ed)., *The University as an Organisation*, New York, McGraw Hill, p. 12.

15

Learning Components in Development Activities

—*Barrie Brennan**

This paper is concerned with the learning components within development activity. Learning components consist of the teaching and learning strategies, and the settings and methodologies designed to achieve learning objectives in development activities.

In one sense the paper's focus may be considered as the micro-level of the debate about development. At the macro-level, the debate has concentrated on the grand theories of 'flow-down' development, or 'human capital' development. While one might argue that discussions about learning components are relegated to the level of micro-issues, the counter-argument can be put forward, and it is the point of view of this paper, that having the right theory and practice with regard to the learning components of a development project may be as crucial for the success of the project as having the proper development theory, at the macro-level, for the overall development project. In a development project related to health or nutrition or literacy or agricultural production, unless the target group of mothers or farmers really learns what the project is about and what the benefits may be to them and their community, then the project does not succeed. The learning

**University of New England, Armidale, Australia.*

components of a development project are not secondary or ancillary: they are central. That is my first point.

My second point is that learning is culturally determined. If there is one lesson that is clearly evident from decades of development activity, it is that Western culture is very arrogant. Westerners, and those from developing nations who have been socialised into Western culture, have been very culturally arrogant. They have completely disregarded local culture and its learning styles because they have shown by their actions that they know that Western methods are better; Western methods must be right for every situation. In forcing the Western school and the Western classroom and the Western-style teacher on cultures of Africa, Asia, South America and the Pacific during the colonial period, and more recently, educational technology on these and other cultures, they have shown an arrogance equal to that of any other form of intellectual imperialism.

Even those Westerners or Westernised indigenous people who try to break away from this practice that the West is best find it difficult to scrape off the educational barnacles. Why? Because learning is culturally determined. Andragogy or human resource development (HRD) or self-directed learning (SDL) or simulation—these techniques, developed in the context of Western society, are applied in other cultures in the belief that because they work in the West, they must be equally useful in other societies.

Some may suggest that the above picture is an extreme position. I fear not. The lessons have not been learned. The mistakes are repeated. If lectures or gaming or CAL are being used in a development activity, and if the process of evaluation indicates that the rate of progress is not what was planned or expected, then the participants in the development project (the learners) are given some remedial work in the method or some extra coaching. The participants must be wrong. Such is the cultural blindness of many Westerners to the degree of their own socialisation and to the possibilities of learning within other cultures.

The learning styles, the conditions for learning, the preferred and the taboo methods are culturally determined. To overlook this fact and to maintain a myopic, Western view of techniques and strategies has a two fold effect: Western styles are over valued, despite their inappropriateness and traditional styles are under valued by neglect. Further, in relation to the development project the results of over-concentration on what might be culturally-inappropriate teaching/learning strategies may be complete failure of the project, or at best, less than maximum success. Another consequence, usually completely unanticipated, is a lack of continuity of the project's objectives beyond the period of the project. Certainly, the project can be maintained beyond its time with additional support to maintain Western teaching/learning methods, but the impact of continuance in those circumstances results in another blight on development activities, the continuation of dependence of Western aid.

If there was an acceptance that learning is culturally defined and that Westerners are so well socialised in their own learning methodologies that they find it difficult to accept that there are other, quite appropriate methodologies in the cultures of the communities being serviced, and if development is to be delivered and maintained in ways that evelop locally, rather than maintain a relationship of dependence, then there are three possible solutions:

a) those involved in devising learning components for development activities must be aware of the cultural roots of Western-developed learning strategies, and be sensitive to the potential impact of the strategies in other cultures.

b) those involved in devising learning components for development activities must be sensitive to the learning styles, activities and appropriate settings of local culture, and be prepared to look in the right places and discuss the question with the appropriate people to ascertain where to look and ask.

c) those involved in devising learning components for development activities must look for those possibilities of merging the traditional with the Western, not with a compromise mentality, but in the development of a new style identifying the most appropriate from the two cultures or others as may be appropriate.

The solutions are not easy. However, those involved in developing learning strategies in projects now and in the future have the results of a number of studies that have been, and are being, carried out to identify the learning components of various non-Western societies.

Before examining research on traditional learning styles, one study, noting the potential impact of Western technological methodology, will be cited. Conboy and D'Cruz (1988) examine what they term the 'secondary order consequences', or those effects not immediately apparent, of the use of technology in distance education and rural development. Though their prime focus is a project in the Australian state of Victoria, their argument is related to other societies because they stress the role of culture. In relation to Victoria, they note the possibility of a second order consequence being 'the loss of rural autonomy' (1988, 15). The article is not anti-technology but it cautions that the use of technology should be analysed in the particular social and cultural context in which it will operate. For example, certain technology used in distance education may have a second order consequence on interpersonal communication. The impact may be detrimental where the cultural emphasis is on the collective rather than on the individual or where the culture is concrete as compared with a more individualistic and impersonal abstract culture. The cultures of many developing countries have the qualities of collectivism and concretism.

The Conboy and D'Cruz study refers to broad social and cultural relations rather than specific learning components. However, the study highlights the possibility of problems being created by ignoring the cultural context in which the learning is desired to take place.

For just 200 years, Australian whites have been trying to educate the indigenous people, the aborigines, in the traditional white methods, and have had only limited success. Only recently has there been an interest from both whites and aborigines in traditional aboriginal ways of learning, after all they lived very successfully on that dry continent for thousands of years before the white man come without the benefits of Western education. Stephen Harris in a study of aboriginal people at Milingimbi in North-east Arnhem Land identified five important learning strategies in that aboriginal community. In his report (Harris, 1980) he expresses these strategies (in a very useful way for the white educator here or in the Territory) in a series of contrasts between traditional Western and traditional aboriginal learning. His five strategies are:

1. Learning by Observation and Imitation versus Verbal Instruction
2. Learning by Personal Trial-and-Error Versus Verbal Instruction and Demonstration
3. Learning in Real-Life Activities Versus Practice in Contrived Settings
4. Context-Specific Learning Versus Generalisable Principles
5. Person-Orientation Rather than Information-Orientation: Absence of the Institutionalised Office of 'Teacher'. (pp. 77-102)

An illustration of the contrasts between learning in the two cultures, as well as an elaboration of one of the general strategies, is contained in the following quotation. The illustration gives an example of the second strategy: learning by personal trail-and-error versus instruction and demonstration.

> L, a young man of about twenty-one, had a reputation for recognising the footprints of many Milingimbi people. He claimed that he learned to be such a good tracker during training received under the Boy Scouts. The Boy Scout

> Movement at Milingimbi had lasted for only one or two sessions. Games of tracking had been played, and L had done very well at those games. Actually, it appears that L had learned his tracking skill by personal observation and trial-and-error over many years, and through spending a lot of time in the bush with his father. When I asked L, who is one of the better speakers of English, to teach me how to track or explain to me how to track, he could not even begin. "I just do it", was as close as he could get, yet there is no question about his knowledge. (p. 88).

Supposing, for example, there was a development project for the Milingimbi people that involved, as many do, skill development. What would be the likely success of the whole project if the teaching of skills was carried out in the normal Western way—blackboard/classroom theory, followed by instructor demonstration and supervised practice? With some sensitivity to the traditional culture, there is the possibility of exploring the potential relevance of learning components that may be generally classified in Western terminology as 'discovery' methods.

In another Australian study, Eve Fesl (1982) discussed with the aboriginal people in three communities their attitudes to literacy education. The Western white assumption is that literacy is absolutely necessary for adequate functioning in modern society. Fesl's study concludes (1982, 48-49) that aborigines showed little or no interest in literacy tuition.

Five sets of reasons were given for this lack of interest. There was a reaction against, forced tuition in youth, what might be termed a negative 'school inheritance'. Secondly, it was noted that in a culture based on oral transmission, prestige was accorded to the storytellers, rather than the readers. Since so much of the printed word was non-aboriginal and even anti-aboriginal in context, there was little relevance in reading. A related reason was that jobs which aboriginal perceived as being available to them did not require literacy, e.g., labouring, cleaning or gardening. Finally, in a culture where the emphasis was on the extended family unit, there was not a need for everyone to be able to read and write provided that someone in the unit had these skills.

While this study is not primarily concerned with learning strategies, it does illustrate the point that providing a literacy programme with materials focused on Western culture would be highly unsuccessful.

The African continent has witnessed a range of projects seeking to identify the patterns of learning, or learning components, of traditional African societies. Jakayo Ocitti, for example, has identified (1988) two categories of learning:

> (1) personally-initiated learning strategies which were characterised by the processes of observation, imitation and practice through positive involvement in the day-to-day living activities of the family, the community or in short the entire society. More details of this category of learning patterns remain yet to be researched;
>
> (2) and socially-initiated learning strategies which comprised the processes of questioning, demonstration, explanation, and task assignments. This category of learning patterns involved extensive use of folklore, ceremonies, festivals, job performance, symbolic materials, masks and other learning support systems as media (p. 356).

Care must be taken with the adoption of traditional learning components, as with any methodology, and it is important to heed Ocitti's warning that more details of his first category need to be researched. The process of dealing with traditional, learning strategies is best described as an exploration, using the local people as the chief resource.

Ocitti's two categories emphasise that traditional learning strategies use a wide range of methods, many of which are normally excluded from Western methodological lists. His work is very useful for those seeking to develop meaningful teaching components in a cross-cultural situation because he relates traditional methods to the language and structure of Western instructional design, e.g., he notes that socially-initiated learning strategies are in fact learning support systems and fill a role of equivalence with Western instru-ctional media.

The importance of culture to learning strategies has been emphasised in the examples from Australia and Africa. The potential for normal Western-learning components in development activities in these societies is evident. The dissociation of theory from practice, the emphasis on the abstract rather than the concrete and on learning for its own sake, and the divorce of the content or learning from local life and traditions will result in the failure to achieve the objectives of the development project as far as learning is concerned.

There have been attempts to develop a modern indigenous learning strategy in developing countries, that is, where a synthesis is attempted between traditional cultural elements and learning and Western approaches. The Thai concept of Khit-pen is an example of this attempted synthesis. In the simplest terms, the approach seeks to define the goal of the Khit-pen man as one whose orientation to life, and learning, is based on problem solving or problem overcoming. The Khit-pen learning style is founded on both Western humanistic adult education philosophy and practice and traditional Thai Buddhism.

In a recently published, short volume on Khit-pen (in English), Oonta Nopakun (1985) has explained the importance of 'harmony' as a central focus of the Khit-pen philosophy. To achieve harmony a person has:

i) to adjust oneself to achieve harmony with society or the environment.

ii) to adjust society or the environment to achieve harmony with oneself.

iii) to adjust both oneself and society to environment to achieve harmony.

iv. to evade the existing society and environment for a society and environment which is appropriate for oneself.

There is a clear link between the conditions for achieving harmony and the four truths of Buddhism: life is suffering; suffering can be cured; to cure the suffering, the origin of suffering must be identified; then can the right way be found to alleviate the suffering.

Kowit Vorapipatane, who first used the term Khit-pen, described the process of Khit-pen as follows:

> A man who has mastered the process of Khit-pen will be able to approach problems in his daily life systematically. He will be able to examine the causes of his problems. He will be able to gather the widest range of information on possible courses of action and weigh the merits of each option, based on his own values, his own capabilities, his personal situation, and the degree of each solution.

Since further elaboration has defined the sort of information required for the Khit-pen man, namely, information on self, information on society and the environment, book knowledge or technical information (Nopakun, 1985, 13), insights are given into the content of the educational programme. Guidance is also given as to learning techniques because of the emphasis on problem-solving, research, values clarification and the emphasis on the individual.

In another geographical region, the Pacific Islands, the writer has discussed methods that can be adopted to discover the techniques and practices of traditional education in the many cultures of the area (Brennan, 1987). Two methods were advocated. The first involved taking a long-range, historical view of the relationship between the two educational styles. The following table suggests some of the important features in the changing relationship:

The relationship between traditional and western education

Time	*Stages in western education*	*Stages in traditional education*
Nineteenth century	Missionary education	Degrees of resistance (open or undercover)
Early twentieth century to 1960s/70s	Education as a support to colonial goals and the western economic system	Gradual devaluation by being ignored
Early independence period	Viewed as a means to nationhood and development in Western terms	Undervalued by new national leaders as neither modern nor developmental
1980s to the 21st century	Questioning of value of traditional Western education in the West; of the basic structures, outcomes, costs, alternatives being proposed and attempted	Some questioning of the ultimate value of Western education: some searching for alternatives

In exploring the Western tradition, foci for the search can be the Western historical records, particularly the diaries of the observations of early explorers, settlers and missionaries. The way they recorded their impressions and the interpretation placed on their observations can give insights, from the advantage of present-day historical perspective, into traditional learning styles. Due to the importance of the oral tradition for the traditional culture, the stories, songs and dances can be investigated particularly for what they can reveal about learning strategies and methods.

The second approach has some similarities with the method of presentation used by Harris in presenting the learning strategies of Milimgimbi. The approach consists of trying to define the contrasting characteristics of the Western and traditional systems.

Constrasting traditional Pacific learning with western education

	Western education	*Traditional Pacific learning*
i)	sequential	Spontaneous lifelong learning
ii)	progressing from level to level	Lifelong learning
iii)	reward system in grades, certificates	Intrinsic personal and social value of learning
iv)	competition	Cooperation: collaboration
v)	formalised	non-formal
vi)	delivered by educational institutions	social group basis
vii)	bureaucratically controlled	Community controlled
viii)	professionalised teachers	Volunteer, part-time teachers
ix)	discipline-based, specialised knowledge	Problem-centred, cross-disciplinary knowledge
x)	knowledge-cognitive logical	Knowledge intuitive
xi)	based on an essentially material view of and response to the natural world	Based on an essentially spiritual view of and response to the natural world
xii)	based on a power system from the top to the bottom	Based on a collaborative/shared power system within social hierarchies

While isolating the contrasting positions may encourage the emergence of extreme views and features that may be difficult to justify, the exercise does allow for a general profile to be developed. From such a profile, some judgements can be made about learning components that may be appropriate or inappropriate. For example, the table of contrasts suggests that strategies that are informal and based on cooperation and collaboration may be preferable to formal techniques that rely on competition.

The argument of this paper has been that learning and the learning components used to promote learning are culturally determined. In development programmes inspired or managed from the West, there is an assumption that Western learning strategies are not really part of the Western culture but rather universal. Their use to achieve the educational aspects of the development programme are likely to be detrimental to the long and short-term objectives of the programme.

In addition to the on going failure of the educational component of development programmes—failure that has not necessarily prompted the questioning of the educational techniques used or the basis on which they are used—there has been a recent interest in research into the traditional learning styles of the indigenous people. There is 'therefore' a greater possibility of discovering alternative learning components than relying solely on Western techniques.

An important aspect of the recent research is that the indigenous people have been heavily involved in the research, with the possibility of the important 'second order consequence' that the continuity of projects may be achieved and dependence, created by Western methodologies, reduced.

In seeking to discover or re-discover traditional learning styles and techniques, so that they can be used, and valued in their use, several potential approaches have been suggested in the articles discussed. The techniques can be divided into the large-scale and small-scale. The large-scale techniques involve the examination of systems in an historical or comparative way. A notion or culture's history can be examined to detect the modes of teaching and learning used at various times. Comparisons can be made between historical periods and between neighbouring or distant cultures, particularly, for example, in their reaction to imperialism as an economic, political or religious force. Such an examination can be directed to the printed word and books or the search can be made through the oral tradition, where it exists and has cultural significance.

The small-scale approach is no less important than the large-scale, just different. A complete picture, particularly of learning techniques, will require both approaches to be made. In the small-scale approach the emphasis is on local factors, what happens in this village or on this island. While general social relationships and work patterns are of interest and potential value, the learning components of a single craft activity or significant skills, of a dance or a song, of a festival or shelter-building activity may provide central clues to an understanding of the learning style of a particular group of people.

Let it not be thought that such a process is only of value in developing countries. The educational institutions of developed nations would also be well advised to look at the way people in rural communities or the large metropolis learn, because I suspect it is not exclusively through the formal programmes of these institutions.

The importance of this task of discovering how the traditional style of learning operates is evident by examining what has happened in developing countries, not just in relation to development projects that are Western-inspired but in relation to departments and divisions that carry the title Non-Formal Education. Such government instrumentalities with their optimistic objectives and large bureaucracies have tended to use Western-developed learning components and have not seen as a major objective to discover which are the preferred methods, the traditional ways, of those who are supposed to become literate or more productive or enthusiastic to adopt a new approach to farming or fishing or to reduce their family size. In a recent paper, Sarfraz Khwaja (1988) has described the problems of Pakistan in seeking to eradicate illiteracy. Quite appropriately, the paper lists the departments and programmes, the policy statements, the programmes for training teachers, of building facilities, of using the mass media. In this, as in other reports, there is no mention of an attempt to discover what are the views of those for whom literacy is being prescribed, like the Australian aborigine, and if they really want it. Nor, however, is the time and effort being devoted to seeking to define what are the means by which literacy or farming skills or new health procedures can be traditionally learned.

A significant difference between development projects, and NFE programmes, before and after the mid-1980s, may be that those of the present and future may take seriously the concept of developing learning components that are consonant with the traditional learning values and styles of the people for whom the programmes and projects are designed. To continue to neglect traditional learning styles, in favour of the so-called superior Western techniques, is to invite on going failure or at best only a modicum of success and only limited long-term gains, with the possibility that dependence will be retained because of the use of non-traditional learning components.

REFERENCES

Brennan, B., 1987, "Traditional Education . . . The Pacific way", *Adult Education and Development,* 29, October, 71-78.

Conboy, I. and D'Cruz, J.V., 1988, "Distance Education and Rural Development", *Unicorn,* 14, 1, 10-16.

Fesl, E.D., 1982, *Bala Bala: Some Literacy and Education Perceptions of Three Aboriginal Communities,* Australian Government Publishing Service, Canberra.

Harris, S., 1984, *Culture and Learning: Tradition and Education in North East Arnhem Land,* Australian Institute of Aboriginal Studies, Canberra.

Nopakun, O., 1985, *Thai Concept of Khit-pen for Adult and Non-formal Education,* Chulalongkorn University and the Asian and South Pacific Bureau of Adult Education.

Ocitti, J.P., 1988, "Indigenous African Pedagogy", *Adult Education and Development,* 30, March, 347-357.

Sarfraz Khwaja, 1988, "*Eradication of Illiteracy in Pakistan: An Analysis 1947-1987*", Australian Journal of Adult Education, 28, 1, April.

16

Ecocentrism, Leader Compassion and Community

—*R. Swann**

Drawing on results of critical incident research into the compassion shown by school leaders and on writings in areas such as deep ecology and ecofeminism, connections are made for possible ways forward in thinking about both leadership and community.

COMPASSIONATE LEADERSHIP

Earlier research (Swann, 1996, 1998a, b 1999) investigated the compassion of leaders in schools. A conceptual framework was developed that linked eleven elements of compassion in a matrix with four leadership frames. Leadership was interpreted from the successful framing model of Bolman and Deal (1991). Appendix I shows that matrix from which was developed a questionnaire on leader behaviour. This was tested in schools deemed, by expert opinion, to be run by compassionate leaders. Much quantitative data flowed from this questionnaire including strong statistical confirmation of the robustness of the model. However, this quantitative work was seen as an adjunct to the qualitative, which involved

**Environmental Science, Victoria University, Victoria, Australia.*

many, hours of semi-structured, critical incident interviewing of school leaders and others in the school community. Together, the synergy of the two methodologies advanced understanding of three questions: What do leaders do in exercising compassion in schools? How is success in the school affected by compassion on the part of the leader? How have leaders developed compassion?

COMPASSION

Compassion is a feeling of sympathy and resultant action, directed towards the relief of suffering by another. The understanding of compassion in this research, based upon both my own thinking and the works of others, particularly, Matthew Fox (1979) moves compassion beyond feelings. Compassion involves a sharing of solidarity with the suffering of others and not an at-a-distance attempt implicit in pity. Compassion involves celebration (rejoicing at another's joy) and grieving at another's sorrow. It is about suspended egos, feelings of togetherness and the feeling of kinship with all fellow creatures. Compassion is not sentiment, that is, it is not a mental feeling, but involves action in the relief of the pain of others. Compassion is a public not private action that is intent on justice. There exists a clear distinction between the care for another person (personalism) present in most schools and universities, and compassion. Sentimentality, not compassion is present in most educational institutions. The action of compassion is missing in the sentimentalist approach. Rationality and reasoned argument cannot totally remove compassion from people but such argument can harden us to suffering so that we do not act on our emotions. It is the intuitive trusting of emotions, the willingness to let others be their creative selves, that marks the compassionate leader. Apart from the highly influential work of Fox (1979), other writers in the area of compassion include Eckhardt (1972), Miller (1981), Nouwen, McNeill and Morrison (1982), Purpel

(1989), Prior (1989), Noddings (1992), Gyatso (1993), Birch (1993)), Jones (1993), Nouwen (1994) and The Dalai Lama (1995).

A sifting of the literature on compassion resulted in the distillation of contributors to compassion into 11 elements: celebrative, passionately active, benevolently loving, creative, non-elitist, networking, transpersonal, pain relieving, transcendent, fun-filled. Links between some of these and ecocentrism are explored later.

VALUES IN LEADERSHIP

Several writers have commented upon the lack of recognition in leadership studies of those concerns of leadership that are not always neatly qualified or measured in the model provided by a positivist science approach. They have, instead, insisted on the investigation of ethics, morals, values, feelings, actions, beliefs and the will of individuals as inexhaustible sources of information regarding leader behaviour. Leadership as an art and as service to others, not as a science, is emphasised.

There is a commonality of ideas emerging between, on the one hand, writings to do with values and service in leadership and ecocentrism (see p. 4) on the other. A brief overview of some of those leadership writings follows.

Blumberg (1989:18-19) reports a "gnawing feeling that (he) may have been missing the point" in his many years of behavioural/rational research into school leadership and was "thinking more and more about the unquantifiable 'somethings' of the person or people who administer schools that seem a bit out of the ordinary in their goodness." Greenfield (1984) also wrote of the impersonal way that organisations are too often researched in terms of' leadership and along with Hodgkinson (1991) and Noddings (1984), stresses the importance of morality and ethics in leadership. Wheatley (1992) sees the breakthroughs in ways of viewing the world experienced by physicists, and later other scientists, as having much to give as a way of understanding organisations and their leadership, and Sungaila (1990) explains how chaos theory, with its understanding of far from equilibrium, dissipative structures may point to new ways of developing leadership. Starratt's (1991:186) ethic of caring has much to do with compassion. He writes of the sacred nature of the human relationships within a school, and Beck (1994:20) also writes of an ethic of caring and emphasises the importance of mutual dependence and community.

> Caring proceeds in the context of interdependent relationships in networks that might be labelled communities (where) the welfare of each (person) is inextricably related to the welfare of others so that one caring for others in fact cares for herself or himself. The commitment between people who care is not conditionally dependent on merit or whim, but is unconditional and marked by acceptance, nurturance and grace.

Dance (1991) relates the story of rejuvenation of a Canadian community college through leadership that he concludes as a performing art is aesthetic and not logical. He also expands the Bolman and Deal symbolic frame to include the spiritual, and writes that if leadership is ultimately however, about bringing out the best in people, that best is tied to one's sense of one's deepest self, to one's spirit.

This requires a leader to be in touch with his/her own spirit and core beliefs—in touch with a credo or personal guidance system for functioning in uncertain times.

Vaill (1989:213) also writes of the way that much management literature has avoided the spiritual aspects of people's experience in the workplace whilst Wong (1996:18) suggests that much about leadership might be learned from the Confucian ideas of service which emphasise groups rather than individual leaders. Nouwen (1989:43) writes that "somehow we have come to believe that good leadership requires a safe distance from those we are called to lead," and cautions against the individualism and resultant spiritual loss that influenced much of his working life as a prominent Catholic academic in prestigious universities. Nouwen recognised the extent of his own giving-in to the temptation to be powerful when he left academia to work in a community, of mentally handicapped people. No longer were Nouwen's (1989:56—57) "beautiful words and convincing arguments" sufficient as the people with whom he had come to live made him "aware of the extent to which my leadership was still a desire to control complex situations, confused emotions and anxious minds." It led to him "getting in touch with the mystery, that leadership, for a large part, means to be led." In a similar vein, Greenleaf (1977:14) writes of leaders being servants first and leaders second. That is, the order is important. Those who are great leaders begin with the natural feeling of wanting to serve which then brings them to leadership. Jaworski (1996:182) was strongly influenced by Greenleaf's servant leader idea and sees leadership as far more about being than about doing—who we are in the sense of our being open to truly listening to others and our inner self and being there for them and ourself, so that they/we feel empowered to act. De Pree (1987:3) thinks that it is fundamental for leaders to "endorse a concept of persons" which begins with understanding people's gifts, talents and skills. He sees leadership as tribal rather than scientific and "more a weaving of relationships than an amassing of information." Using the metaphor of dance, Duignan (1997:14) recognises the importance of uncertainty, chaos and complexity to leadership and writes of authentic leadership as having ethical, moral and spiritual foundations while Bogue (1994:146) writes of leaders having "spiritual scars and calluses on their characters, the evidence of their having struggled with difficult moral issues."

One of the most useful leadership models to emerge in recent times has been the work of Bolman and Deal who write of ways of looking at both change in organisations and leadership. They use the concept of frames—ways of making sense of organisations and suggest four frames, each of which is based upon one of the four major schools of organisational theory and research. These frames are labelled as structural emphasis upon formal roles, policies, rules, hierarchy, *human resource* (individuals must be matched by the form of the organisation), *political* (recognises competition for power and resources) and *symbolic* (cultural, non-rational where ritual, myth and symbolism are valued). Only when all four frames (they also use the analogy of four overlapping, lenses) are used will the depth and complexity of organisational life be appreciated and simplistic solutions avoided. Knowledge of one's own preferred frame is also critical so that the other frames are not ignored and can be allowed for in decision making. This was the basis for my understanding of school leadership, with the crucial addition that Bolman and Deal's four frames must also be underpinned by compassion.

The metaphor of a healthy, growing tree (see Appendix 2) can aid in understanding compassionate leadership. The Bolman and Deal leadership frames are the four important roots to the tree but a fifth frame beneath (and essential to the survival of) all of them is compassion. The leadership frames seen as Bolman and Deal leadership imply circularity and sharply defined boundaries whereas tree roots are more amorphous and this quality better represents the inherent uncertainty of the bounds of the frame and of its content and so better allows for the complexity of a living concept like leadership within a living organisation like a school. The frames are seen as overlapping rather than separate to indicate the interconnectedness of the different 'bits' of leadership-emphasising that leadership is much more than can be contained in just two axes or four frames–and is much more than the sum of the 'bits.' No hierarchy of outcomes is implied by the relative positions of the branches, and the crown of the tree has no metaphorical significance. However, the metaphor can be extended into thinking about the changes in outcomes (branches) that occur when the mix of the frames at the roots is altered—and about the fragility of the system—if one of the main roots is severed, that is, one of the frames is missing, certain outcomes will be missing or their growth will be impaired.

The significance of having compassion at the base is that all frames lead to it or from it and from that strong compassionate base grow the outcomes sought in the vision of the school. The uniqueness of each tree also signifies the uniqueness of each organisation with no two having precisely the same inputs (represented by differences in frames) or the same outputs (branches).

Such a metaphor is one way that ecology may contribute to understanding of leadership. Ecocentric philosophy is another.

ECOCENTRISM

'Shades of green' might be one simple way of thinking about the diversity of environmental perspectives because not all environmentalists agree with one another. The answer to the question, "Why are you concerned about this issue?", gives some understanding of a perspective. Some might be keen to conserve resources (such as trees) solely for their economic potential whilst others will identify with the plight of caged hens kept under appalling conditions to supply human food. Others will see as their main focus the preservation of tropical rainforests in developing countries to alleviate the enhanced greenhouse effect—and others will want to preserve those same forests for their 'cathedral' value—their spiritual ability to be uplifting to people—or simply for their intrinsic worth—because they are. Robyn Eckersley (1991) employs the helpful analogy of an environmental spectrum of thought to explore difference in environmental positions. At one end of the spectrum (the anthropocentric end) is resource conservation and at the other end, ecocentrism. In between are human welfare ecology, preservationism and animal liberation. This is not a linear progression and there is overlap between the arguments for non-adjacent parts of the spectrum. As I want to concentrate on the ecocentric end, I'll briefly outline the other parts. Resource conservation (or "wise use") is human-centred, economistic and utilitarian and seeks to reduce inefficiency in the use of non-renewable resources and maximum sustainable yield in the use of renewable resources (soils, trees, fish). The intrinsic worth of other species or the aesthetic value of wilderness are not considered. Human welfare ecology considers physical and social limits to growth and challenges the technological fix idea–that we can eventually fix all problems of our interference with natural systems. However, it is still anthropocentric in seeing value in the non-human only in terms of its usefulness to humans. Preservationism stems from a spiritual and aesthetic valuing of the non-human and so calls for wilderness preservation. But the use of wilderness to restore jaded Western souls is still anthropocentric. Even the very notion of wilderness is criticised by ecocentrists as lending weight to a false divide between humans and nature. Animal liberation developed independently of the three streams of environmentalism mentioned. Based upon Jeremy Bentham's utilitarianism and with considerable recent input from Australian philosopher, Peter Singer, it challenges anthropocentrism but is ecologically narrow in its focus upon sentience as being the only criterion for moral consideration. Ecocentrism uses insights from all of the foregoing streams of environmentalism, but is an ecologically-wider version of preservationism. Ecocentrists want protection for nature irrespective of its value in aesthetic or spiritual terms to humans. They are also concerned with the valuing not just of individual organisms but with populations, species, ecosystems and the ecosphere. So the fundamental difference between ecocentrism and the other parts of the spectrum is the recognition in ecocentric thought of the moral standing of the non-human world, or as Eckersley (1991:26) writes, it is a contrast between "a human-centred orientation toward the non-human world with an ecology-centred orientation." Within ecocentrism are several kinds of approach, two of which are deep ecology and ecofeminism.

DEEP ECOLOGY

Norwegian philosopher, Arne Naess, coined the term 'Deep Ecology,' in 1973 to distinguish between shallow, (or reform) ecology which asks shallower questions such as, "How do we clean up the waste from this industrial process?" and deep ecology, which asks more fundamental questions such as, "How should we live so that such ail industrial process is not needed?" The word 'deep' in this context does not mean 'difficult to understand' but refers to the depth of the questions asked.

Reform environmentalism began during the nineteenth century in response to the ills of industrialised societies—the air and water pollution forest and soil loss toxic chemical dumping—but always, as Naess (1973) noted, with the goal of "the health and affluence of people in developed countries." There was little or no questioning of why such a society should continue to develop. The dominant worldview, assumes a boundary between individual persons and their surrounds leading to the ecological destruction now so evident. Deep ecology counters that view.

Following the success of Rachel Carson's 'Silent Spring' 1962, the science of ecology became more widely understood and appreciated. Carson, along with Spinoza and Gandhi, influenced the early deep ecology writings of Naess. The Deep ecology movement also developed during the 1960's and 1970's both through academic philosophical writings and as a social/ political movement. Sessions (1995: ix) writes that the main concern of deep ecology "has been to bring about a major paradigm shift—a shift in perception, values, and lifestyles—as a basis for redirecting the ecologically destructive path of modern industrial growth societies." And that it is "characterised philosophically by a move from anthropocentrism to ecocentrism, and by environmental activism." It used ecology (the study of natural interrelationships) as a science base, with many ecologists going beyond the narrowness of data to think more broadly (and deeply) about their own personal links with nature. An example was the change in thinking of Aldo Leopold (1949) from resource manager to his development of a most influential ecological consciousness. But as Devall and Sessions (1985: 80-108) and Devall (1988) detail, deep ecology was informed by many other areas of thought. These included: the perennial philosophy idea of Aldous Huxley—that we are intimately connected with natural processes; some Christian sources such as St. Francis of Assisi, who in the early 1200's wrote of the equality of all creatures; the 'new' physics that began in the early 1900's and that goes beyond seventeenth century Newtonian/Descartian mechanistic reductionism to an understanding both of energy flows, uncertainty, probability and of the illusion of objectivity; feminist writings that began to explore dominant patriarchal worldviews; the philosophies of primal peoples such as native Americans and aboriginal Australians; the pastoralist/naturalist literary tradition beginning with Rousseau and including Goethe, the Romantic poets (Blake, Wordsworth, Coleridge, Shelley) and Whitman, Emerson, Thoreau, Muir and more recently, the poet Gary Snyder; and lastly, some Eastern spiritual traditions—Taoist and Buddhist writings. Other writers with a deep ecological perspective include: Seed (1988). Foreman and Haywood (1987) and La Chapelle (1978).

ECOFEMINISM

Ecologically, ecofeminism (Francoise d'Eaubonne first used the term in 1974) has much in common with deep ecology in its advocacy for a huge shift in thinking and acting with regard to the relationship between human and the non-human world. But ecofeminists (who explore connections between the feminist and ecological movements) argue that deep ecology is rooted in patriarchy and suffers from androcentrism. Strong links exist, say ecofeminists, between the domination of women and the domination of nature. "How can we humans use science and technology to 'conquer' nature" has strong echoes with "How can men continue to subdue and oppress women?" The same logic of domination applies, write Plumwood (1993) and Warren (1994), who see the need to counter our culture of dualistic thinking which leads to domination of: "masculine over feminine, human over nature, reason over emotion, mind over body, objectivity over subjectivity" (Des Jardins 1997: 243). Other writers in this area include Merchant (1983). Plant (1989), Mies and Shiva (1993), Birke (1994) and Salleh (1997).

CONNECTIONS BETWEEN ECOCENTRISM AND COMPASSION

Despite the differences that emerge within ecofeminism and between ecofeminism and deep ecology, this ecocentric end of the environmental spectrum of thought has much to offer those educators who are concerned with leading in a more caring and compassionate way.

Some commonalities between ecocentric thought /action and the compassion seen as crucial to leadership include holism, interconnectedness, relationships, creative input of a minority, the place of the spiritual and of the sacred, the avoidance of patterns of domination and an ethic of care, mutual dependence and community. These are now viewed through some of the compassion elements used in the leadership research.

Passionate action-ecocentrists, like compassionate leaders, experience strongly-felt emotions that are not left at the stage of feeling and which results in doing something to help others in a way that does not necessarily seek attention, akin to the 'wu-wei' or 'not forcing' of Taoist thinking. Compassion is not sentiment. Sentimentalism is an opposite to social justice and is described by Fox (1979:6) as 'a flight from action', that involves abstractionist thinking resulting in an apathy, a coldness, an abstractness that prevents love of neighbour or is indifferent to it.

Justice-making: Action directed towards equity and even-handedness, moral rightness, fairness and impartiality. Justice is not merely arbitration but is the deliverance of moral decision-making. Ecocentrists believe in fair and equitable treatment for the non-human world. They believe also in distributive justice between countries in terms of the world's resources.

Benevolently loving: Affirming of both the self and others, seeing the beauty, value and quality of others and ourselves and accepting of the admirable qualities along with the imperfections; the opposite of egocentricity. Fox (1979) notes that compassion is not altruism in the commonly understood meaning of loving others instead of loving ourselves, but rather loving others as we love ourselves. This relates to compassion being based on the insight, expressed by Friedman (1966:363) when writing of Martin Buber, that the other and I are one. Buber distinguished between two relationships—the 'I-Thou' and the 'I-It'—on the basis of the difference in meaning attached to the 'I', where the 'I-Thou' relation is direct, mutual and present and the uniqueness of the other (Thou) is recognised. This is the sense of relationship between self and other intended in benevolent love, as opposed to 'I-It' where the other (It) is treated as a detached independent object. In the same vein, Noddings (1984:14) writes ". . . although I can never accomplish it entirely, I try to apprehend the reality of the other." Similarly, Koestenbaum (1991:167) writes of the importance of love to leadership in these terms:

"Love means that you really care about people, whether you are a mother or a general. To love is to communicate intimately in the sense of establishing an inter-subjective field, a joint ego or communal self. Love establishes a higher unity, a spiritual connection, an emotional bond."

"The sort of love that is considered as benevolently loving is unconditional and unlimited and goes further than affirmation, support, encouragement and sympathy."

All of those expressions of love for another can be withdrawn, resulting in feelings of betrayal and loss. Deep ecologists and ecofeminists have this sort of love for the uniqueness of other species (and ecosystems) that prevents them from seeing the other as an independent, unimportant 'bit.' Naess writes in *Sessions* (1995-466):

> "What we propose is not a shift of caring away from humans and towards non-humans, but rather an extension and deepening of overall caring. It is unwarranted to assume that the human potential for caring is constant and finite, and that an increase of caring for some creatures necessarily reduces caring for others."

Non-elitist: A brotherly or sisterly approach to relationships with other beings and opposition to unfair privilege. Ecocentrists adopt that philosophical position because they care deeply, not only for other persons but for other species acknowledging their intrinsic value and not abusing the power they hold over them. More recent 'third wave' or transformative feminism (Plumwood, 1993: Warren, 1994) is pluralistic and inclusive in its respect for diversity and difference and aims to deliberately avoid hierarchies. Noddings (in Beck. 1994:ix) writes of attention to our relationships through showing caring that is non-elitist and helps us to refocus our attention on clients and those over whom we hold power. The tendency in highly bureaucratised systems is to attend most diligently to those above us in the hierarchy; much of all administrator's time goes into compliance. When we evaluate our work through the perspective of caring, we experience a motivational shift toward those who need us and to whom we must now respond.

Part of non-elitism involves listening skills which were identified strongly through interviews in the compassionate leadership study as an important part of the way each of the leaders works—the ability to truly listen to others, not in a superficial way, but with the deep attentiveness characteristic of ecocentrists. Valuing people in an organisation, such as a school community by relating to them as you would to a brother or sister, can be shown by deeply listening to the other and not merely going through the motions of giving attention whilst your mind and attention are planning your next comment or concentrating upon what you will do when this person leaves.

Networking: A realisation of, and a consequent acting upon, the importance of' mutual dependence (between all beings) and of connections, one with another. Environmentalists generally, and ecocentrists in particular, appreciate the importance of mutual dependence and networking that occurs between the billions of seemingly insignificant microscopic decomposers in soil. According to King (1989: 19), one of the principles upon which it rests its networking—that "Life on earth is an interconnected web, not a hierarchy. There is no natural hierarchy; human hierarchy is projected onto nature and then used to justify social domination." Similarly, Fox (1979) thinks that compassion involves an amongness-consciousness, or consciousness of interdependence. Those who are overly object-conscious are likely to miss this amongness element of compassion precisely because it is an action, a verb, not an object.

Beck (1994:27) writes of the need for educational administrators to respond to those in the school community as people, not objects.

In Buber's words, they will recognise teachers, students, parents and other administrators as 'Thous' rather than as 'It's'. They will seek to understand the perspectives of those with whom they work and to consider those perspectives as their own when making decisions. They will recognise and delight in the interdependence of all within their school or school system, and they will continually search for concrete ways to encourage caring relationships between those whom they lead.

Transpersonal: A belief that goes beyond individuality to something more inclusive than the individual person; beyond the personal sense of self to a deep-seated realisation that we and all other entities are aspects of a single unfolding reality. Deep ecologist, Warwick Fox (1990:198), provides a clear description of transpersonal in an ecological sense of self that extends beyond one's egoic, biographical, or personal sense of self. Transpersonal ecocentrists realise their 'ecological, wider or big self', where the uppercase 'S' (a symbolism of Naess) signifies a "wide, expansive, field-like, or non-egoic sense of self" as distinct from lowercase 's'—a "narrow, atomistic, particle-like or egoic sense of self', (Fox, 1990: 106).

Pain relieving: Action leading to relief of physical and mental suffering or distress. In general, environmentalists react to alleviate the pain of the suffering planet (or parts thereof, Ecocentrists go further than most down this path with a wide encompassing view of what is in need of pain relief.

Transcendent: A belief that recognises that there is more than only the material, more than the human body, and that a higher level of consciousness, the spiritual dimension of humankind, must also be considered. Many ecofeminists oppose what is for them a "dual denigration of women and nature" (Des Jardins, 1997:241) that they see in much mainstream Western religion. That as women they lack the "special spirituality that would qualify them as priests, rabbis, ministers, popes . . . ." Instead, they are renewing pre-Christian, earth-as-mother/goddess religions (such as the Greek goddess Gaia) and see beyond the ecological reasons for care of the earth to the spiritual. Deep ecologists refer to writings of Christian mystics, to the biocentrism of St. Francis and the Taoist classic, the Tao Te Ching and the Buddhist writings of Dogen. Apart from the ideas of organic unity and biocentric equality expressed in Buddhism, the transcendent process of "awakening from illusion and delusion" (Devall and Sessions, 1985: 100) has been influential in deep ecology. O'Murchu (1997), Tacey (1995) and Tacey (2000) offer depth in understanding the connections between the increasing importance of the spiritual and ecocentric philosophy. The compassionate leaders studied showed an on going struggle with the transcendent. They all looked inwardly and had in common a searching for what is good for others (the students primarily) and what they should do inwardly about themselves to better serve the educational needs of their community. And now briefly to 'community'—a word that, like 'sustainable', seems somewhat tarnished through misuse.

Vanier (1979: 13) suggests that "community is a place of belonging, a place where people are earthed and find their identity." The compassionate leadership study showed clear evidence of relationship building, interdependence, collaboration and other features of community. Those school leaders showed a love for others by listening deeply to their needs; they showed a strong sense of what is morally right which supported others in the community, so encouraging them to give more to the school; they showed humour which breaks down barriers and elitism, and a selflessness which acts as a model for others to follow; they relieved pain, first through listening that detected it and then by providing services to reduce the level of pain; they celebrated so as to strengthen a sense of belonging to community; they were creative and prepared to take risks and they cultivated their own spiritual beliefs to help them in their work.

Community in an ecological sense means populations of all species living and interacting in an area at a particular time. It is about relations, interdependence and collaborative effort, not the competition of win-lose individualism. In his insightful and passionate book, *The Courage to Teach*, Parker Palmer (1998:96) writes that "Ecological studies offer a picture of nature less focused on the terrors of combat than on the dance of communal collaboration." Palmer has much to say that is relevant to our understanding of community, and that draws on both compassion and ecological insights. He outlines negative forces that inhabit the inner landscape of teachers' lives—forces that lead to our lack of connection with students subjects and importantly, ourselves. Parker then critiques three models of community—therapeutic, civic and marketing—all with deficiencies, and suggests that to teach is to work in what he calls a "community of truth" which is circular, interactive and dynamic, rather than linear, static and hierarchical.

"The first step toward understanding the community of truth is to understand that community is the essential form of reality, the matrix of all being. The next step takes us from the nature of reality to the question of how we know it: *we know reality only by being in community with it ourselves*" (Palmer 1998:97).

As teachers, Palmer suggests we need periodic conversations with each other about teaching over an extended period of time—we need involvement in a community of pedagogical discourse. Contrasting the openness in practice of lawyers and surgeons with the private world of teaching, Palmer (1998:144) comments, "If surgery and law were practised as privately as teaching, we would still treat most patients with leeches and dunk defendants in millponds."

Two intuitions developed for me during the compassionate leadership work—one, that perhaps 'transcendent' was not the right word to use for that particular element of compassion because the questioning included the spiritual as well as the soulful, and two, that strong community was evident at each school. By 'soulful' I mean the more mundane, ordinary everyday experiences linked the spiritual. This meaning is explained well by Moore (1996a:25-26) who writes that soul is broader than we tend to think and is, to him, inclusive of the spiritual.

It encompasses not just the higher or transcendent level of consciousness, the realm that we traditionally call the spirit, but also what we might refer to as the lower level of consciousness—the soul in ordinary experience, the soul of everyday life. What I mean by this lower level is the value of living one's day-to-day life with attention to essential everyday qualities such as beauty, intimacy, community, imagination.

Connected with this apparent search by leaders for soulfulness was that strong sense of community at each school. I got the sense that there were deeper meanings within the schools than even the interview material could expose. The unstated, but palpable feeling that each school held a strong sense of meaning for each leader, for example, with garden plots commemorating the lives of the dead—their spirits living on in the school community. There was a feeling that each leader was integrally connected to the place—that their experiences and memories of the people and the place give it meaning for them beyond that of a job. The place itself, land, buildings and space—all were sacred. This has strong resonances with deep ecologists, views of bioregions—'life' and 'territory' combined—a love of, and a sense of, place.

CONCLUSION

In conclusion, ecocentric philosophies have much to offer our coming-to-grips with the 'slippery', ecological subject of leadership, especially if we are going down those sparsely-explored roads of compassionate-, servant-, ethical- leadership. Moore (1996b: 123) puts it into perspective well when he writes:

"When we all, leaders and participants in community, discover the sheer joy of creating a way of life that serves families, ennobles work, and fosters genuine communal spirit, then we will begin to touch upon the sacredness that lies in the simple word *polis*, which is not just a city defined in square miles, income, or population, but a spirit that arises when people live together creatively."

Appendix I

Conceptual Framework Matrix

Elements of Compassion	*Bolman and Deal Leadership Frames*			
	Structural	*Human Resources*	*Political*	*Symbolic*
Celebrative uses ceremonies to rejoice and grieve together	supports celebrations of events, both good and bad, in the life of the school	uses school events to lift the self-esteem of individuals	supports funding to function that include all groups in the school community	acts to maintain a strong school culture
Passionately active strong emotions that lead to actions that help others without being egocentric	influences school policies so as to maximise service to others	acts so as to properly utilise the talents of people for the benefits of the school	manages conflict to ensure interests of all are met	organises events to lift the spirit of the school community
Justice-making equitable, fair and impartial	uses processes that are fair	develops high levels of trust between members of the school community	is fair in balancing the demands of different groups within the school community	builds a school culture that reflects the different values within the school community
Benevolently Loving loving others and self; not egocentric patient and listening	uses the strengths and accepts the limitations of individuals when involving them in the work of the school	has a comforting presence to those in need	accepts the limitations and strengths of those in the school community	tells stories that affirm the value of people in the school community both from the past and in the present

Creative during linkage of ideas that can involve loss	is creative in developing structures to get tasks done	is supportive in giving people a chance to try out new roles	devises creative ways of involving opposing groups in the school where appropriate	encourages events that are innovative
Non-elitist opposes privilege	opposes misuse of authority	responds to any problem by listening first.	avoids imposing top-down change, except where appropriate	ensures that people in privileged positions are not singled-out for special treatment
Networking mutual dependence and connections	uses communication methods that show them to be appro achable	ensures that individuals get an opportunity to contribute to the workings of a group	effectively . builds networks of support for the school	encounts stories of the school that emphasise the importance of mutual dependence between school community members
Transpersonal beyond the personal sense of self	contributes to flexible policies that enable school community members to work together	encourages individuals to view an issue from a perspective that is beyond that of their own immediate needs	effectively divides resources to serve broader interests rather than only those with power in the school community.	encourages a school culture that takes the school community beyond itself to a world perspective
Pain relieving relieves physical and mental pain	helps develop school structures that reduce suffering	acts to relieve the pain felt by an individual who does not fit well into a group	supports people as they learn about their own areas of ineffectiveness	uses events that lift those in the school community with low self-esteem

Transcendent apiritual dimension of humankind	encourages structures that allow groups in the school to pursue their belief in spiritual (not necessarily religious) matters	encourages those in the school to explore the non-material aspects of their lives	allocates resotuces so that memebrs of the school community can address the spiritual (not necessarily religious) side of their lives	rewards the efforts of people in the school community to pursue spiritual (non necessarily religious) matters
Fun-filled values humour	organises meetings so that laughter with others (not at others) is seen as acceptable	encourages individuals in the school community to see the funny side of situation, where appropriate	uses humour to break down the barriers of differences and so lend value to interdependence	incorporates humour as a part of the way things are done in the school

Appendix II

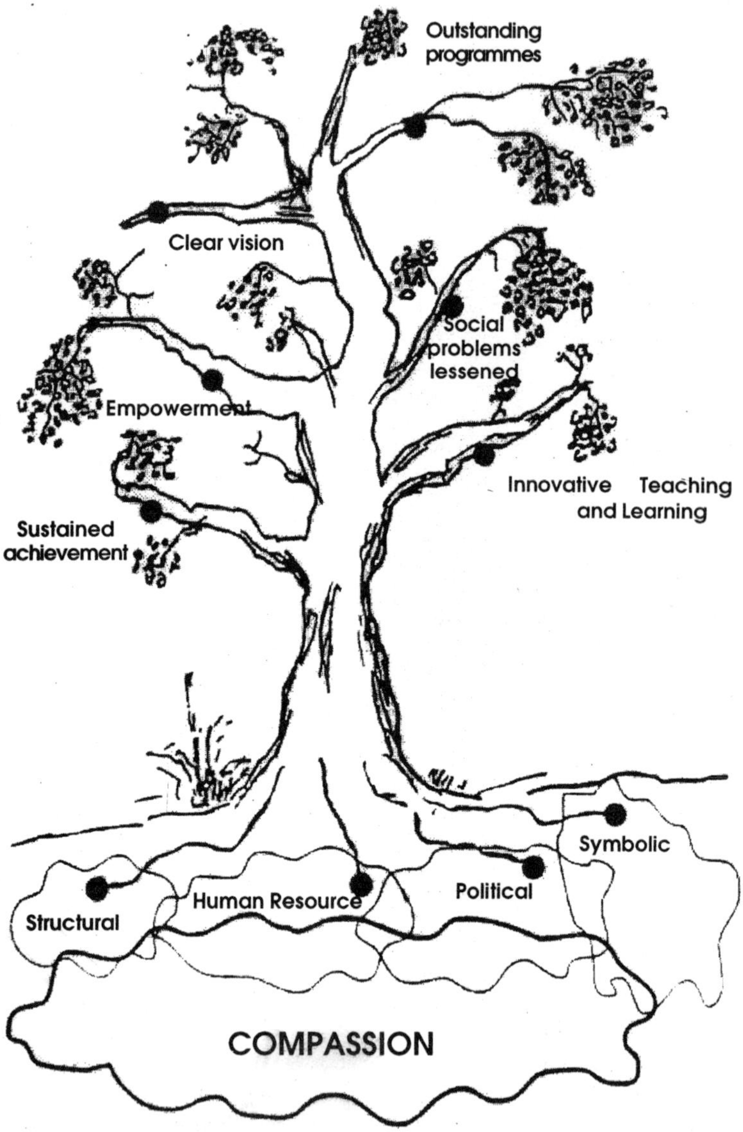
Outstanding programmes
Clear vision
Social problems lessened
Empowerment
Innovative Teaching and Learning
Sustained achievement
Symbolic
Political
Human Resource
Structural
COMPASSION

REFERENCES

Beck, L., 1994, *Reclaiming Educational Administration as a Caring Profession,* New York: Teachers College Press.

Birch, C., 1993, *Regaining Compassion for Humanity and Nature,* Sydney: New South Wales University Press.

Birke, L., 1994, *Feminism, Animals and Science: The Naming of the Shrew,* Buckingham: Open University Press.

Blumberg, A., 1989, *School Administration as a Craft,* Boston: Allyn and Bacon.

Bogue, E.G., 1994, *Leadership by Design: Strengthening Integrity in Higher Education,* San Francisco: Jossey-Bass.

Bolman, L. G., and Deal, T. E., 1991, *Reframing Organisations: Artistry, Choice and Leadership,* San Francisco: Jossey-Bass.

Dalai Lama, 1995, *The Power of Compassion: A Collection of Lectures by His Holiness the XIV Dalai Lama*, London: Thomsons.

Dance, T., 1991, 'Leadership and Spirit: Rejuvenating an Organisation from the Bottom UP', Paper presented at the Annual Conference of the Association of Canadian Community Colleges, Winnipeg, May.

De Pree, M., 1987, *Leadership is an Art,* East Lansing: Michigan State University Press.

Des Jardins, J., 1997, *Environmental Ethics* 2nd edn., Belmont CA.: Wadsworth.

Devall, B., 1988, *Simple in Means, Rich in Ends: Practising Deep Ecology,* Layton, UT.: Gibbs-Smith.

______________, 1985, *Deep Ecology: Living as if Nature Mattered* Layton, UT.: Gibbs M. Smith.

Duignan, P., 1997, *The Dance of Leadership: At the Still Point of the Turning World,* Hawthorn, V.C.: Australian Council for Educational Administration.

Eckersley, R., 1991, *Environmental and Political Theory: Toward an Ecocentric Approach,* Albany: State University of New York Press.

Eckhardt, W., 1972, *Compassion: Toward a Science of Value,* Ontario, Canada: CPRI Press.

Foreman, D., and Haywood, B., (eds.), 1987, *Ecodefense: A Field Guide to Monkey-wrenching,* Tucson, AZ.: Nedd Ludd.

Fox, M., 1979, *A Spirituality Named Compassion and the Healing of the Global Village*, Humpty Dumpty and US, Minneapolis: Winston.

Fox, W., 1990, *Toward a Transpersonal Ecology: Developing New Foundations for Environmentalism,* Boston: Shambhala.

Friedman, M., 1966, in P. Nash, A. Kazamias and H. Perkinson (eds.), *The Educated Man: Studies in the History of Educational Thought,* New York: Wiley and Sons.

Greenfield, T.B., 1984, 'Leaders and Schools: Willfulness and Non-natural Order in Organisations', in T. Sergiovanni and J. Corbally (eds.), *Leadership and, Organisational Culture: New Perspectives on Administrative: Theory and Practice,* Urbana and Chicago: University of Illinois Press.

Greenlead, R.K., 1977, *Servant Leadership: A Journey into the Nature of Legitimate Power and Greatness,* Ramsey, N.J.: Paulist Press.

Gyatso, Geshe Kelsang, 1993, *Universal Compassion: A Commentary to Bodhisattva Chekawa's "Training the Mind in Seven Points",* London: Tharpa Publications.

Hodgkinson, C., 1991, *Educational Leadership: The Moral Art,* Albany, NY: State University of New York Press.

Jaworski, J., *Synchronicity: The Inner Path of Leadership,* San Francisco: Berrett-Koehler.

Jones, K.B.m, 1993, *Compassionate Authority: Democracy and the Representation of Women*, New York: Routledge.

King, Y., 1989, 'The Ecology of Feminism and the Feminism of Ecology' in Plant, J. (ed)., *Healing the Wounds: The Promise of Ecofeminism,* Philadelphia: New Society.

Koestenbaum, P., 1991, *Leadership: The Inner Side of Greatness,* San Francisco.

LaChapelle, D., 1978, *Earth Wisdom,* Silverton, CO.: Finn Hill Arts.

Leopold, A., 1949, *A Sand Country Almanac,* New York: Oxford.

Merchant, C., 1983, *The Death of Nature: Women, Ecology and the Scientific Revolution,* San Francisco: Harper & Row.

Mies, M. and Shiva, V., 1993, *Ecofeminism,* Melbourne: Spinifex.

Miller, J., 1981, *The Compassionate Teacher: How to Teach and Learn With Your Whole Self,* Englewood Cliffs, N.J.: Prentice-Hall.

Mooore, T., 1996a, 'Embracing the Everyday' in R. Carlon and B. Shield (eds.), *Handbook for the Soul,* Moorebank, NSW: Doubleday.

_______________, 1996b, *The Re-enchantment of Everyday Life,* New York: Harper Collins.

Naess, A., 1973, 'The Shallow and the Deep, Long-Range Ecology Movement', *Inquiry*, 16 95-100.

Noddings, N., 1984, *Caring: A Feminine Approach to Ethics and Moral Education,* Berkeley, CA: University of California Press.

Noddings, A., 1992, *The Challenge to Care in Schools: An Alternative Approach to Education,* New York: Teachers College Press.

Nouwen, H.J.M., McNeill, D.P. and Morrison, D.A., 1982, *Compassion: A Reflection on the Christian Life,* London: Darton Longman and Todd.

____________, 1989, *In The Name of Jesus: Reflections on Christian Leadership,* New York: Crossroad Publishing.

____________, 1994, *The Wounded Healer: Ministry in Contemporary Society,* London: Darton, Longman and Todd.

O'Murchu, D., 1997, *Reclaiming Spirituality,* Dublin: Gill & Macmillan.

Palmer, P., 1998, *The Courage to Teach: Exploring the Inner Landscape of a Teacher's Life,* San Francisco: Jossey-Bass.

Plant, J., (ed.), 1989, *Healing the Wounds: The Promise of Ecofeminism,* Philadelphia: New Society.

Plumwood, V., 1993, *Feminism and the Mastery of Nature,* London: Routledge.

Prior, W.J., 1989, 'Compassion: A Critique of Moral Rationalism' in R. Taylor and J. Watson, (eds.), *They Shall Not Hurt: Human Suffering and Human Caring,* Boulder, Co.: Colorado Associated University Press.

Purpel, D.E., 1989, *The Moral and Spiritual Crisis in Education: A Curriculum for Justice and Compassion in Education,* Granby, Mass.: Bergin and Garvey.

Salleh, A., 1997, *Ecofeminism as Politics: Nature, Marx and the Postmodern,* London: Zed Books.

Seed, J., Macy, J., Fleming, P., and Naess, A., 1988, *Thinking Like A Mountain: Towards A Council of All Beings,* Philadelphia: New Society.

Sessions, G., (ed.), 1995, *Deep Ecology for the 21st Century,* Boston: Shambhala.

Starratt, R.J., 1991, 'Building an Ethical School: A Theory for Practice in Educational Leadership', *Educational Administration Quarterly* 27(2), p.185-202.

Sungaila, H., 1990, 'The New Science of Chaos: Making a New Science of Leadership', *Journal of Educational Administration* 28(2). p.4-23.

Swann, R., 1996, 'Compassionate Leadership Schools', Paper presented at British Educational Management and Administration Society Annual Conference, Coventry, England, 20-22 September.

_____________, 1998a, 'Leader Compassion in Schools', Paper presented at the 25th Australian Council for Educational Administration International Conference, Gold Coast, Queensland, 27-30 September.

_____________, 1998b, 'Compassionate Leadership in Schools', *International Studies in Educational Administration* 26(1), p. 21-29.

_____________, 1999, 'The Role of Compassion in School Leadership', Paper presented at the Association for Teacher Education in Europe Annual Conference, Leipzig, Germany, September.

Tacey, D., 1995, *Edge of the Sacred,* Melbourne: HarperCollins.

_____________, 2000, *Re-Enchantment: The New Australian Spirituality,* Melbourne: HarperCollins.

Vaill, P.B., 1989, *Management as a Performing Art: New Ideas for a World of Chaotic Change,* San Francisco and London: Jossey-Bass.

Vanier, J., 1979, *Community and Growth,* London: Darton, Longman and Todd.

Warren, K., 1994, *Ecological Feminism,* New York: Routledge.

Wheatley, M., 1992, *Leadership and the New Science: Learning about Organisation from an Orderly Universe,* San Francisco: Berrett-Koehler.

Wong K., 1996, 'Early Chinese Thinking and the Moral Education of Educational Leaders', *International Studies in Educational Administration* 24(2), p.17-24.

17

Management of Women Education for Gender Equality in India

—*Arun Kumar Kulshrestha**

The country now stands on the threshold of the twenty-first century. Those who are being born now will finish their elementary schooling at the turn of the century and enter into a new world. Only education can imbue people with the knowledge, the sense of purpose and the confidence essential for building a dynamic, vibrant and cohesive nation as well as for creating better, fuller and more purposeful life. In human terms, democratic development implies availability of equal opportunities to all people, irrespective of caste, creed, sex and religion to develop their personalities. Development of the community and group concerned in all its aspects should be directed towards reshaping the existing literacy, imparting of vocational skills and income generating capabilities. These are essential means and an integral part of the process of planned socio-economic development. We should develop a broad framework of issues, around the basic understanding of citizenship building.

In India, the increase in the educational facilities and opportunities for women and the removal of traditional bars on the entry of women to particular branches and levels of education, came to be supported by all advocates of women's

**Deptt. of Pedagogical Sciences, Faculty of Education, D.E.I. (Deemed University), Dayalbagh, Agra, India.*

emancipation from the 19th century onwards. However, the Indian reformers of the 19th century wished to educate women to perform their role as good wives and mothers and not to make them as direct active participants in the process of national development.

After independence, the Constitutional guarantee of equality changed the conceptual thinking, even of the traditional man in India, and invited women to play multiple roles in the polity, the economy and the social functions. The educational development of women began in that direction. This is amply evident in the government's policy, the reports of various committees and commissions set up for this purpose and in the objectives of developmental plans formulated after independence. The expansion of education and health services in the 20th century, however, precipitated a need for women teachers and doctors which results in the incorporation of these two vocations in the programme of women education.

Researches available on the education of women in India points a number of socio-cultural and socio-economic factors that influence the participation of women in the system of education. The prevailing cultural norms of gender behaviour and the perceived domestic and reproductive roles of women tend to adversely affect the learning and retention of girls in schools. The effect of gender bias varies in different social and economic groups and is particularly harsh on communities which suffer discrimination. The gender biases existing in society and domestication of girls have a direct bearing on many aspects of the educational system. Educational policy must, therefore, address itself to the larger socio-economic and cultural context that affects education of girls. These are the propositions rendered to improve upon the inequalities among boys and girls.

The Education Commission (1964-66) endorsed the recommendations of all committees and commissions about the equality in the educational development of women. The Government's National Policy (1986) also laid down that "The education system must produce young men and women of character and ability committed to national services and development. Only then education will be able to play its vital role in promoting national progress, creating a sense of common citizenship and culture and strengthening national integration".

In spite of the Constitutional provision and the recommendations of the committee and commissions about the provision for the same type of education for women as for men, the traditional, limited viewpoint of women's education with a separate role of women in the society has had a great influence on the planning for women education. The new policy of education was proposed to bring "basic change in the status of women". It did not discriminate a man from a woman on the nature of education that was to be given in order to neutralise the prevailing distortions and anomalies. It was well considered an edge in favour of women. The national education system was to play a positive, interventionist role in the empowerment of women. It was a considered act of faith and social justice that women's studies will be promoted as a part of various courses and educational institutions encouraged to take up active programmes to further women's development.

The last quarter of this century is marked by a series of efforts towards raising women's status, enhancing their quality of life, bringing about gender equality and gender justice. The first effort on the global level was made in 1975 the year which was observed as the International Women's Year and it has its motto, "Equality, Development and Peace". During the year meetings, rallies, seminars, symposia and conferences were held in all the states of India and almost all the countries of the world. As a part of the IYW programmes an international conference on women was held at Mexico in 1975. As a follow-up of the conference United Nations declared 1976-1985 as the International Decade of Women.

The National Policy on Education with modifications undertaken in 1992, on equality of women's education stipulated the principle removal of women illiteracy and obstacles inhibiting their over riding priority, through provisions of support services, setting of time targets and effective monitoring. Major emphasis was laid on the following points:

1. In lieu thereof recognising the holistic nature of child development, viz., nutrition, health, social, mental, physical, moral and emotional development, early childhood care and education (ECCE) will receive high priority and be suitably integrated with the child development programme.
2. Wherever possible, day-care centres will be provided as support services of universalisation of primary education to enable girls engaged in taking care of siblings to attend school and as support services for poor working women.
3. A new thrust in elementary education will emphasise three aspects (i) Universal access and enrolment, (ii) Universal retention of children up to 14 years of age, and (iii) A substantial improvement in quality of education to enable all children to achieve essential levels of learning.
4. In the total literacy campaigns the theme of empowerment of women is receiving special focus, since the female literacy rate in the country is strikingly lower than for men. Also in the adult education and post literacy education centres, special attention was given to enrolment of women.
5. The *Mahila Samakhya* was formulated in pursuance of the NPE 1986. Its overall goal is to create circumstances to enable women to better understand their predicament, to move from a state of abject disempowerment towards a situation in which they can determined their own lives and influence their environment. This presupposes that education can be decisive intervention towards women's equality.

6. There has been phenomenal expansion of educational opportunities for women in the field higher education–both general and technical. Emphasis was laid on enrolment and retention of girls in formal and non-formal schooling.
7. Women education at the university and college levels has been diversified and re-oriented in tune with the changing requirements of the society, industry and trade. The University Grants Commission has been providing financial assistance to universities for promoting studies, programmes and setting up of centres or cells for women's studies.
8. The policy of non-discrimination will be pursued vigorously to eliminate sex-stereo typing in vocational and professional courses and to promote women's participation in non-traditional occupations in existing and emergent society.

Moreover, several attempts have been made at the regional, national and global level by which the basic concept of education and equality became acceptable to the policy makers and others. The volume of resources now being devoted to development of women and children in gratifying institutional mechanism like the National Commission on Women and others have become available. A variety of training programmes and training institutions are being implemented. There are specific schemes directed to target groups among women in respect of health, nutrition, child welfare, education, employment, self employment, etc. Womens education for gender equality is the agreed agenda for action. Hence a rational approach has clearly stated that focusing on improving the daily life conditions of women's existence and to enhance the status in family, community and society.

REFERENCES

Agrawal, S.P., and Agrawal, J.C., *Women's Education in India Historical Review, Present Status Perspective,* Concept Publishing Company, Delhi, p. 41- 42, and 87, 1992.

Anderson, M., *Improving Access to Schooling in the Third World: An Overview.* Hardward University, Cambridge: 1988.

Apte, J.S., 1996, "Educational and Women's Empowerment", *Indian Journal of Adult Education.*

Bhandari, R.K., *Educational Development of Women in India,* Ministry of Education and Culture, Govt. of India, New Delhi, Pub. No. 1378.

Kulshrestha, A.K., 1994, "Eradication of Sex-Discrimination in Education", *Bhartiya Shikshan,* Vol. IV, No. 4 and 5.

______________ , "Elevating Women Education in India", Communicated for Publication, *In Quest of Bhartiya Shikshan,* Mumbai.

Mazumdar, V., ICSSR, 1981, *Women and Educational Development,* New Delhi.

Report of the committee for review of NPE, 1986, "Towards and Enlightened and Human Society", *NPE, 1986—A Review,* (Final Report), Dec. 1990.

Singh, T., "Literacy, in Women's Development", *Indian Journal of Adult Education,* April-June 1996.

18

Education: Contributing to Community Development

—*B.C. Patil**

INTRODUCTION

All of us have accepted that education has a crucial role to play in bringing about systematic, orderly and peaceful socio-economic and political change for the good of all people. A large number of countries which have traditional society on the verge of modernisation has accepted the significance of education as the basic instrument for radical transformation of social values and ideals. The traditional ideas on education emphasise mainly on three functions, namely, of securing knowledge for individual, enriching, the cultural thought of the people and preparing every individual for a profession for which he has an aptitude.

The 21st century has seen the dawn of revolutionary advances in the quantum of knowledge and the corresponding role of education in the universe of phenomenon and this assumes social importance. This knowledge explosion enables an individual to understand and regulate the environment to augment his material welfare.

**K.L.E. Society's College of Education, Vidyanagar, Hubli-Karnataka, India.*

Education is a means to the end of human enlightenment— in all the three domains, i.e., cognitive, affective and connative ultimately resulting into human betterment, and life worth living.

Education is a process of human enlightenment and empowerment for the achievement of better and higher quality of life. Education worth the name should result in the unfoldment of the learner's potentialities, enlargement of their competencies and transformation of their interest, attitude and values. Quality education for all is the cry of the hour all over the world.

Ignorance of our dormant and hidden powers is a major stumbling block in the path of self-progress and prosperity. Self-discovery is the first step in the fuller unfoldment and development of human possibilities. Every individual, wherever he is born, has some talents or capabilities which an earnest evolution of himself will reveal. One may not be an intellectual giant or a brilliant one but has in oneself the possibility of limitless expansion.

True education is a system of self-realisation, a plan whereby one has assisted to take inventory of one's resources. Self-discovery and self-improvement go hand in hand. The ability of every individual, gifted, brilliant, talented, dull, must be mined by self-effort. Intensive and persistent work alone will guarantee success in life, something will be accomplished.

If every individual is impressed from the earlier days with the wonderful and marvellous possibilities of life, with the giant strength, power and success awaiting, if he will only keep an eye on ambition and struggle hard to realise that combination, a lot of human gold i.e., education would succeed in instilling in all individuals that they are made for triumph and not for failure. If this is to be realised, everyone should gear up for toil, sacrifice and perseverance, in spite of all obstacles and discouragement. Success must be earned individually. No one should think that success comes just by gift or inheritance. Downright hard work and persistent endeavour are the only legal tender that success recognises.

SOCIAL CHANGE

Social change is one of the most dominant characteristic functions of social reality in the contemporary world. Social change is antecedent as well as consequential in its impact on the changing individual, changing group or society. Consequently, realistic perception of social change is founded upon the canons of individual and group dynamics. It also takes into account the entire flow of person to person relationships. In any such understanding of social change, the role of interaction and communication becomes meaningful.

Indian society today stands in the uncertain zone between tradition and modernity. Social scientists and educationists are not very clear about goals of social change. Indian's rich cultural heritage casts its influence on them and on occasion they tend to re-emphasise the pristine values of a traditional way of life. At the same time, they are aware of tremendous advantages of technological modernisation in terms of human welfare.

"Indian society is classified as a hierarchical social order. We are still in a closed system in many aspects of life. Stratification necessarily implies a graded scale in inequalities. The higher the stratification in a society, the greater the hierarchical inequalities in the social system," opines Humayan Kabir. In such a social system vertical mobility becomes not an easy task. An individual born in a lower structure encounters all sorts of hurdles in the task of self-advancement. An individual's social status gets fixed with his birth and the individual socially higher in the stratum maintain their distance from those lower in the hierarchy. Hierarchy-based description is anti-ethical to the high values of democracy, socialism and a temper of science that emphasise a reasoned search for truth. The stratified structure of Indian society mitigates against the cardinal tenets of democracy. Democracy implies freedom, justice, rule of law and equality of all, irrespective of sex, creed and race. An ascriptive society undermines all these values sacred to a democratic way of life. In Indian society religion plays a very dominant role. Most issues are viewed from the touchstone of religion at the expense of secular approach to those problems. In such a process reason and logic are sacrificed at the altar of superstition and dogma.

In a developing country like India where the hold of custom, dogma and superstition is preponderant in the lives of people, meaningful social change becomes hazardous proposition. The ancient and modern coexist but exercise their divergent pulls in different directions. The heavyweight of the past lingers in the present, making the task of planning for a hopeful, all the more problematic. Real change is possible only if far-reaching changes are effected in the structure of society, political and economic institution and in the culture of the people.

SOCIAL CHANGE THROUGH EDUCATION

Education is an investment in human resource as well as important social service. As a social service it involves catering to the requirements of the individual in society. The inculcation of such qualities as courage and endurance, honesty and interest, selfless devotion and patriotism, passion for truth and clarity against emotionalism and hidebound ideas appears to be the primary task before the Indian education system. Moulding the psychological aspects in human begins in a systematic manner becomes necessary for rapid social change. Individuals are not automation but are live, vibrant personalities who think and feel. The greatest weakness of Indian education is that individuals are considered and not as thinkers, creators and producers.

"One of the important principle to be emphasised in the socialistic pattern of society which the nation desires to create, is that individual fulfilment will come, not through selfish and narrow loyalties to personal or group interest but through dedication of all to the wider novelties of national development in all its parameters" (*Report of Education Commission 1964-66*, p. 4.).

Education must prove a harbinger of social-cultural revolution by assigning higher importance to the quality of education through equality of educational aspiration of all. The creation of technically competent and skilled manpower is the *sine quo non* for increasing productivity and promoting economic self-sufficiency. If the Indian educational system continues to turn out indifferently and inefficiently educated products, a social crisis may be created, leading to hampering, of economic development. Judging from this wider perspective it becomes very evident that a radical shift away from the present structure and content of education is necessary to create the conditions of fundamental social change. Our educational system creates a white-collared class as it is a suppressing, unnatural and enslaving system. This rigid dogma-ridden, subject-centred and office motivating system needs to be discarded and replaced by an educational system that is in tune with the realities of modern world.

Education must serve as a liberalising force by a proper emphasis on such values as tolerance, team spirit, toil and compassion for the neglected and downtrodden. Any meaningful system of education must tackle the problem of rural poverty, hunger, disease and ignorance in order to bring about a multidimensional social change.

A high rate of illiteracy is still flourishing even after more than a half century of independence. Illiteracy and abject poverty smash the dome of democracy. Democracy remains a myth as long as illiteracy and poverty are the reality of the society. The fabric of such a society to be the least is broken and defaced. In such a situation community development remains a dream. In the Indian present context, the crucial elements are those of functional literacy, economic efficiency, citizenship responsibilities, health, hygiene and family planning. Unless these and other equally important aspects of nation building are not attended to with utter sincerity and diamond-hard integrity, the nation has no future worth the name. Keeping millions and millions of people in the dark and making them suffer human degradation and keeping them away from a respectful life pattern is nothing but a crime on the part of people who often claim that they have saved the destiny of India by their sacrifices. Being one of the most corrupt countries in the world order, we have failed to recognise the worth of human dignity and decency. The fact of not reaching education worth the name to millions and millions of people of the land has resulted in the invasion of violence instead of non-violence. A country like India which almost created non-violence in the birth of great religions dedicated to non-violence in the teachings of Gautama Buddha, Basavanna, Mahatma Gandhi, is being ravaged by violence, any day and every day, here and there and almost all over the country.

The present-day education system has utterly failed in contributing to the social good of the people of the land. Community development in its right spirit is a far cry. Education that does not cater to the needs of the entire population of the land should be discarded right away and new and realistic thinking based on facts and realities must be thought of and implemented before it is too late. The time bound distractions, decays and degeneration are ticking every fraction of a second and it may explode and blast the Indian social fabric. Violence is a real threat to our country, to our so-called democracy, to our future and to the future of the millions of people who are claiming that they are Indians, and the multi-million who are born every year. The so-called leaders telling fellow people to live peacefully is nothing less than hypocrisy.

Everyday we come across statements, advice by a section of people to solve problems peacefully, be in peace with yourself and in peace with those with whom we see the problem. But very little is done providing a system of education which will develop that type of personality that always thinks of peace. Education for peace should be the goal of the 21st century. Education should help the younger generation and elders as well, to eschew violence. Eradicating violence should be given top priority in the education system. Anger is the base for all types of violence which is survived by ill-will, hatredness, prejudice and inhuman behaviour. The education system must be successful in inculcating human values that are ensured in Indian culture for more than 3,000 years. India's culture was great and we are ashamed to claim that greatness today. When we see all around the country and peep into the depth of the reality of life lived by the brute majority of nearly 85 to 90 per sent of Indians life, we get enraged at the system of education that is prevalent today. An Indian gets angry every time he sees or come in contact with poverty, deprivation and the unhappiness. Educational system that does not bother about these hard facts cannot be labelled as an education system of any country.

Education for community development should give top priority to the following:

1. *Eradication of illiteracy*: Where there is a will there is a way. Enough is enough, 52 years of independence and illiteracy still prevalent. What a shame!
2. *Education not merely for white-collared jobs*: Education is for dignifying living by earning for his own living.

Experiments in this direction have failed. The reason is that we failed them. The vested interest must be uprooted so that an individual born in this country feels that he is an Indian and feels happy to be called an Indian.

3. Economic efficiency is related to the quality of life, if not wholly, at least to a greater extent. Hunger is the breeding ground of all the evils that we see all around. In a drama of ugliness, the educational system should be able to switch off the lights of ugly drama of character of evil design.

4. Community development can take place efficiently where there is goodwill, understanding, harmony and peace. Education should provide opportunities day in and day out- for the development of these finer qualities of life.

5. Health for all by A.D. 2000 has remained a slogan. A country that is lost to a slogan is a country lost forever. Deceased individuals cannot build a great social order and a great country. Health care should be an all-important area of education.

6. Childrens and mother's health, not merely physical health but the social, emotional, ethical, spiritual, etc., are not to be lost sight off in education.

7. Environmental and ecological problems are to be specially taken care of. Ecological problems are symptoms of careless use of natural wealth. Indiscriminate application of technology has only hastened the process of ruination. Community development may be nearer if we sincerely take care of the environmental and ecological problems. Education should enrich itself in tackling these problems of environmental and ecological realities.

8. Pure drinking water is a luxury in our country. Community development cannot be successful if education fails to make every individual aware of the

importance of pure drinking water and its proper usage. Under ground water level is going deeper into the earth crust. Drinking water is a problem all over the world and becoming acute in India. The education system should help develop the importance of preserving the under ground water and making the right use of the same.

9. Industrialisation had led to urbanisation. This has resulted in the increase of the number of slums. Life is miserable in slums. The education system should throw a light about effective management of slums so that life in slums and around the slums has a better meaning.

10. Poor communication facilities have hampered the growth of society in the right direction. Lack of roads, rails, bridges, etc., have kept millions of rural folk in drudgery.

11. Special attention to girls, education, at least up to 12th standard, should be given. This should become a reality and not another slogan.

12. Sincere efforts to help and motivate women to become entrepreneurs and start their own small scale industries and village crafts should be made.

13. Folk schools of Denmark should be taken as models and institutions that suit our development programmes, started by non-governmental organisations and people who are committed to make community development a reality. Such institutions should be started in rural areas keeping in view the congenial atmosphere for effective functioning of such institutions. The rural leadership should also be kept in view while starting institutions. The 21st century may be described as informational Technology era. The fruits of information technology should be easily accessible to the rural folk—young and

old. Advancement in all the areas that take place all over the world should reach the doorsteps of all, specially the rural population.

14. Population explosion is a fact, and if this is allowed to continue, the future is black. Nature will take revenge in its own way against the onslaught of man against it. Population explosion should be controlled irrespective of caste and religion. The concept of secularism should not allow any section or sections of community to produce a large number of children as they please. National interest and world peace should be uppermost in their minds. Hence the urgent need to put an end to population explosion. Vested interests, specially the power managers, have nearly ruined the country's future, let alone community development.

15. Any development in the country and community can take place only when people work hard in that direction. We belong to a non-working era and in a way non-working is being is encouraged for reasons best known to people who claim to be the leaders of the nation. Working philosophy is a must. Learn, learn and learn. Work, work and work should be the life- breath of the people of the land. Education should encourage this philosophy. Only those who accept this philosophy should find a place in the field of education. This is for the common social goal and community development.

16. Education, having a programme like NCC, NSS, Scouts, etc., should be encouraged to become living programmes.

17. Corruption is rampant. Hence development is at a standstill. Peoples, specially the youth, should be educated of the criminality of the corrupt people and impact of corruption on the future of humankind, not merely on Indians. Education is a major weapon to fight corruption.

CONCLUSION

Therefore, education system should not fail hereafter to educate the young and old to tackle successfully the above-mentioned areas, and should bring a ray of hope for a bright future for the entire community. Community development will not remain a mirage, if the education system is redesignated keeping in view all the failures. Peace and prosperity should be a reality. Peace and humaneness should flourish.

Education should be able to generate modern ideas, secular values and liberal philosophies to mould the social, economic and political institutions of the nation. The hold of customs, religions and dogmas are still dominant in our traditional society. Education for the 21st century should be able to instil modernising values and forces which will become the prime vehicle of social change. Skill and manpower are necessary to meet the requirements of a modern, technical society. The rural youth should not be denied the opportunities to develop in themselves the required knowledge, attitudes and skills. Community development will be a reality, only when the youth, from both urban and rural, get opportunities of education that is expected to meet the manpower requirements for the development of a newer social order. Education should succeed in providing intellectual leadership-action for the uplift of the community. System of education should be able to liberate the energies of the people, unleashing the creative power. This implies sincere democratisation of education.

The concept of welfare state combined with the spurt in the hopes and aspirations of the people, certainly calls for a new role of education.

Community development, with all the best of efforts, has still remained a mirage. The rural society has a large number of gaps in the vital areas of endeavour. Programmes like rural road building, provision of drinking water facilities, catering for the needs of rural health and hygiene, inculcation of scientific temper and modern attitudes in the rural population, adoption of rural improved techniques in agriculture along with a comprehensive programme of social education will help community development. Education should not fail in its role.

19

Creative Insubordination at Your Service: The Mayfield Accelerated Schools Project

*—Rob Andrew**

The project has been underway at Mayfield for over three and a half years. It is the only school in Australia to have trialed the Accelerated Schools Project (ASP) school-renewal model and the only school in Tasmania to have received a waiver of the mandated Assisted School Self-Review (ASSR) requirements. Mayfield's ASP process has been taken through one year of establishment, a further year of early implementation, and a year and a half of full implementation. In all, it represents a piece of participatory action research spanning four years from inception to its current status.

The ASP is one of a dozen school-wide reform models endorsed by the US Department of Education as exemplary in addressing the learning challenges faced by schools of highly disadvantaged communities. The study probes the thesis that changes in governance can generate positive conditions for changes in teaching and learning. It has tracked change in the school community over nearly four years. The results suggest, for the players and for those working with academically disadvantaged communities, that democratic, inclusive

**Department of Early Childhood and Primary Education, University of Tasmania, Launceston, Tasmania.*

whole-school governance can help us in generating optimal conditions of learning. The study's findings have much to offer systemic school development and review processes, particularly in its explanation of effective priority-determination and collective inquiry/action procedures.

CONTEXT

Mayfield Primary School is a K-6 government school. Just under 80 per cent of its population receives government school levy assistance, i.e., eight of every 10 families have incomes below the 'poverty line'. There are currently 285 students enrolled, making it an 'average' size in Tasmanian terms. A majority of households are headed by a single mother, unemployed, living in rented (assisted) government housing.

In 1995, Mayfield's plight was highlighted in the book *Making the Peace at Mayfield* (Breheney, Mackrill and Grady, 1995) which told the story of the staff's efforts to turn around a school culture rife with oppositional behaviour and violence. In the following year, the suburb of Mayfield was a long-term source of newspaper headlines. Vigilante groups were forming to contend with the increasing incidence of property crime and assault, much of which was slated home to youth gangs and family rivalry.

Tasmanian schools are funded and staffed according to an 'educational needs index' which factors in household incomes (as a socioeconomic status measure) and enrolment numbers showing eligibility for 'loan issue' status (which exempts families from school levies). Mayfield's Educational Needs Index standing was 87 in 1999, positioning it in the highest 5 primary schools in the state in respect of educational 'needs' and recurrent support eligibility. Academic performance as measured against norms developed in state-wide testing has shown Mayfield to be among the lowest five on aggregated numeracy scores at Grades three and five, and in the lowest five of aggregated literacy scores at Grade five level. State-wide, literacy scores improved across the state in 1998, with Mayfield making greater gains than many of the previously better-performing schools of the district.

Of the approximately 250 families in the school community in 1996, prior to the implementation of the caps project, only seven parents, all but one female, contributed to any levels of discourse between parents and senior staff. In one early questionnaire-survey for the ASP project conducted in 1997 there was a response rate of eight out of 250 (3.2 per cent). When I later attempted to insert questionnaires into newspapers at the local shop, I was laughed at by the shopkeeper who told me, "Nobody reads newspapers around here."

Teaching and Learning at Mayfield Prior to 1997

When in 1990 Tasmania's system was reviewed by a consultancy firm specialising in system rationalisation, CRESAP, it was claimed that Tasmania's education system was too concerned with the process and not enough concerned with product. This marked the beginning of a new accountability-driven management in Tasmanian public schooling. For Mayfield and schools like it with high levels of students experiencing chronic failure, the shift to outcomes -dependent accountability left them in no better position than they had been in a learner-centred process dealing with large numbers of dysfunctional and dependent learners. The staff knew the dilemma they were in. A majority of families were, however, largely unaware that education trends or 'orthodoxies' had changed over time from transmission methods with mandated curricula to facilitation methods with school-based curricula. They had been left uninformed apparently as a result of their non-involvement in direct school-learning activity.

When in 1997 parents were informed by Mayfield staff that their children's scores were well below par in statewide literacy and numeracy measures, families were shocked. Mayfield's relative performance on numeracy tests at ages 10 and 14 (N10; N14) and reading tests (R10; R14) had declined quite markedly both against its own scores of the 1970s and 1980s (when a number of parents had actually been students at the school) and against the statewide averages.

In 1996, I was asked by my supervisors at the University of Tasmania to take a role as 'coach' for one or more Tasmanian trials of the Accelerated Schools reform model, established since 1986 in urban San Francisco as a process (not a programme of fixed content or routines) to help deliver democratic, inclusive governance and authentic learning experiences to high poverty communities. Mayfield Primary School had a new principal incoming. He was keen to work in a bottom-up, democratic and consensual way. Another 'tough' school was approached and given all the required information upon which to 'buy into' the project, but the principal chose instead to go the ASSP pathway. Hence our project became a single-school case study.

My role of 'coach' for the project involves several responsibilities: change agent, introducing the concept to all stakeholders and clarifying their respective input; guide on procedures and ensuring that the school community undertakes the ASP change model with sufficient fidelity; and participant observer in an interactive, open-ended piece of participatory action research. No one is better placed to see a change model from both inside and out, but no one is as compromised as the researcher-coach. Spending at least a day a week in the school over four years, I have, of course, built working friendships with staff and families in the school community. Always feeding back to these partners, always directing ownership into their hands, this professional intimacy allows the 'coach' to access more candid perceptions from the players. In this way, objectivity is not false; one sees things through the eyes and hearts of the real decision makers.

The Political and Socio-cultural Context of the Study

No central government can risk criticism that, under its control, public education is failing to enhance the employability and productivity of a nation's 'human capital'. Yet the unemployment rate in Tasmania remains static, with very high rates among school leavers, beyond 40 per cent in some areas. Serious questions surround the outcomes of public education for those most affected by joblessness, the rising cost of tertiary education and the issue of how schools can advance the future prospects of those with the least apparent advantage from the experience of public schooling.

How does a system with a competitive end-point in both the job market and tertiary entrance ensure equitable outcomes under the conditions of limited public expenditure? In a political climate which pits international competitiveness against welfare and compensatory education, governments don't know whether to tighten up and dumb down—through highly structured and narrowly academic school programmes or to give head to the logical consequence of devolution and the free market—a loosening of controls and a ceding autonomy to local bodies (schools, community health and the like). The two positions are potentially mutually contradictory. Nevertheless, the current mandated model of school development planning in Tasmania, Assisted School Self Review (ASSR) attempts to do the seemingly impossible: to give genuine autonomy to the local school community (through 'Partnership Agreements' between communities, schools and district offices) while framing for the community certain compulsory domains of accountability—largely literacy, numeracy, information technology and student behaviour. This is systemic reform.

In Australia the potential for individual schools or districts to undertake 'models' of reform in their own right faded significantly in 1996 when the Disadvantaged Schools Program (DSP) was dismantled by the incoming Liberal conservative government. DSP equity funds allowed individual schools to innovate in areas deigned by their local school communities to promise more equitable outcomes for the schools in which disadvantaged learners were being educated, The difference between whole school reform and curricular reform becomes clearer under such a regimen. Citing Simon (1991), Bill Stringer asserts that "no two schools are so alike in their circumstances for prescriptions of curricular action to adequately supplant the judgments of those who work within them" (Stringer, 1992, p. 67). While officers of central authorities may be able to conceive of 'fair' distribution process for Commonwealth funds, the empowerment of school level educators and their communities in significant curricular and organisational decision making is fundamental to effective schooling for learners with little family history of advantage from education.

Until recently in the US, school renewal has been initiated at local levels, in partnership usually with change agents from university education faculties. However, the US Department of Education has recently reviewed its Title I compensatory programme and has set up a Comprehensive School Reform Demonstration initiative to promote school-wide, long-term reform in disadvantaged schools through the use of federal funds. The ambiguity of the term 'school reform' is only a lexical problem. A line is being drawn in US educational management theory between top-down systemic, mandated reform, and the bottom-up, context-embedded *renewal*. The distinction is becoming "abundantly clear in contemporary school improvement movements . . . [between] school reform and school renewal" (Goodlad, 1999: 575).

Three dimensions can be noted, across which such renewal models function: *school-wide* in so far as they include and enfranchise each stakeholder group or level, be it staff, parent or student; *comprehensive,* in addressing the several domains of governance, school programme structures, curriculum and instruction (including assessment), which are frequently dealt with in isolated fashion by schools or systems; and *school-based* in that the locus of decision making, imple-mentation and accountability is at the level of the school.

The tension in and around Tasmania's educational politics is brought into fine focus by this study. The processes of ASSR purport to give sufficient autonomy to the local school community to achieve an effective voice in the education of their children. Some developments in the US, such as the Chicago Schools programme have, through legislation, given the balance of power to families. This was done under the rationale that only under such conditions would schools of black and minority communities have the will to transform. Tasmania hasn't the same underlying history of race riots and class struggle, but it does have a dilemma. In each district there are several schools whose students have chronically occupied the bottom percentile of statewide test outcomes, reflected in the other end in the weakest school leaving records. These schools represent too perfectly the lowest socio economic sector and all the associated variables: 'housing commission' homes, sub-sidised school fees, youth crime and alienation, and continued ignorance among the majority of families concerning the wherewithal of schooling, the how-to-do-its of success in the learning game. The parents are scared to take bigger roles in the teaching and learning process for fear they will replicate in their children their own 'failed' school experiences. To empower such communities and the staff who work with them, alter-natives to the ASSR/Partnership process need to be explored. We have a saying in Tasmanian educational orthodoxy school that students must take responsibility for their own learning if they are to become real learners. The professional learning of teachers in low-socio-economic communities and families' educational development alongside them should operate no differently. This study probes the synergy of responsibility and learning at the whole school level.

The Accelerated Schools Model

The Accelerated Schools Project (ASP) is a 'school self-renewal' movement focused on disadvantaged populations. The thesis driving the ASP movement is that participatory democracy (on the part of the whole school community) combined with a thorough praxis review of teaching and learning in the school (largely along constructivist and inclusive curriculum lines) will result in improved student learning outcomes. In the lingo of the project, *empowerment plus powerful learning = improved student outcomes.*

The Stanford University originators of the ASP programme called it 'Accelerated Schools' to connote the desired function of speeding up learners' progress to literally undo the disadvantage met by them. Ambitious curriculum, not back to basics methods, was needed; all children were to be treated as gifted, and were to learn through engaging, authentic, context-honouring activity (Levin, 1996). The implication is that schools can begin not from a deficit idea of their conditions, but from a strength and challenges position, in which they design and pursue a desired future, rather than spending their educational energy 'making up shortfalls'. Paulo Friere's (1972) 'conscientisation' notions underpin the localism and contextuality which dignifies struggle, rather than stigmatising it.

The ASP process is undertaken by each ASP school. It sees school communities compare their strengths and challenges through a 'taking stock' phase, agree on a vision statement to express their collective ideal and goals, establish their own priorities, and set up a non-hierarchical governance arrangement that uses a consensual benchmark of 87 per cent agreement. The heart of ASP process is in the 'cadres' which are mixed-membership group teams comprising voluntary parents and self-selected staff (sometimes, also students). The cadres, organised around three or four priority areas (such as 'School Climate' or 'Instruction') meet regularly to attack the school's priorities through an action research model called the 'Inquiry Process'. After rigorous objective investigation of the facts, action plans are agreed and roles assigned in trailing and evaluating innovations. All school actions under the ASP aegis must move the school towards its agreed vision and priorities. The priorities and cadre domains are reviewed at least yearly. Central also to the overall impact is a commitment by the school community to develop 'Powerful Learning' methods in teaching and teaming which build on strengths inherent in the students and community.

RESEARCH

I differentiate the project at Mayfield from my study and its report. The project has its own life, and will exist or not independent of my writing about it. I write here about the project, not as a piece of reflection for the project's several member groups which collectively make up the School-as-a-Whole (SAW or whole school community–students, teachers, parents, active friends, district and university contributors). Nevertheless, the SAW members will receive a copy of this as a piece of tangible transparency, which has been a necessary condition of participatory action research from the start.

My thesis is the telling of the story of whether and how it works in a Tasmanian community as an insider/participant/agent, and it is the critical analysis of dynamics at play in school reform of a democratic nature. Working with teachers and educational laity in families, I have come to view my 'audience' as those on the ground in the field. I lean upon 'relatability' (Sanger, 1994) of the results and conclusions, rather than quasi-scientific reliability and validity. Sensible use of triangulation renders my inquiry more accessible to 'truth-testing' but the story of the players yields generalisable lessons because the stories and explanations are largely from teachers who have worked in other schools, and from families who have rich contacts with friends who have children in other so-called 'disadvantaged' schools. So long as the circumstances and influences are well described, readers can filter the noise from the true code.

The specific questions which have informed the data-gathering and analysis are:

1. To what extent has the ASP process been implemented at Mayfield?
2. How has the implementation of the process influenced outcomes in the areas of (a) school governance and organisation and (b) teaching and teaming?
3. What implications can be drawn from the Mayfield ASP experiences for comprehensive school reform in the Tasmanian context ?

Data Gathering and Analysis

Data has been gathered through yearly repeated series of interviews, focus groups, survey, documentary analysis and video observation. Quantitative data has also been made available through the school's own monitoring/testing as has data from Tasmanian statewide testing at years three and five ,over the past four years.

As a blend of reflective ethnography and action research, the 'thesis' of the study is not dependent on test scores to measure outcomes. Such scores will remain of some interest to distal stakeholders such as Esk District Office. But my focus for this part of the overall research is upon the implementation phase. Hence the outcomes lie in indicators of coherence and data which relate to the overall school culture. The researched hypothesis is that change in school governance and organisation has a discernible positive impact on student learning (not to mention institutional learning as a community of learners). I attempt to involve as many of the school members in 'collective analysis' of whatever data we receive, because they are the ones making directional decisions regarding priorities, school organisation and curriculum towards priority outcomes. The main task is to first describe and interpret the changes that have emerged from the early years. Only after some six or so years can a school make serious claims that its reforms or renewal have translated into sustained end-point student outcomes (Woods, Jeffrey, Trotman and Boyle, 1997).

At this stage, the Interview and Survey data is largely complete, but a collective analysis of this data has yet to be conducted on year-to-year comparisons on testing results, nor have the SAW been interviewed for their summary viewpoints regarding the whole implementation process. We needed to reach the true consolidation and operation stage before making judgements or critical reflections of a summative nature. What is reported here will inform some of those players' reflections. But they are in this instance the perceptions of a 'coach' who has stepped back from the fray and attempted to ascertain the changes, the surprises, the challenges and the potential benefits to the field raised by the project.

OUTCOMES

Changes

a) The ASP project gave staff a sense of autonomy which led it in 1998 to undertake a time-buying adjustment to school hours which, by adding 15 minutes to the in-class days of Monday, Tuesday, Thursday and Friday, freed up an hour from 2:00 on Wednesdays for cadres meetings, school-as-a-whole meetings, professional development and collaborative curricular planning. The staff meet every Wednesday (with parents every other week) from 2:00 pm to 4:00 pm while those students who can't go home directly are given extra-curricular activities and instructional technology opportunities. An all-family vote achieved 99 per cent consensus on the change. Since this time, other schools in Launceston have reorganised their schedules to free up planning and 'PD' time.

b) The cadre/inquiry process gives ownership of the action to the range of players. One danger in school communities is that despite lengthy consultation (though usually it is all too hasty) among all stakeholders, it is teachers who bear the brunt of the work. The week-by-week monitoring of interventions in action research, the collection and analysis of data, all fall to staff. The initiative inadvertently is wrested from the broader community. Because involvement in the cadres is self-selected, there is no sense of parent or community 'elites' getting the lay voice.

c) In each of the past two years only two staff members have opted to transfer to other schools, and those transfers have been at the end of long stints in 'hard-to-staff' schools. Prior to the implementation of ASP, the staff of 14 had at least one-third of its members turning over. Mayfield has become a favoured placement for teachers-in-training and has developed a reputation of excellence among the educational community for its supportive learning environment. Its 'Hall of Fame' has spread by the year along its corridor in an expression of pride by the school community;

d) Suspensions and high order behaviour interventions have quartered over the period 1997 to today. Vandalism has gone from being a maintenance nightmare to occasional damage.

e) High levels of staff satisfaction with the democratic and inquiry-based decision-making model introduced and operating for over three years; and broad community support for the new school programme.

f) The support from families was due in part to the early commitment to transparency that was part and parcel of multi-stakeholder collaboration. Early in 1997 it was agreed to communicate directly to the PTA the poor academic standing of students at Mayfield. The staff had discovered, from results released to them on the previous year's statewide reading and maths testing, that Mayfield's scores were among the worst in the state. The families went through the stages of grief towards acceptance of something they hadn't really comprehended, unaware as many of the families were of 'standards' against which schools and their students were being compared. But the upshot of it all was a clear sense of trust between parents and staff. Partnership could begin with realism. It is interesting to note that the emphasis on 'basics' expressed by families in the 'taking-stock' was at first rejected by staff as narrow-minded but discourse over time has resolved the issue to centre on the explicitness of teaching and a review of any staff's temptation to take students' learning for granted.

Surprises

a) It was unexpected that so few families were neither confident nor willing to respond to written questionnaires sent home in the (popular) weekly newsletter. As a consequence, using research support funds from the University of Tasmania, videos were taken in 1998 of classroom practices. These were distributed to all families on a roster basis along with a two-page questionnaire concerning parents' perceptions of teaching and learning at Mayfield. One hundred and sixty responses were received (a response rate of 64 per cent). Compared to previous rates of response, this was astounding. A further confirmation of the value of video as a stimulus to community response was seen in a follow-up of the video/survey exercise in the next year. This video on the topic of opportunities for family participation in Mayfield's school affairs elicited another 150 responses.

b) Early cadre meetings engaged students as participants because of the novelty experienced by students as they sat, talked and voted alongside their adult 'new equals'. However, the more grinding aspects of hypothesising, cross-checking tentative solutions, piloting, action researching and data analysis slowly but surely lost the students' active interest and input. I witnessed this same 'burnout' in experienced Californian and Texan ASP schools in a 1998 visit (Andrew, 1998). With this in mind, a Student Representative Council was established to give a voice to students at their own pace and level, while maintaining lines of communication to the cadres through the teacher/convenor. For some time students were working on both the SRC cadres. The SRC has proved a winner. For similar reasons, the PTA has been retained by families as a forum for action that is not encumbered by methodology as much as the cadres

When offered funding support to trial the Program of Additional Support for Students (PASS) using a template of dedicated literacy blocks for related language arts of speaking and listening, reading and writing, Mayfield staff undertook to implement a more structured programme than it had previously. The PASS processes sit in creative tension alongside Mayfield's version of integrated curriculum—the Multi-layered Integrated Curriculum which is planned within a matrix of multiple intelligences and Bloom's levels.

c) My clear expectation before the Mayfield ASP process had become established was that families would derive the most empowerment from the project. After all, they were the least enfranchised in school decision making, and had little to no understanding of how to value-add to their school's inputs. However, over time, it has become clear that the teachers have gained more, and that the reality had been that the teachers were actually just as disempowered by conditions as parents. Instructional coherence at Mayfield had been lost in the years of head-to-head behaviour management battles. As a result, the staff who had significant curricular knowledge and instructional skills were denied the ability to use them. The governance structure of ASP afforded the staff a chance to focus on curriculum, to have a definitive say in the direction taken by the school, and to establish credibility before families. Interviews with teachers at the end of 1998 showed they had generalised confidence in the cadre process, and questionnaire responses showed they believed the management profile in the school was democratic and 'flat'.

Challenges

Several challenges have emerged in the fourth year of Mayfield's ASP implementation:

a) The school is heading towards a succession in its principalship. The current principal has been with the project from the start and has supported the model in action. However, there is no certainty that the incoming principal will take up the project as a long-term priority. The succession will be a test of the school community's commitment and valuing of the ASP process.

b) Parents and students are two member groups which remain hard to reach. Complexity is a withering factor for both groups when engaging in data based action research (Inquiry, as the ASP term has it). The process is slow and cautious, but strong—when initiatives are designed by cadres in response to school-agreed priority challenges, the implementation is not thin, rarely needs going back over, and invariably has broad-spread support through the consensual and inclusive decision-making system. But this strength is also a frustration to families who may only have one year left of their child's involvement in the school. Students have much to offer schoolwide renewal. Their voices speak volumes about the lived learning experiences that ultimately, in all paradigms, give education its purpose. But it takes a long time to build real capacity in students for the task. It takes thorough work in all classes and a *savoire faire* among all families (all is used deliberately here) to make sense of giving the most disadvantaged a better chance through an empowering, effective education.

c) The US has given schools the capacity to spend compensatory money on school renewal (comprehensive schoolwide reform). Unless schools such as Mayfield have discretion over their compensatory funds, no real comparative basis will be afforded in respect of state-mandated school development planning. One example is the need to support partially or wholly a renewal 'coach'. I am now about redundant in the scheme of things, but a new need has emerged for community liaison staff member who can advance family and student participation. Commonwealth money would be suitable and long-term change processes like the ASP or even home-grown partnership models would constitute funds not frittered away on fad initiatives.

CONCLUSION

Mayfield's school renewal model attracts considerable interest from like schools. It is seen as an outrider from the state wide review programme, with a real track record and results from the study are being directed toward District and Central offices to inform ASSR schools in their own implementations of priority actions. Contributions from maverick schools have been characterised as creative insubordination (Bryk, Sebring, Kerbow, Rollow and Easton, 1998: 12). Mayfield's experiences are important for other schools in the same circumstances in Tasmania, despite differences such as size or transience rates, but equally important for system level planners in Tasmania. A very rare opportunity exists for central leaders to hear the voices and read the responses of one community that has taken its situation seriously and has explored a deeper tissue of autonomy than mandated processes can support.

Chicago schools have recently reported one of the most community-empowered reform programmes in US experience. The report's closing statement highlights a need for stories such as that of Mayfield to inform many equity-seeking communities: "The common rhetoric today, that states and districts set the goals and leave it up to schools to achieve these goals, glosses were over the very real consideration that how to get there is the problem" (Bryk et al., 1998: 269).

REFERENCES

Andrew, R., 1998, Reversing Disadvantage: Lessons From a Foray into Successful High Poverty US Schools, *Leading and Managing,* Vol. 4, No. 3, p. 219-229.

Breheney, C., Mackrill, V., and Grady, N., 1996, *Making Peace at Mayfield,* Armadale, Victoria, Australia: Eleanor Curtain Publishing.

Bryk, A.S., Sebring, P.B., Kerbow, D., Rollow, S., and Easton, J.Q., 1998, *Charting Chicago School Reform: Democratic Localism as a Lever for Change,* Boulder, Colorado: Westview Press.

Freire, P., 1972, *Pedagogy of the Oppressed,* New York: Penguin.

Goodlad, J.I., 1999, "Flow, Eros and Ethos in Educational Renewal", *Phi Delta Kappan,* Vol. 80, No. 8, p. 571.

Levin, H.M., 1996a, 'Accelerated Schools: The Background', in Finnan, C., St. John, E.P., McCarthy, J. and Slovacek, S.P. (eds.), *Accelerated Schools in Action,* California: Corwin. p. 323.

Sanger, J., 1994, Seven Types of Creativity: Looking for Insights in Data Analysis, *British Educational Research Journal,* Vol. 20, No. 2, p. 175-185.

Stringer, W., 1992, "Education Policy, National Curriculum and Schools", In Stockley, D., (ed.), *Rationalising Education,* Melbourne: Melbourne Studies in Education, Latrobe University Press, p. 63-70.

Woods, P., Jeffrey, B., Trotman, G., and Boyle, M., 1997, *Restructuring teachers: responding to change in the primary school.* Buckingham, UK: Open University Press.

20

School Education in Maharashtra (India): A Bird's-Eye View

*—Smita Kakan**

According to the Constitution of India, education is the subject that is on the concurrent list. It means that it is the subject on which the central government and the state government can take policy decisions jointly. With the advent of independence, education of the masses was perceived as one of the guiding principles of the Indian state.

In the post-independence period some dedicated efforts were taken with zeal and total commitment. The efforts were recognised even by the international agencies like UNESCO. They awarded efforts of the state with ' Mohammed Raza Shah Pahelvi Award'. However, the zeal and the enthusiasm were lost in the course of time. The literacy percentage went sliding down steadily. The alarming fall in women's literacy was one of the big concerns before the educational planners. At the same time the primary or elementary education also was facing the problem of dropout from the schools in the state.

The national government also took serious note of the problems. Various commissions such as the Mudaliar Commission and the Kothari Commission were appointed for suggesting remedies in the matter. Suggestions of these commissions were implemented but with little success. Though

**Bal Bhavan, Mumbai, (Maharashtra), India.*

the real problem was identified but ignored was the social cause. With the result the Government of India, with the adoption of the New Policy on Education, in 1984 expressed the determination to achieve the goal of Universalisation of Elementary Education (Universalisation of Elementary Education) for all children in the age group of six to 14 years by the year 2000. The school curricula have been revised in the light of National Educational Policy. The Programme of Action, 1992 (POA) reaffirms the nation's commitment to universalisation of elementary education. The real problem identified but ignored was again the social cause.

The national experience to achieve universalisation of elementary education had established:

a) Universalisation of elementary education is contextual.

b) Contextual approach needs local area planning with desegregated targets and decentralised planning and management.

c) Resources though are important but not sufficient condition for achieving universalisation of elementary education.

d) The strategy for universalisation of elementary education till now emphasised mainly access in terms of construction of classrooms and appointment of teachers. This was inadequate and needed to be supplemented by:

    i) A holistic planning and management.

    ii) Should corporate a gender prescriptive in all aspects of planning and implementation process. It should be an integral part of all measures needed to achieve universalisation of elementary education.

    iii) Addressing the more difficult aspects of access, particularly access to girls.

    iv) Stressing the participative process, particularly local community.

The District Primary Education Programme (hereinafter referred to as DPEP) is based on the above experience at the national level.

DPEP

1. It is a primary education programme that aims at providing quality education.
2. The world bank provides financial backup and monitors the DPEP.
3. The programme has been implemented in Maharashtra from 1994 for seven years in five districts and from 1997 for five years in four districts.
4. DPEP is being implemented in the districts with low female literacy rate, hence has special focus on girls' education.
5. It is participatory, decentralised and need-based.
6. Provides for capacity building of individuals and institutions.

OBJECTIVES OF DPEP

To increase enrolment rate. To reduce dropout rate. To improve achievement levels.

DPEP plan is an outcome of series of deliberations right from the village, cluster, and block levels to the district level.

It is an undeniable fact that the school cannot be treated as an independent and isolated unit from the wider social system. The strengthening of this linkage between school and community would mean local community improving, managing and developing the school.

COMMUNITY MOBILISATION AND COMMUNICATION

The District Primary Education Programme stresses upon sustainability for which community participation is a crucial factor. The efforts under DPEP are to establish a strong linkage between the school and the community resulting in community ownership of schools and the schooling process.

The literacy profile according to the 1991 census of our nation (total 52 per cent women 39.4 per cent) and that of our state (total 65 per cent women 52.3 per cent) shows that half of the population is still illiterate. At every level and act in the home and society the male child is treated with preference resulting in giving the girl-child a secondary status. The mentality of the girl-children was so moulded that they had accepted mentally this status. This gender disparity needed to be eliminated. The National Policy on Education (1986) and its Programme of Action (1992) makes education for women's equality, the cornerstone of all endeavours.

STUDIES ON GIRLS' EDUCATION

Baseline studies were undertaken in project districts to provide inputs into the formulation of plans for girls' education and women's empowerment. The study focused on perceptions of causes of continuing girls in the schools, of non-enrolment, of dropout and of gender inequality in communities.

FINDINGS OF STUDY

The problem of access exists in small-sized villages and scattered habitations. Availability of educational and other infrastructure such as health, water, roads, electricity, etc. are scarce in villages with population less than 100.

a) Parents of unserved villages do not want to send their children, especially girls, for schooling outside the village.

b) Early marriage is a big constraint.

c) Most of the girls left school on account of domestic compulsions of work and poverty.

d) Mothers are mostly illiterate.

e) Drop out girls belong to large-sized households.

f) The national trend of a declining sex ratio is seen vividly at the district level. (Aurangabad District sex ratio is 9:22).

g) The status of women varies in different socio cultural groups, casts and communities within and among districts.

h) Parents were reluctant to send their daughters to single-teacher/male-teacher schools as they felt that their daughters were not safe, especially if the teacher was absent.

That is why a gender perspective has been incorporated in all aspects of planning and implementation of the DPEP. Thus it is an integral part of the programme. A wide variety of programme inputs included were:

a) Alternative schooling.
b) Flexible school timings to accommodate the needs of girl children.
c) Gender sensitive curricula and textbooks.
d) Recruitment and development of women teachers.
e) Improved school buildings with separate toilets for girls.
f) Educational incentives, and
g) Gender sensitisation for teachers and project managers are often considered, depending on the need and circumstances.

In Maharashtra, the Mahila Prabodhan Programme (MPP) has been evolved as a gender intervention under DPEP. The Mahila Prabodhan Programme has picked up relevant points.

The various programmes and activities envisaged and implemented under the Mahila Prabodhan Programme can be broadly divided into the following five categories:

i) Environment building activities.
ii) Training
iii) Curriculum, textbooks, pedagogical issues and classroom
iv) Monitoring access and retention
v) Development of media material and document.

MAHILA PRABODHAN PROGRAMME STRUCTURE

Under the Mahila Prabodhan Programme Structure, the state has created a post of District Gender Coordinator at the district level, Block Gender Coordinator at the block level, Mahila Prabodhan Programme Cluster Coordinator at the cluster level. Teachers from primary schools are village coordinators. At the state level, the state level gender coordinator is appointed under the guidance of the State Project Director. The core committee under the chairmanship of the chairperson of the society guides on different programmes and issues.

The present paper is mainly aimed at understanding and assessing the extent and process of participation of mother-teacher associations (MTA), which is promoted by the District Primary Education Programme in order to develop a sense of ownership amongst the local people for the village school and girls' education in particular and primary education in general, so as to achieve the goals of the programme. The broad objectives of the paper are as follows:

a) To assess the process of Mother-Teacher Association and its participation with reference to various interventions.
b) To identify the strength and weakness of the process in relation to the articulated strategies, implementation and impact.

MOTHER-TEACHER ASSOCIATION: CAPACITY BUILDING

A mother should initially realise the various qualities and skills she herself possesses. Hence, schools should outline such a programme to identify the same and develop those which are beneficial to the process.

The programmes in the school should be organised in such a way as to facilitate easy involvement of mothers. Festival meets such as Raksha Bandhan, Holi, Nagapanchami, Mother' Day and National Days should be encouraged.

The Mother-Teacher Association brings about a constructive change in the set-up of the school and comes to terms with the needs and problems of the school as well as the children.

Members of the Mother-Teacher Association realise that working for the school is as important as working for their own home.

MOTHER-TEACHER ASSOCIATION COMPOSITION

a) It is free from hierarchy and wheel communication.

b) Involvement of money in the form of fee or donations is curbed and avoided.

c) No social or political interference.

d) The teacher or *sahayogini* coordinates the programme as Secretary of Mother-Teacher Association to keep the updates of meetings.

e) The head of the school acts as the Chairman of the Mother-Teacher Association and works as caretaker of it.

f) No rigidity about the number of members.

g) The structure develops on its own in the natural course of time.

Role of Mother-Teacher Association

a) To contact parents for the enrolment of their child, especially girl(s).

b) To guide and help the parents and ultimately to reduce the rate of dropout.

c) To help children to raise their achievement levels.

d) To help provide teaching learning material and to organise supervised study for the children.

e) To help the school by contributing their skills in various fields like reading, writing, storytelling, experience narrating and sports, etc.

f) To keep school surroundings clean and hygienic by carrying out various cultural activities such as *rangoli*, planting trees, etc.

g) Help in providing basic amenities such as drinking water, toilets for children and other facilities with the help of community.

h) To participate in co-curricular activities organised by the school.

i) To keep an eye on the anti-social elements and make proper arrangements to keep them at bay.

j) Most importantly, to identify and understand the problems faced by the girl-child and find means to overcome them.

Achievements and Impact of the Mother-Teacher Association

A beginning has been made to address the issue of girls' education and equity through the Mother-Teacher Association.

While reviewing the programme and its impact, it cannot be denied that a general awareness and concern about girls' education has been created among teachers, administrators and planners. It has contributed in improving (the classroom climate) the rate of enrolment, the retention of pupils and of the girl-child in particular. Women's effective participation in the decision-making process and in community development activities through village education committee and the village school has been significant.

The Mother-Teacher Association functionaries have been trained and have developed clarity regarding their roles and responsibilities. They have been playing a vital role as catalysts to bring about the expected reforms and changes. The Mother-Teacher Association has helped sustainability to project.

BOTTLENECKS

It is true that the DPEP and its Mother-Teacher Association alone cannot be an answer to the issue of gender inequality and girls' education. As the problem is closely linked to socio-economic factors, a proper coordination among different bodies/departments/local NGO(S) is essential for the programme to be effective.

The rural woman responds better if activities are linked to income generation. Therefore, the programme should intervene to provide this facility.

The Mother-Teacher Association has a great potential, as it is a link among the planners, the executives and the beneficiaries. It can contribute in a big way to achieve the objectives of access and retention. However, this potential is unfortunately not recognised and this programme is given a secondary status. This indifferent attitude and marginal participation of the other functionaries not only dampen the enthusiasm of the workers, they also fail to create adequate motivation among them.

FUTURE PLANS

DPEP plans to initiate follow up activities in the following areas:

a) To initiate steps for evaluation of the performance of the Mother-Teacher Association.

b) Preparation of handbook of case studies.

c) Preparation of handbook for teachers of early child care and education.

d) Compilation of works of eminent women from districts.

e) Establish close and meaningful liaison with other agencies resulting in avoiding duplication of activities.

f) Video film on girls' education emphasising gender equity.

21

Education of Scheduled Tribes: Current Scenario and Challenges

—Hemlata Talesra, Shima Sarupria***

The tribal community occupy a unique position in Indian society. Being the earliest inhabitants of the country, they have for centuries maintained a distinctive lifestyle. Unfortunately their isolation has kept them out of the mainstream of the nation and made them easy prey to exploitation. This paper makes an attempt to discuss the current scenario of tribal education in Rajasthan and analyse the challenges related to their basic needs and structural changes. The paper also suggests some strategies for promoting education of STs.

The Directive Principles of the State Policy of the Indian Constitution provides free and compulsory education for all the children up to the age of 14 years. Article 46 of the Constitution also says, "The state shall promote with special care of education and economic interests of weaker sections of the people, particularly the scheduled tribes and the scheduled castes and shall protect them from social injustice and all form of exploitation".

**Secretary General, RCEAM, Professor and Head, Deptt. of Edu. Planning, Management and Administration, Vidya Bhawan G.S. IASE, Udaipur.*

***Professor of Education, Vidya Bhawan, G.S. Institute of Advanced Studies in Education, Udaipur (Rajasthan), India.*

The tribal education situation has to be analysed in terms of the social conditioning of the people in the past. It would not be wrong to say that in the long period of history the non-tribals have created some myths about the people. These have become stereotypes. Tod, writing in 1839 about Western India, observes, "the Bhil will feed a vermin of any kind, foxes, jackals, rates... yet in moral degradation their followship is complete. The non-tribals would call them cow-eaters. The tribal is said to be dishonest and ungrateful".

If we look at the problems of tribal education within the 'shadow' of non-tribal prejudices and stereotypes your scientific analysis of these people is likely to be obsessed. We would, therefore, only argue that let us look at the tribal educational situation as is found today in the context of the historical social conditioning, namely, subsistence economy, isolation, hill and forests, feudalism, exploitation and stereo-types developed by the non-tribals, especially the high caste Hindus.

After independence the framers of our Constitution have given certain special safety and security to the tribals. These safeties and securities provide some protective discriminations to the tribals against the non-tribals. Besides the Constitution, the main basis of educational policy in India is emphasizing the rcommendations of the several commissions and committees appointed from time to time to suggest reforms in the educational system so as to meet adequately the new demand of the country.

The education commissions' policies and programmes which include University Education Commission (1949), Secondary Education Commission (1952-53), Kothari Education Commission (1964-66), National Policy on Education (1986), Programme of Action (1990) and Yashpal Committee (1993) emphasised the need-based education for tribals.

CURRENT SCENARIO OF ST'S EDUCATION

According to the 1991 census the general population of the country comes out to be more than 88 crore and on the basis of news of TV on 1994 September it comes to 90,655,735. According to the 1991 census the total tribal population percentage was 8.08. They have been concentrated mostly in Central India across the state of Orissa, Bihar, Madhya Pradesh, Arunachal Pradesh, Maharashtra, Gujarat and Rajasthan. Literacy rate among the tribals comes to 16.35 (males) and 8.04 (females).

The Constitution has made provision that compulsory education would be made for children in the age group 6-11 years. (4.62 lacs). The population of students enrolled in the schools in different age groups shows that the number of non-tribal students far exceeds the number of tribal students at all the levels of age groups.

The enrolment of tribal students at the levels of primary and secondary education shows that the percentage of their dropout increases with each higher level of school education. In other words, at the state level it is found that the higher the standard of school education the smaller the size of tribal student's enrolment. Actually the tribal educational system as we find today is the result of multiple factors. The whole region of the erstwhile state of Rajputana was characterised by Rajput rule for several centuries. The Rajputs anyhow had accepted that getting education for themselves and their children was below their status. It was meant only for Brahmins and the Baniyas. Such a doctrinaire approach to education discouraged the opening of schools in the state.

The social condition generated through feudalism, the practice of forced labour, subsistence economy and untamed environment came in the way of creating a favourable situation for education. The tribal groups being a different racial and ethnic stock were kept encapsulated in hills and forests.

On the basis of collected data for the project completed in 1987, out of the student sample (at the secondary level) 300, 32.3 per cent belong to the Bhil tribe. The Minas numbering 143 account for 47.7 per cent. The Damor and Garasia, who have numerical size in sample of 22 and 38 constitute 7.3 and 12.7 per cent.

Out of 12 major tribal groups found in Rajasthan, Mina, Bhil, Garasia, Saheriya, Damor and Bhilmina constitute the major tribal groups in the state. The Minas were once a force to reckon with as they held power over a large part of Rajasthan previous to the advent of the Rajputs. Literacy among them is low. While there are 9.6 per cent males who are literate the corresponding figure for female is only 0.3 per cent, in other words, one out of 10 males and one out of 362 females are literates.

The Bhils who have a numerical strength below the Minas are an ancient tribe. Literacy in the community is very low. Put broadly one out of 20 males and one out of 408 females are literates.

The Garasias have extremely low literacy. Female literacy is negligible while amongst the males also it is as low as 2.5 per cent. The rate of literacy among the Damor is 6.5 per cent for males and 0.4 for females.

Saheriyas are the most backward among all the scheduled tribes of the state. Only 2.3 per cent males and 0.2 per cent females are literate in this community.

Among all the scheduled tribes of the state, literacy is the highest among the Bhil-Mina. It is 14.9 per cent among males and 5.8 per cent among females.

In the state of Rajasthan all tribal students are staying in three types of educational institutions, namely, common government schools, Ashram schools and schools run by voluntary agencies including mission schools.

Challenges Regarding the Basic Needs of the Tribals

The tribal society's basic needs are twofold. They want to get rid of poverty. Poverty has been their plight for the last several years. The tribal land situation has become the worst today. Their problem today is to say goodbye to agriculture and seek employment in off-the-farm occupations.

The second need of tribals is to maintain their ethnic identity and at the same time integrate themselves in the mainline of regional and national culture. It requires some elaboration in the light of empirical reality. The ashram schools which began a new experiment in helping the students to prepare their lessons at home, having no educational background at home, have isolated the tribal boys from the interaction of the non-tribal students. Educationally, the working of ashram schools is helpful in raising the standard of tribal boys but it keeps the tribals away from the wider society. In the way to educate the tribals there are the challenges regarding how to maintain their ethnic identity, how to integrate themselves in the mainline, what type of education to be provided to the tribals for their interaction and link from the wider society.

Challenges Regarding the Structural Changes in the Tribals

Among the factors bringing tribal structural changes in education is a crucial causal factor. It is found that the tribals have succeeded in establishing political networks with non-tribals right from Panchayat Raj institutions to parliament. As a result of education those who have migrated to the plains have started living in compact villages. They are in various degrees competing with the non-tribals.

Recently, the traditional tribal Panchayats have issued some of the resolutions saying that bride price should be abandoned, drinking of liquor should be prohibited, taking of non-vegetatian meals should be taboo, and girls should not dance with the boys in the fairs. These are some of the reformative aspects which characterise the new social structures. In this aspect the challenges to education is how to meet out different networks and keep balance between the traditional and modern structure of the tribals. What type of methodology should be used to educate the tribals with structural transformation? What type of methodology of education will be helpful to integrate the tribal students with non-tribals, and which model of education would help the tribal students?

Strategy for Challenges and Promotion of Education of STs

A number of strategies have been used in India and other countries to meet the needs and structural changes of tribal students. These refer to organisation of schools, employment of teachers, use of method and material, participation of community, shortened schoolday or the night. Some of the strategies are described below:

1. Relaxation of existing norms in opening of schools

In many countries the norms for opening schools for tribals are quite liberal as compared to general norms. In India, the national norms of 1.5 km of walking distance for opening of primary schools should relax in the case of hilly and remote areas where there is concentration of tribals.

2. Opening of special schools

In the form of special school Ashram schools are most common in India. They intend to serve the needs of tribal areas where habitations are so small that schools become not only financially infeasible but also academically non-viable. These schools serve the needs of several habitations. They are located in the natural environment of tribes. The teachers are specially chosen for those schools and live with the children in residence. All boarding, lodging and educational facilities are provided free of cost to children. Pedagogy is supposed to emphasise dignity of labour and respect for cultural life and tradition of tribes. The experiment is only partially successful since the schools have failed to translate the philosophy into practice.

3. Mosque schools

In remote areas of Pakistan, mosque schools enrol children in classes first and second. The schools make use of mosque structures. Leaders and local literate persons teach in these schools. At the beginning of class second, children go to the nearest primary schools. In India also, in certain regions maktab structures are being used for universalisation of elementary education and modern education in science and mathematics. Similarly, in areas where Buddhism is predominant, mompas (Buddhist monasteries) are utilised for promoting education of children.

4. Mobile schools

For nomadic population groups, mobile schools have been established in certain countries. Here the teacher is attached to the group and moves with it. He gives lessons where and when appropriate. Such teachers are also known as parapetic teachers. In India, such schools are known as 'tent' schools. In Thailand, the mobile school concept is a little different. There the group of teachers proceed to slum areas and select a place as 'temporary school'. Teachers go from house to house recruiting pupils; incentives are provided to the children in the form of learning material and clothes. In this model, schools go to the pupil while in the tent school, the concept moves with the pupil.

5. Alternate intake sch ols

This concept is relevant for scattered school population. The school has grade one intake every alternate year. One teacher is responsible for two classes. Hence, in a six-grade school only three teachers are required. The method reduces cost and is suitable for the areas where population is scattered and very few children are available for each grade. The system is in vogue in Thailand.

6. Non-graded schools

Here, children are not grouped by age and grade and they proceed at their own pace. Children, who enter primary school late may rapidly complete their units, and are not forced to go through all five grades. The non-graded concept is based on continuous evaluation. End-term exams are therefore not necessary. There are no pass and fail in the system, hence, children do not drop out because of failure situation. Many states in India have adopted the system and thus have increased retention rates.

7. Learning post schools

This strategy is adopted in Pamong School System in Indonesia. It is based on the use of available village structure for schools and local people as instructors. The focus is on use of self-instructional materials. A primary school serves as the focus for the scheme and learning posts are established around it. The flexible nature of the scheme makes it attractive for poor children who can interrupt their studies. They are encouraged to drop in at learning post again and take up their studies from where they left. Meher UPE project in Bangladesh is also based on this approach of use of community structure and local persons as teachers.

The strategies outlined above have certain commonality. Common to all the strategies is a flexible approach, "a more efficient use of facilities, teachers and time", and consideration of child's need. Therefore, if the child cannot go to school, take the school to the child. Basic to all the strategies is a non-formal approach.

Some other strategies may be adopted to promote tribal education. These are:

1. Provision of schooling facilities.
2. Teacher training and orientation about tribal needs and educational programmes.
3. Re-orienting curriculum, content and medium of instruction.
4. Provision of teaching learning materials.
5. Innovative methods to be developed for supervision of schools.
6. Microplanning and effective implementation.

22

Administration in Education: A Process Driven Approach

*—P.K. Dashora**

Educational administration is different from administration in any other field. Educational administration is a process. It is a process of monitoring the efforts of educators in developing the coming generations as useful citizens. It is a process of helping the educators in finding out a common ground for people coming from varied contexts. It is a process of producing materials and generating ideas, keeping in view the purpose of social reconstruction and individual emancipation. In short, it helps the educators to effectively initiate the process of self-unfoldment of the student in the mini-society created in the institution.

Before exploring in detail the role of administration in education, the field of education and the aims and objectives of education need to be critically examined.

In fact, education should ensure three basic functions:

**Associate Professor, Rajasthan College of Agriculture, M.P.U.A.T., Udaipur (Rajasthan), India.*

i) Transmission of cultural values and traditions.

ii) Education for self-emancipation, self-actualisation and aesthetic appreciation.

iii) Education for social change in the changing time and context.

These three broad functions of education can be termed as 'Classical humanism', 'Progressivism' and 'Reconstructionism' respectively.

'Classical humanism' is knowledge-oriented. It apprises the individual with the store of knowledge mankind has accumulated, synthesised and experienced in the past. It is concerned with promoting intellectual and cultural values. It aims at the transmission of knowledge, culture and value system from one generation to another. Subject-centred and content the driven syllabus in this ideology is teacher-directed. Subject matter is analysed into its constituent elements sequencing them from simple to complex. It is based on the transmission of basic rules governing the basic phenomenon in a homogeneous class in terms of ability. Educational research relating to curriculum development in this value system is determined by university or board and the evaluation by the administrative authorities.

'Progressivism' is concerned with the development of individuals and the value of diversity. It recognises the aspirations of an individual, his curiosity, his creativity, his experiments and his experiences. Education is not seen as a process of transmission of closed truths but as a way of enabling the learners to learn how to learn. Learning is envisaged as a continuum, which can be broken up into several broad developmental stages. In this ideology the process is more important then the product and there is always enough scope for improvement in an individual. It makes the learner responsible to work at his own level and evaluate his own achievements. Teachers are continuously refining their procedures and working out the solutions of the problems they encounter in the process.

The ideology of 'Reconstructionism' is society-oriented. It is concerned with mutually agreed social conduct. It assumes that man can improve himself and his environment. Education is seen as an important agent for bringing about social, economic intellectual and spiritual advancement through rational planning. Goal centred approach of this ideology derives its objectives from the social needs and needs of an individual as a social being. The behaviour of an individual is aimed at making him useful for the society. The emphasis is on the graded mastery in learning and each step is based on the preceding one.

The process of education starts with the first breath an infant inhales and continues till the last breath. It is a continuous process through the span of cradle to grave undergoing the phases of confrontation with the moment, accumulation of data, modification in the context of past experiences, consolidation of already acquired knowledge and assimilation of conclusions. Every learner gets education with reference to his context. A teacher teaches the whole class uniformly but the gain in terms of learning among learners varies because of their individual contexts. In fact, education is a multifarious activity operating on different dimensions and getting support or obstructions at the individual level. The interesting thing to note is that this all happens simultaneously. Due consideration of these facts is required for effective administration in the field of education.

Education is not a mechanical activity. It is not to tell the learner what he doesn't know. It is in fact to make him behave as he doesn't behave. It is to make him think as he does not think. It is an attempt to mould his being to a pattern which is conducive to a normal process of the extension of his subjective consciousness to the level of cosmic consciousness. Any endeavour in this direction will ensure the dawn of wisdom.

Talking about the wisdom in the modern times T.S. Eliot has said:

> Where is wisdom?
>
> We have lost it in knowledge?
>
> Where is knowledge?
>
> We have lost it in information.
>
> I would like to add to this,
>
> Where is information?
>
> We have lost it in examinations, guides, grades, coaching classes and so on.

Education today seems to have failed to accomplish any of the objectives or fulfil any of the functions mentioned above. Preservation of cultural values, persistent quest of the truth, self-actualisation, aesthetic appreciation and emotional refinement seems to have been replaced by bankruptcy of intellectual integrity, emotional barrenness and moral depravation. Commenting on the present state of education in our country Nani Palkhiwala has said that our universities and educational institutions are content with producing a large number of degree holders who are ethical idiots and moral illiterates. The function of education has limited itself to a weapon of earning easy money without any urge for aesthetic creativity, personal emancipation and social responsibility.

These days education is reduced to only a means of making an opportunistic career. Skills are developed mainly for enhancing the employability of the people. Though employability is essential, yet it cannot be the end of education. In fact, for leading contented life, a person may have capabilities and sensitivities which may not have anything to do with his employability. The system of education which focuses only on enhancing the capabilities for better employment is doing more harm then any good to the people at large for leading full, happy and contented life. No system of education can be termed as a purposeful, meaningful and satisfactory system if it cannot make people realise their potential for exploring the world, experiencing the joys of living, unfolding the mysteries of universe, understanding human mind and developing a sense of aesthetic appreciation.

It has to be a very judicious administration in the modern context as present-day students are exposed to a variety of complex and complicated situations. The influences of family, friends, society, culture, and media with the advent of information technology and close interaction with the world is so vital and varied that it is difficult to ascertain what really shapes their personality. Often these varied influences are so diagonally opposite and at conflict with each another that the students are completely lost in utter confusion.

It is the greatest challenge to educational administrators to provide courageous and effective leadership so that children are taken out from this mire of confusion, confrontation and conflict. They are made socially responsible on the global level and their potential is fully utilised for the upliftment of the downtrodden, distressed and deprived, otherwise degrading dissipation and disaster will follow.

Educational administration needs to find out ways to equip students with such an outlook or value system that they are able to respond to the environment they are living in without becoming victims of wrong notions, forged values and fallacious judgements about the things and happenings. It is the task of educational administration to imbibe in the students the basic moral sense of doing the right thing, which may not be necessarily pragmatic or personally profitable. The basic moral sense of doing the right thing means striving to be better as human being and make the world a better place to live in.

23

Value of Education: A Study of Parents of Children Studying in Vadodara Municipal Corporation Primary Schools

—*Sarjoo Patel*, Maneesha Shukul***

INTRODUCTION

Education is the need of the day. It is a very powerful instrument for change, for achieving intellectual and social development of the people. It is in the interest of individuals and societies to expand and improve the education of children and youth in order to better meet their basic learning needs. Education leads to individual creativity, improved participation in the social, economic, cultural and political life of society and hence to a more effective contribution to human development. In fact, education is a prerequisite not only for the full exercise of the individuals rights but also for understanding and respecting the rights of others (Dahama and Bhatnagar, 1998).

**Ph.D. Scholar*

***Reader, Department of Home Management, Faculty of Home Science, M.S. University of Baroda, Vadodara.*

PRIMARY EDUCATION

Primary education forms a very important part of the entire education system as it forms the base of the individual's comprehensive development. It is a stepping stone on which one's entire future depends. It is the base which is needed to be strong enough so that the entire structure does not collapse. Primary education is an important period in which the child learns crucial things which he carries forward in life. It leads to better family health, lower fertility and thus slower population growth. It is a sound base for secondary and higher education too. Hence, it should be given the highest priority as it leads to development of competence of average worker and increases national productivity.

Primary education rightly understood and sincerely implemented has the potential to function as an empowering experience for all. There is a need to bring back the emphases on its goals, contents and processes which have become distorted and submersed in recent times. Primary education as it is known is education that caters to the basic language needs for all the young students irrespective of what they are going to become later in life. These needs comprise both essential language tools and basic language content such as knowledge skills, values and attitudes. This will help them to develop their full capacities to improve the quality of their lives and to continue learning.

The education in such an important phase of life is certainly influenced by the values that the parents hold about education. The parents views and opinion about education is very important in the child's educational attainment.

Values were once the prime concern of philosophy but today they pertain to many fields, which include, anthropology, sociology, economics, management and home economics. They are however defined and expressed differently by all these disciplines. The term value is therefore of great importance in the present era because of its permeation in all spheres of life. (Chatterjee, 2000)

An individual learns his values from varied sources. These may include his closest associates, his religion, culture and his experience. Hence, one's way of life and thinking is manifested by the values he holds. It can therefore be concluded that behaviour is intricately blended with the values held by the individual. It can also be said that values of an individual can be identified by placing him in a conflicting situation permitting more than one cause of action. Values of individual are very important and the underlying force by which they take decision (Varghese, Ogale and Srinivasan,1985). If the values are positive it will greatly influence their views and opinions about education. Also it is seen that if the views of the parents regarding education are positive and they rank education high among the values held by them they will motivate and encourage their children to study well. But if they hold a negative opinion and low value of education that will certainly affect their decision regarding education. Therefore, an exploration of values underlying education was felt to be essential to comprehend the vital role of management and their operation in education. Hence, a study to explore and identify the values underlying education was planned. The knowledge in this area will help to increase the understanding of how values play a significant role in determining our behaviour and lifestyles.

Objectives and Field Procedure

The study was conducted with the following objectives.

1) To find out the opinion of the parents regarding the importance of education.
2) To find out the place of education among the various values held by the respondents.

Interview schedule was used as an instrument for gathering data which consisted of three sections. Section one contained questions regarding background information of the respondents. In section two projective technique was used to find out the opinion of the parents regarding importance of education. Section three contained a list of values which the respondents had to rank. Content validity and reliability of the scale was established (r = 0.56).

Two municipal schools, one from Sayajigunj area and the other from the Fatehpura area, were selected purposively for the study. The sample of the study comprised 120 respondents (mother of children studying in the municipal school of the two localities) selected through systematic random sampling method. A separate list of parents of boys and girls studying in fifth and sixth standards was prepared from both the schools and then a sample of 60 was drawn from each school.

Major Findings: The data collected revealed that the mean age of the homemakers was 34.0 years. A wide majority of the parents of both boys and girls were illiterate. A wide majority of the homemakers and all the fathers of the children were employed. The mean income of the family was Rs. 1,587.50 per month.

Opinion of Parents towards Education of Children

One of the aims of the investigation was to study the opinion of parents towards the education of children. An opinionnaire was developed for this purpose, which was subjected to validity and reliability (r=0.56 sig. at 0.01) It comprised 10 statements each having three options in order of ideal situations which had weighed scores of one through three. The scores were summated to assess the extent of favourable or unfavourable opinion of parents towards education. Gender-based analysis of responses was done.

It was revealed that if there was a financial crisis in the family, majority of the boy child's and the girl-child's mother would discontinue the child's education forever whereas a few of them said that they would discontinue it for sometime.

Further, when they were asked about the child's activities after returning from school a majority of mothers said that the child had to perform household work and a few of them said the child had to complete the homework given in the class.

Statements	Boys		Girls	
	f	%	*f*	%
1) If there is financial crises in the family you would	45	75	38	63.3
a) Discontinue your child's education in the school forever	15	25	20	3.3
b) Discontinue the child's studies for sometime	-	-	2	3.3
c) Continue the child's education in the school	-	-	2	3.3
2) When the child returns from the school they generally				
a) Do household work	37	61.7	34	56.7
b) Play	16	26.7	18	30
c) Do homework given in the class	7	11.7	8	13.3
3) When someone in the family is ill				
a) The child is asked not to go to the school and take care of the sick person	16	26.7	27	45
b) You take leave from your work and take care of sick person	23	38.3	10	16.7
c) Someone else in the family takes care of the sick person	21	35	23	38.3
4) Education for a girl-child				
a) Is not necessary	11	18.3	11	18.3
b) Does not matter if she is not educated	16	26.7	30	50
c) She should be educated	33	55	19	31.7
5) Education for each child				
a) Is not necessary	10	16.7	4	6.7
b) Is necessary to some extent	38	63.3	42	70
c) Is absolutely necessary	12	20	14	23.3
6) It is necessary to send a child to school because it helps				
a) To earn money	50	83.3	39	65
b) People respect the educated person	6	10	9	15
c) To gain knowledge	4	6.7	12	20

(Contd...)

(Contd...)

7) If Gujarat government is providing free education for girls to promote girls, education you				
a) Are not concerned with the idea	1	1.7	3	5
b) Feel thankful to the government	10	16.7	11	18.3
c) Make your daughter study well and take advantage of facilities provided	49	81.7	46	76.7
8) If your child wants to study further you				
a) Discourage him/her to study	3	5	10	16.7
b) Allow him/her but not willingly	28	46.7	23	38.3
c) Allow him/her to study	29	48.3	27	45
9) If you lack resources, you would				
a) Make the child work instead of study	31	51.7	14	23.3
b) Stop the child's study for sometime	25	41.7	33	55
c) Make some arrangement to make him/her study	4	6.7	13	21.7
10) In your opinion spending on education is				
a) A waste	2	3.3	5	8.3
b) Neither a waste nor an investment	31	51.7	22	36.7
c) A productive investment	27	45	33	55

If someone in the family was ill two-thirds of the girl-child's mother said that the girl had to take leave from the school to take care of the sick person whereas in about three-fourths of boy child's family the mothers or other family members take care of the sick persons. When the mothers were asked about their daughters education very few of the girl-children's mothers agreed to that whereas half of the girl-children's mothers did not mind if the girl was not educated.

A majority of the mothers of both the sexes considered that education as necessary to some extent whereas very few of them considered it to be absolutely necessary. Further, when it was asked as why it is necessary to send a child to school majority of them reported that it helped to earn money whereas a very negligible percentage of the boy children's mothers said that it helped to gain knowledge but few of the girl-child's mothers believed that it helped in gaining knowledge.

If the Gujarat government is providing free education for girls to promote girl education, a majority of the mothers of both the sexes would make their daughter study well and take advantage of facilities provided.

When asked that if the child wanted to study further nearly half of the mothers of boys reported that they would allow him to study whereas a little more than one-third of the girls' mothers said that they would allow them but not willingly.

If the parents lacked resources nearly half of them would stop the child's studies for sometime whereas less than one fourth of the girl-children's mothers would make the children work instead of study. Nearly half of the mothers of total sample opined that education was a productive investment whereas very few of them believed that it was a waste.

Overall Opinion of the Homemakers Regarding Importance of Education

The total possible scores on the scale of opinion were divided into two categories as to show favourable, neutral and unfavourable opinion.

Table 23.1

Frequency and percentage distribution of homemakers according to scores obtained for the opinion regarding importance of education.

Scores of opinion	*Range of scores*	*Boys*		*Girls*	
		f	*%*	*f*	*%*
Unfavourable	10-16	40	66.6	33	55
Neutral	17-23	11	18.4	8	13.3
Favourable	24-30	9	15	19	31.7
Total		60	100	60	100

The mean score on opinion of the total sample was found to be 15.7 from a range of 10-30 among the boy children's mothers and 13-8 among the girl-children's mothers which showed that the opinion was unfavourable regarding education.

It was observed that on the whole, a majority of the boys, mothers were low scorers which revealed that they had unfavourable opinion regarding education and two-thirds of the girl-children's mothers scored low which also revealed the same result. Very few mothers had neutral score for import-ance of education.

Various Values held by the Respondents

The section was mainly designed to get a view of the importance of education given by the homemakers. A list of values were provided in this section to the homemaker and she was asked to identify the most important five values in order of importance according to her. The main purpose behind this was to trace out the position of education in a particular family. Based on the percentage of respondents who considered certain values as important a list in descending order was made.

It was observed that on the whole in the boy-child's family the first place is given to health, then to work, education, leisure and knowledge. Thus place of education was third among other values in the boy-child's family (Table-23.2). It shows that among the first five important values education holds a place. Further, it can be seen that some percentage of respondents valued safety, comfort, economy, family unity, equality, responsibility, security and achievement but none of them valued beauty, determination and privacy at all.

Further, a look into the girl-child's family values reveal that work is given the most importance followed by health, comfort, education and convenience. Here, education holds the fourth position. It is noticed that knowledge, leisure, safety, economy, family unity, responsibility, security are also given some importance but very few of them consider efficiency, prestige, team, spirit and sharing important and none of them hold value of beauty, determination and privacy.

Table 23.2

Frequency and percentage distribution of respondents according to the values held for the family

Values	*Boys*		*Girls*	
	f	%	*f*	%
Health	51	85	47	78.3
Work	47	78.3	51	85
Education	31	51.7	27	45
Knowledge	22	36.7	21	45
Leisure	25	41.7	24	40
Convenience	18	30	25	41.7
Safety	19	31.7	16	26.7
Equality	11	18.3	4	6.7
Economy	17	28.3	15	25
Family unity	14	23.3	15	25
Comfort	19	31.7	32	53.3
Responsibility	9	15	6	10
Security	8	13.3	9	15
Achievement	5	8.3	3	5
Efficiency	1	1.7	2	3.3
Prestige	1	1.7	2	3.3
Beauty	-	-	-	-
Determination	-	-	-	-
Team spirit	2	3.3	1	1.7
Privacy	-	-	-	-
Sharing	1	1.7	1	1.7
Total	60	100	60	100

The t-test was used to find out difference in the opinion of the parents regarding importance of education due to age, education, and occupation of the respondents. The testing of hypothesis revealed that opinion of the parents varied with the family income (t = 3.00 Sig. at 0.01) but age, education and employment status of the parents did not cause any variation in the opinion regarding importance of education.

CONCLUSION

On the basis of the present study it can be concluded that the majority of the homemakers had unfavourable opinion regarding education which depicted that they did not give importance to education. The place of education in most of the boy-child's family was found to be third whereas in the girl-child's family it was fourth amongst all the values they held. The opinion of the parents regarding education varied with the family income.

Implications

Since it was revealed through the study that a majority of the parents had unfavourable opinion towards education, there is a clear need to change the opinion of the parents. Educational institutions such as home science, and social work can play a significant role in influencing the opinion of the parents.

REFERENCES

Chatterjee, P., 2000, "Challenges in School Education in 2000", "Value Education: Integrated Approach", Paper presentation, Faculty of Education and Psychology, M S. University of Baroda.

Dahama, O. P., and Bhatnagar, O. P., 1988, *Education and Communication for Development*, Oxford and IBH Publishing Co. Pvt. Ltd.

Varghese, M. A., Ogale N. N., and Srinivasan, K., 1996, *Home Management,* New Delhi: New Age international (I) Ltd., Publishers.

24

Educating Homemakers for Time Management

Veena Gandotra, Maneesha Shukul**, Neerja Jaiswal****

Management has existed throughout history. It can be traced as way back as time when people started forming groups to achieve those goals, which they could not achieve as individuals. Hunting of a large animal can be cited as an example of such a group activity. There managing was essential to assure coordination of individual efforts, ever since then informal groups were formalised and then arose institutions/ organisations or enterprises. Management is universal. It is the same in business enterprise, social organisations, government and in the home. Management in home, as in any other institution or organisation, is planning, organising, controlling and evaluating the use of resources at the disposal of the group to achieve their set goals. Management is a means of reaching goals.

The family is the oldest institution. As soon as a man and a woman is married, a family is established and they begin

*Head, Department of Home Management, Faculty of Home Science, M.S. University of Baroda, Vadodara.

**Reader, Department of Home Management, Faculty of Home Science, M.S. University of Baroda, Vadodara.

***Lecturer, Department of Home Management, Faculty of Home Science, M.S. University of Baroda, Vadodara.*

together setting and working for achievement of common goals. They develop plans; delegate responsibilities, organise and control the use of available human and non-human resources. Generally, the resources at their disposal are limited whereas the goals to be attained through resources are multiple, competing with each other and complex in nature. In relation to these, innumerable problems are to be solved and therefore decisions have to be made constantly.

Moreover, when in today's world, environment has become more complex, the resources are more varied, sophisticated and scarcer, and the families are increasingly confused with many possible uses for the resources. It is only management, which helps the families to find a way out of such confusion. Hence, today management has become even more important than what it was in the past.

MANAGEMENT AT HOME

Management takes place in every home. It is essential and applicable to almost all aspects of family living. Very aptly cited by Gross, Crandall and Knoll (1980.): "Management in the homes is a part of the fabric of living. Its threads are interwoven because decisions for the use of resources are made whether the family is at work or play."

The manager in the home is the homemaker, i.e., wife, mother in the family. She can be compared with the manager of an enterprise. "Managers must establish an environment in which people can accomplish group goals with the least amount of time, money, materials and personal dissatis-factions, or where they can achieve as much as possible of a desired goal with available resources" (Koontz, O'Donnell, Weihrich, 1984).

In the home situation, it is the homemaker, better addressed as a 'home manager', who is responsible for a smooth running of activities aiming towards the achievement of family goals, from the given limited resources.

Amongst all the resources, the limits of time can be easily recognised. Time is one of the resources available to each one in the same quantity. Everyone has 24 hours a day to use in some way. This is the one resource we share alike (Nickell and Dorsey, 1960).

Every individual has certain demands upon his time. These "Demands may be met or avoided; enjoyed, accepted or despised. Nor is a difference to be found here whether one is a homemaker or a teacher, an industrialist or an artist, a man or a woman, a child or an adult" (Moore, 1957).

Though time is an individual resource largely used separately by each family member, time can also be used jointly, and if it is so used, it becomes an important family resources. The homemaker's role in the inventory of family time is quite different from that of other family members. The time of the homemaker is much used for the entire family. In that sense it is family time. For her, conscious decision making for the use of time becomes more and more important as the number of choices grow. Such a balance is hard to achieve especially by Indian women.

Time management is highly essential for the home manager, especially the one who is gainfully employed or self-employed as she has to accomplish several activities at home as well as the work phase. It is only through proper time management can she achieve a balance between her work, rest and leisure time.

TIME USE PATTERN OF HOMEMAKERS

As shown by researches, the workday of a rural woman ranges from 12 to 17 hours out of which five to seven hours are spent in household work. Women work three to four hours a day more than the men do in the same society. Women get very little leisure time if they work outside their home also.

Analysing the total time spent on various activities, it is revealed that, among Indian women, food preparation takes the maximum time; other activities on which women spend their time are care of house, dishwashing, care of family members, washing clothes and then on personal care.

In rural areas, women have additional responsibilities of agriculture-related activities, care of livestock and that of collecting fodder and fuel from faraway places. They also spend considerable time in milching and preparing milk products. Nearly three hours a day are spent on such activities. Those women who work on farms spend nearly five hours on an average on various activities such as sowing, harvesting, threshing, winnowing, etc.

VARIABLES INFLUENCING TIME OF HOMEMAKERS

A number of variables influence the use of time available to homemaker. They can be categorised as (a) Socio economic and demographic variables (b) Work-environment-related variables (e) Worker-related variables.

The socio economic and demographic variables which influence time use pattern of women can be the type, size and composition of their family, family occupation, income of family and the like.

Many researchers have reported that homemakers belonging to nuclear families spend less time in household work. (Grewal, 1980; Kamalamma, 1981; Munjal, 1984; Sandhu, 1985; Singhal, (1989).

A direct linear correlation between the amount of time spent on all household tasks with the size of the family was also reported by many of these researchers. Family occupation plays a role in time spent by women of rural area in livestock and farm activities.

A direct linear correlation is found between the amount of time spent on all household tasks and on the percapita and yearly income of the family. As reported by Chauhan (1981) women from middle income group families spent 250 hours per month on household work whereas those from low income group spent 227 hours. On the other hand, 197.50 hours were spent by women from high income group. It becomes evident that women with high socioeconomic status spend less time on household work compared to women with lower socioeconomic status.

Among the work and environment-related variables are daily and seasonal activities, meal type, equipment available, help received and the like. Research conducted by Rajkumari (1971) has shown that time costs of meal preparation varied with the quantity of food cooked, the type of fuel used and the type of utensils used. Chauhan (1981) found that time spent by women on household tasks decreased with the availability of help. She reported that paid help performed 5.4 per cent of the household chores. Kamalamma (1981) found that even in the households with two or more adult women, the household work was allocated to one women, the housewife.

Some of the significant variables associated with the worker herself that are age, education and occupation of homemakers influence their time use pattern. Saraswathi (1962) and Munjal (1984) found that time spent on household activities decreased with increase in the age of homemaker. Kaur (1986) reported that husbands and daughters of middle-aged homemakers assisted in household activities followed by those of old and young homemakers.

A significant relationship was found between time spent by women on work and their educational level by Bafna (1979), Sandhu (1985) and Singhal (1989). The time spent on household work is also influenced by the employment status of homemakers. Saraswathi (1962) and Sandhu (1985) found that working women spent less time on household work as compared with the full time homemakers. Grewal (1980) reported that in urban as well as in rural areas, irrespective of employment status, the homemaker was the prime performer of household tasks. Singal (1989) found that women's work status affected time spent by them on work as well as sleep during the peak season in rural areas. Saini (1983) reported more time spent by farming homemakers than non-farming homemakers.

Apart from the variables reported by various researchers, certain other factors also influence the time use pattern of homemaker such as stage of family lifecycle, presence of small children, help of family members in sharing the household work, her own attitude towards household work and her likes or dislikes towards specific household tasks, her physical fitness, etc. Researchers in these areas need to be carried out from time to time and at various places to have a clear picture of time use pattern of homemakers.

However, one fact emerges from the researches, that since the homemaker is the main performer of household tasks and her time use becomes more complicated by different factors, it is only through proper time management that she can accomplish maximum activities during the day.

MANAGERIAL PROCESS APPLIED TO TIME

The management process remains the same in relation to time as it is for any resources. The process comprises goal setting, planning, implementing and utilising feedback.

a) Goal setting is logically the first step in the sequence of the managerial process. The goals stem from the values of individuals. The goals specific to time management and common for each individual are:

   1) The use of time so that it will mean the most in the attainment of individual and family goals.
   2) Achieving satisfaction with the use of one's time.
   3) Accepting the limitation of time and achieving balance among work, rest and leisure in its use.

4) Minimising of work time may be the goal for some individuals.

If the goals of time management are set very clearly then only proper planning of time can be done and then other steps can be followed. If careful consideration to goals has not been given to a time plan, the plan may defeat its own purpose.

b) *Planning* : "Planning saves some work time," is true for the use of all resources, so it is for the use of time. A time plan shows what one expects to do in a given period of time. It also indicates the sequence of the various activities and the time allowed for each one.

Most homemakers follow some sort of time plans. Standing plans or routines exist for the day's activities in almost everyone's life, and metaplans, (Miller, Galanter and Pribram, 1960) exist for varying these somewhat as well as for generating new plans (Gross, Crandall and Knoll, 1980). Plans are not usually developed 'from scratch'.

Time planning can be done in mainly three ways, based on increasing amount of details involved, viz.:

a) simple list
b) series of projects
c) schedule

The simple list is just a memo of decisions as to what is to be done, often listed without any particular order of importance or without noting time when each activity is to be done.

The series of projects is more complex and in detail than the simple list of jobs. This may include time sequence but not time limits. It is directed toward the time when an activity is to be performed and/or the order in which activities are to be carried out.

The schedule is the most detailed one, which includes approximate amount of time allowed for each activity included in it and the sequence of these activities. As a technique in time management it forces fitting together what is to be done in time available. Truly a scarcity device, it is valuable when a person experiences a time pressure. It is appropriate for a relatively short period of time. Some parts of the schedule consist of known routines; other parts may require fresh decisions and planning, and some parts of the day may be left unplanned. These may act as 'Catch-up period' where the activities which could not be accomplished at the decided time, could be completed. Such periods also become helpful if the planned activities are to be shifted in time but keeping the sequence as it is. Some flexibility is desired in the schedules.

For the household work, written schedules are quite uncommon. Mostly homemakers do some mental scheduling. Younger homemakers tend to prepare schedules more consciously than older homemakers do. One must be realistic in allotting time for doing the activities. A record of time taken for doing a particular work should be maintained for oneself, if one wants to be realistic in making time schedules.

For making a time schedule one must:

1) list activities to be included in the time available.
2) establish priorities.
3) estimate time needed, both quantity for an activity and the time when to be carried out finished.
4) bring total time needed and total time available into harmony.
5) establish a sequence of activities.
6) check meshing with other people's plans where essential. (Gross, Crandall and Knoll, 1980).

Carefully thought out time and activity plans are useful tools in saving time and energy and relieving the tensions of indecision and uncertainties.

Pert (Programme Evaluation and Review Technique)

For a Dinner

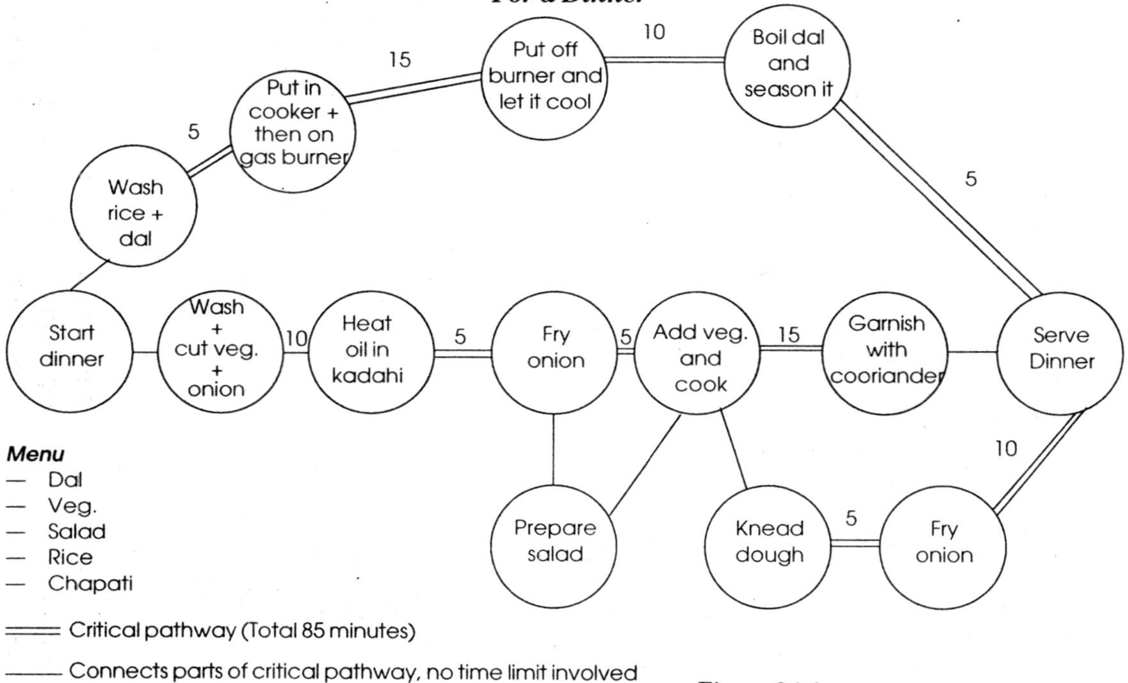

Figure 24.1

PERT (Programme Evaluation and Review Technique) is a special device for scheduling time, which was developed in the industry. Hill (1965) defines it as a "management control system for defining integrating and interrelating the work to be accomplished in completing a complex programme on time."

PERT is an outgrowth of the housewives system of preparing a meal, starting the different paths of it so that all foods will finish at the same time (Hill 1963). An example is shown in the accompanying figure. PERT is useful for a complicated household task such as preparing and serving a meal. It is also very helpful for scheduling a group activity. It helps to identify the peak load. To even it out certain activities can be started and finished ahead of time so that the way for later activities can be cleared. Sometimes certain activities can be delegated to others.

c) *Implementing:* Plans once made but not implemented are of no value. The exercise done for making a plan becomes a waste of time and effort. Hence, it is essential that after a time plan is made it must be implemented, which means it must be initiated and carried to completion. Implementing is heavily weighed with the performance. During the implementation, many a time, fresh decisions are necessary. Adjustments become essential either in activities or the goals behind them if emergencies arise. The homemaker's skill in adjusting her time planed when inter-options arise helps control many situations. Various aspects of the plan need to be coordinated while carrying out the activities as planned.

The success of implementing plans into practice depends to a great extent on the realistic time allotted to well-thought out parts of a large activity. A larger activity must be broken down in smaller parts which helps to perceive the activity in advance and to estimate the time required to complete each part of the activity leading to the completion of the whole.

Checking of each part of the plan must be done frequently so that adjustment in the situation can be done if need arises. If PERT is made one can see immediately in the diagram, where the person is and whether the work is being done according to the schedule or not. The plan or PERT call be put on a bulletin board for easy and constant view.

d) *Utilising Feedback:* Feedback is that portion of the output of a system which is returned immediately or later to the input of the system. It is of two types: the immediate one leading to action, the other, to learn through evaluation.

Action feedback is during implementing and co-exists with it. It is immediate. It modifies the plan quickly if needed. It may be positive or negative. The positive feedback will result in changes in the original plan. The negative feedback will result in changes needed to stick to the plan.

Learning feedback occurs later than action feedback. This is in fact an evaluation of time plan. Evaluation is a flexible mental tool in time management. A device developed in industry (Gnatt Chart) provides the learning types of feed back in time plan. The Gnatt Chart consists of four column record of time use according to the plan. The details of time and activities are:

Date........................Day............

Time	*Use planned*	*Schedule use accomplished*			*Un schedule*
		Yes	*Partially*	*No*	
7.30-7.30 a.m.	Prepare breakfast and serve	√			
7.30-8.00	Sweep and mop the house		√		Read newspaper & then work
8.00-8.30	Shop for vegetables & sundry		√		Started late from home,
8.30-9.00	Visit mother while returning	√			
9.00 - 10.00	Return Home and prepare lunch		√		Spend more time at mother's place
10.00-10.30	Wash utensils			√	Take more time in preparing lunch

Use planned are filled in the first two columns. In the third column information for evaluating accuracy in time allowed is filled in. In the fourth column the 'Unexpected' events due to which the worker deviates from the planned schedule, are written. It is through these columns that a feedback is obtained, which otherwise, might be overlooked.

Certain subjective questions asked to oneself regarding the overall plan may be another way of evaluating the time plan.

CONCLUSION

A time plan is an important tool of successful time management through which the goals of balanced use of time can be achieved. Time management helps to save time from one task to use it in doing some other task. It helps in meeting time and work demands of daily living. Any plan which makes it possible for the attainment of the individual and family goals to a satisfying degree without wasting the resources available or causing, unnecessary tension may be considered a successful plan. Thus time management is very essential for the Home Manager. Proper formal and/or education in this regard will help them to manage their time in most efficient way and to achieve satisfaction.

REFERENCES

Bafna, K., 1979, *A Study of Use of Time by Homemakers,* Unpublished Master's Thesis, M.S. University of Baroda, Vadodara.

Chauhan, R., 1981, *Time Utilisation for Household Work and its Monetary Value,* Unpublished Master's Thesis, M.S. University of Baroda, Vadodara.

Grewal, N., 1980, *A Comparative Study on Utilisation of Time in Household Activities by Rural and Urban Homemakers of*

Ludhiana District, Unpublished Master's Thesis, Punjab Agriculture University, Ludhiana.

Gross, I.H., Crandall E.W., Knoll M.M., 1980, *Management for Modern Families*, New Jersey, Prentice Hall Inc.

Hill, L.S., "Perspective: Some possible Pitfalls in the Design and Use of PERT Net Working", *Academy of Management Journal*, 8 (1965), 139.

Kamalamma, N., 1981, *Development of a Technique for Establishing Time Norms of Household Work of Rural Families,* Unpublished Doctoral Thesis, M.S. University of Baroda, Vadodara.

Kaur, G., 1986, *A Study of Tasks of Distribution in Rural Household of Ludhiana District*, Unpublished Master's Thesis, M.S. University of Baroda, Vadodara.

Koontz, H., O'Donnel C, Weihrich H., 1982, *Essential of Management,* Tata-McGraw Hill Publishing Co. Ltd., New Delhi.

Moore, B.M.,"Time, Tension and Mental Health", *Journal of Home Economics,* Vol. 49. (Dec 1957).

Munjal, S., 1984, *An Exploratory Study of Rural Women's Time allocated Decisions and Activity Battern in Karnal District,* Unpublished Master's Thesis, Haryana Agriculture University, Hissar.

Nickell, P., Dorsey J.M., Budolfson M., 1980, *Management in Family Living,* Inc., London, John Wiley & Sons.

Rajkumari, 1971, *An Analysis of Job Content and Time Cost of Cooking Breakfast and Lunch in Selected Families,* Cited in Kamalamma, N., 1981, *Development of a Technique for Establishing Time Norms of Household Work of Rural Families,* Unpublished Doctoral Thesis, M.S. University of Baroda, Vadodara.

Saini, H., 1983, *Time Task Analysis of Farming and Non-farming Homemakers,* Unpublished Master's Thesis, Punjab Agriculture University, Ludhiana.

Saraswathi, S.R., 1962, *A Comparative Study of Use of Time by Full-time and Employed Homemakers*, Unpublished Master's Thesis, Queen Mary's College, Chennai.

Singhal, S., 1989, *Women's Work Pattern and Economic contribution of Family Resources: Development of Rural Household in India*, Unpublished Doctoral Thesis, M.S. University,Vadodari.

Index